PHILIP PULLMAN,
MASTER STORYTELLER
A Guide to the Worlds of *His Dark Materials*

PHILIP PULLMAN,
MASTER STORYTELLER
A Guide to the Worlds of *His Dark Materials*

CLAIRE SQUIRES

continuum

NEW YORK • LONDON

The Continuum International Publishing Group,
80 Maiden Lane, New York, NY 10038

The Continuum International Publishing Group Ltd,
The Tower Building, 11 York Road, London SE1 7NX

Cover art: Title: Northern Lights
Medium: Digital Paint (Photoshop 7.0, Calcomp Creation Station Pro)
Original creation date: August 1, 2005
Artist's name: Laura Diehl
Artist's website: www.LDiehl.com

Cover design: Lee Singer

Author photograph: © Claire Squires

Library of Congress Cataloging-in-Publication Data

Squires, Claire.
  Philip Pullman, master storyteller : a guide to the worlds of His dark materials / Claire Squires.
     p. cm.
  A comprehensive study of Philip Pullman, with focus on the contexts, sources, influences and controversies of the His dark materials trilogy.
  Includes bibliographical references.
  ISBN-10: 0-8264-1716-7 (pbk.)
  ISBN-13: 978-0-8264-1716-9 (pbk.)
  ISBN-10: 0-8264-2764-2 (hardcover)
  ISBN-13: 978-0-8264-2764-9 (hardcover)
  1. Pullman, Philip, 1946—Criticism and interpretation. 2. Pullman, Philip, 1946—His dark materials—Handbooks, manuals, etc. 3. Fantasy fiction, English—History and criticism. 4. Young adult fiction, English—History and criticism. I. Title.
  PR6066.U44Z88 2006
  823'.914—dc22
                              2006019766

Printed in the United States of America

06 07 08 09 10 11   10 9 8 7 6 5 4 3 2 1

◖◗ Contents ◖◗

⟪ Preface ⟫

IN LATE 2003, I published a short reader's guide to Philip Pullman's *His Dark Materials* trilogy in the Continuum Contemporaries series. At the same time, Nicholas Tucker's book *Darkness Visible: Inside the World of Philip Pullman* (2003) also appeared, making these two volumes the first book-length critical studies to have been written on Pullman's master work. Since that time, several other studies with differing critical, theological and intellectual perspectives on the trilogy have been published. These include a volume by popular science writers Mary and John Gribbin entitled *The Science of Philip Pullman's* His Dark Materials (2003); three separate interpretations of the trilogy from varying Christian perspectives, John Houghton's *A Closer Look at* His Dark Materials (2004), Hugh Rayment-Pickard's *The Devil's Account: Philip Pullman and Christianity* (2004) and Tony Watkins's *Dark Matter: A Thinking Fan's Guide to Philip Pullman* (2004); an encyclopaedic fan's guide (Parkin and Jones 2005); and two multi-authored volumes of essays, *Navigating the Golden Compass* (2005) and His Dark Materials *Illuminated* (2005), edited by Glenn Yeffeth and Millicent Lenz with Carde Scott respectively. Three publications relating to the National Theatre's sell-out two-play adaptation of the trilogy also have been produced: Nicholas Wright's script for the stage adaptation (2003), a book about the staging of the trilogy (Butler 2003) and a collection of the associated Platform talks given during the staging (Haill 2004). There is even a quiz book based on the series and its sequel, *Lyra's Oxford* (Gifford 2006). Over the next few months—possibly before this book is published—there are titles promised on *His Dark Materials* by David Colbert, Lois H Gresh and Laurie Frost, as well as another book from Tony Watkins. In addition to these print publications, a host of interpretive material is available online along with a wealth of fan websites devoted to Pullman and his trilogy. Also forthcoming are an educational DVD, entitled *Inside* His Dark Materials, and a multitude of more ephemeral criticism in newspapers and magazines.

Pullman's writing, then, has inspired much secondary writing in the short time since the publication of the final volume of the trilogy in 2000. This secondary writing has been eager to celebrate his success, to comment upon it and even, sometimes, to critique it. This volume adds to the ongoing debate, seeking both to develop further some of the questions I addressed in my initial publication, *Philip Pullman's* His Dark Materials: *A Reader's Guide*, and to offer a more detailed commentary on the secondary material that has grown up around the Pullman phenomenon. It also affords a more critical perspective on what is thought of by many as Pullman's greatest attribute: his storytelling ability. This current volume, *Philip Pullman, Master Storyteller*, therefore examines the power of Pullman's narrative but also critically assesses its implications and its limits.

The majority of the publications thus far devoted to Pullman's work have been written explicitly by fans (although Houghton's volume is a notable exception with its anti-Pullman stance). Watkins's volume goes so far as to declare in its title that it is penned by a fan. I would certainly place myself in the same category: like many thousands of others, I have found myself enthralled, lost to the world around me, as I read the thrilling adventures of Lyra and Will, my only connection to reality the physical consciousness with which I turned the pages of the books. And yet, in the process of writing my reader's guide to *His Dark Materials* a couple of years ago, I also started to ask some questions about the trilogy that I didn't have the space to answer fully at that time. I ended my main interpretive second chapter on the trilogy with a section entitled 'Loose Ends'. This was a suggestive but all too short (two and a half pages, to be precise) meditation on the unexplained in the trilogy, on what I called its 'gaps and silences' (Squires 2003: 63). The book I published in 2003 was short—around twenty-five thousand words—and I didn't have enough space to cover in full detail everything I wanted to write about.

For me, these gaps and silences are what justify the publication of a further critical volume on Pullman's trilogy. As I mentioned in my section on 'Loose Ends', these uncertainties, these gaps and silences, are compelling places for the reader of *His Dark Materials* to consider for two particular reasons. For the fan, and for the critic, the further ventures that Pullman himself has made into the imaginative worlds of his own creation mean that they continue to expand, through the publication of *Lyra's Oxford* and the future publication of *The Book of Dust* and through the various versions of the trilogy on the stage and screen. All of these interventions are assessed in some detail in this book. The second reason is to do with something that I identified at the end of 'Loose Ends' and concerns the engagement made by readers in Pullman's writing and their interpretations of the worlds of the *His Dark Materials* trilogy. The inspiration to write a second volume on Pullman's work only a couple of years after my first, and alongside an array of other critical writing assessing that work, stems from this imaginative engagement made by a legion of readers. *Philip Pullman, Master Storyteller* examines in more depth the narrative powers of Pullman but also has the aim of looking at the ways in which the *His Dark Materials* narrative enraptures, ensnares and sometimes even enrages its readers. In assessing the writing of Pullman, this book defines him as a 'master storyteller'. Such a role carries a weight of responsibility, and this volume debates this role of the master storyteller and in so doing goes beyond the 'fan' reading by developing a critical perspective on the trilogy and its associated texts. Nonetheless, in writing this book I have been inspired by the enthusiastic and engaged responses of readers of the *His Dark Materials* trilogy, and for that reason, *Philip Pullman, Master Storyteller* is dedicated to them all.

In the composition of this new volume on Philip Pullman, I have incorporated some of the material from my earlier book, particularly in chapter 2, which has the function of introducing the characters and plots of the trilogy. However, *Philip Pullman, Master Storyteller* contains substantial new material including a lengthy biographical chapter, more in-depth analyses of *His Dark Materials*, more detailed sections on Pullman's other writing and a fuller bibliography. It also takes into account publications by and about Pullman since the appearance of my first book in 2003.

A note on referencing and editions: the individual books of *His Dark Materials* and *Lyra's Oxford* are referred to within in-text references as NL for *Northern Lights*, SK for *The Subtle Knife*, AS for *The Amber Spyglass* and LO for *Lyra's Oxford*. *Northern Lights*, which was published in the US under an alternate title, *The Golden Compass*, is referred to throughout under its original, UK title. Page references cited in this book are to the UK Scholastic paperback editions.

I have several people to thank for the appearance of this volume. First, to my editor at Continuum Books, David Barker, for commissioning this volume, and for his patience, speed and enthusiasm, all of which make him a pleasure to work with. Also at Continuum, thanks to Amy Wagner and Gabriella Page-Fort for their efficiency and courtesy in the production and design process. I am grateful to the School of Arts and Humanities at Oxford Brookes University for funding a period of research leave during which this book was completed. My thanks go particularly to my departmental colleagues in the Oxford International Centre for Publishing Studies for their support. I also would like to thank all those who have shared their thinking—both positive and negative—on Philip Pullman with me, sent me newspaper cuttings or web references and re-energised me when my spirits were flagging by telling me how fortunate I was to be writing a book on the subject of *His Dark Materials*. In this context, I would particularly like to mention David Fickling; Julia Eccleshare; Nicholas Tucker; the participants of SrafCon 2005; the very well-informed and enthusiastic webmasters and communities of Philip Pullman fan websites; Joanna Braithwaite; Julie, Christine and Michael Squires; and Team Schoolhouse.

⟪ Introduction ⟫

DURING THE NATIONAL THEATRE'S PLATFORM talk session with Philip Pullman to accompany the staging of *His Dark Materials*, one audience member asked a question that temporarily flummoxed the author. The questioner mused, 'When a child is born in Lyra's world, where does the dæmon come from? Does it come out with the baby?' (Haill 2004: 60). Pullman responded, with characteristically dry humour, 'I haven't made a great study of the gynaecology in Lyra's world. The answer is that I don't know. I don't know because I didn't have to write a scene in which anyone was born. If I had, I would have had to think about it. But it's a good question' (Haill 2004: 60).

The fan's question might seem a simple request for more information about the worlds of *His Dark Materials*, a request that would feed the hunger for more knowledge of these unique, involving worlds. It might almost seem that the questioner was trying to catch Pullman out, and indeed the writer's answer demonstrated the limits of Pullman's knowledge of his own fictional worlds or, to be more precise, the limits of those fictional worlds. The conventions of gynaecology in Lyra's world have not been invented; such a question cannot, therefore, be answered. The question, however, not only demonstrates the limits of fictional worlds and the extent of our knowledge of them, but also gestures towards the creative energies that these limits bring into being. Pullman, the creator of the multiple

1

worlds of *His Dark Materials*, does not know—thus far—how dæmons are born. His reply implies, furthermore, that this information does not exist elsewhere, waiting for him to discover it and relay his findings to the waiting audience. But for the questioner it is a point of legitimate curiosity in the attempt to understand and inhabit the worlds of *His Dark Materials*, worlds in which, after all, the themes of being, beginning and knowledge are central.

For in the *His Dark Materials* trilogy—*Northern Lights* (1995), *The Subtle Knife* (1997) and *The Amber Spyglass* (2000)—Pullman has created worlds teeming with multiple lives and characters who have a variety of origins and present a myriad of narrative possibilities. The multiplicity of characters, plots and worlds has undoubtedly attracted readers to the trilogy and left them deeply immersed with the involving worlds they find therein. And yet fans of the trilogy also are left wanting to know what happened before the beginning of the trilogy, what will happen after the end of the trilogy and what happens alongside the timescale of the trilogy but is not narrated in the trilogy itself. They want to know how characters came into being, to have more information about the human/dæmon relationship and to understand more fully the nature of Dust. Pullman himself has answered to this desire for more knowledge with the publication of a sequel to the trilogy, *Lyra's Oxford* (2003), which narrates a short incident in Lyra's life a couple of years after the end of *The Amber Spyglass*. Its inclusion of a fold-out map of Lyra's Oxford, a postcard sent by Mary Malone and an advert for a cruise to The Levant add to the impression that beyond the limits of the worlds written about in *His Dark Materials* and *Lyra's Oxford*, there are many back stories and many further ways of engaging with those worlds. The preface to *Lyra's Oxford* adds to this impression: 'This book contains a story and several other things. The other things might be connected with the story, or they might not; they might be connected to stories that haven't appeared yet. It's not easy to tell' (LO vi).

The preface also mentions stories that 'haven't appeared yet'. This tantalising phrase could well be referring to a projected companion volume to the trilogy, *The Book of Dust*, whose publication date has yet to be confirmed at the time of writing this critical guide. Beyond Pullman's own ongoing creation of his worlds, however, keen readers of the trilogy extend the limits of Pullman's fictional creation through the writing of fan fiction, which is readily available for others to read through a number of fan websites (*See* chapter 4 and the bibliography for further details). There is a well-established online role-playing game (RPG) based on the characters and worlds of *His Dark Materials*. The novels have been adapted for appearance at the National Theatre, and Nicholas Wright's play script has been published. The National Theatre programme included a pull-out history of the alethiometer and instructions on how it should be read. In the future, film versions of the trilogy are promised.

All of these elements would suggest that the boundaries of the fictional worlds created by Pullman in *His Dark Materials* are expandable and that the nature of the worlds within them is still in the process of being created. Furthermore, this ongoing creative engagement with the worlds of *His Dark Materials* signals that knowledge and ownership of them have passed from their initial creator, Philip Pullman, to a much wider sphere of producers, directors, writers, illustrators, game players and readers.

The gynaecological question posed by the audience member at the National Theatre is akin to that satirised by L C Knights in his 1933 essay 'How Many Children Had Lady Macbeth?' (Knights 1945). Knights used this question to poke fun at the tendency of early twentieth-century Shakespearean critics, notably A C Bradley in his book *Shakespearean Tragedy* (1904), to *See* the plays as narrating a portion of a life that somehow had an existence outside the text itself. In his notes to the essays on Macbeth, Bradley has sections entitled 'When Was the Murder of Duncan First Plotted?' and 'Did Lady Macbeth Really Faint?' Yet to this day readers and critics remain fascinated by the elements of a narrative that texts themselves do not fully explain, or leave as insoluble puzzles. We want to know what happened before the beginning of the play (what was the protagonist like as a child?) or after the final page of the novel (did they really live happily ever after?). The recent success of John Sutherland's playful series of books (including *Is Heathcliff a*

Murderer? Great Puzzles in Nineteenth-Century Fiction [1996] and *Can Jane Eyre Be Happy? More Puzzles in Classic Fiction* [1997]) indicates our desire to understand literary narratives fully and our wish to resolve unanswered questions in their texts. The question put by Pullman's interlocutor at the National Theatre is symptomatic of this curiosity, one which is understandably prompted by Pullman's prodigious literary imagination. In the creation of *His Dark Materials*, Pullman is in the business of summoning into being believable, rounded worlds with a clear internal logic which is moral, philosophical, political and narratological. It is precisely this aspect of Pullman's work that calls forth such questions. The teeming worlds of *His Dark Materials* invite encyclopaedic readings: there is already an unofficial companion guide to the worlds of the trilogy, which summarises characters, locations, objects and themes through an alphabetical listing (Parkin and Jones 2005). When Nicholas Wright was preparing the script for the stage version of *His Dark Materials*, he mentions how a friend put together an index of characters, settings and scenes which was invaluable in reducing down the one thousand, three hundred pages of novel into a six-hour script (Butler 2003: 41). Much work has already been done to chart Pullman's terrain, and thought has been put to his character generation. Yet between the lists, indices, unfolding maps and worlds of *His Dark Materials* and its associated creations remain unanswered questions as well as gaps, silences and some surprising paradoxes. It is the aim of this current book to explore both the knowable and the unknowable elements of the worlds of *His Dark Materials*. In so doing, it is both a guide to the worlds of *His Dark Materials* and a critical assessment of them. The remainder of this introduction offers an overview of Pullman's achievement and success, introduces the major themes of *His Dark Materials* and places them in context, and ends with a description of the structure of this book.

The Story of Pullman's Success

Philip Pullman published his first book—a novel for adults—in 1972. By the year 2000, with the publication of *The Amber Spyglass*, the final volume in the *His Dark Materials* trilogy, he had become an internationally acclaimed writer, with his story of Lyra and Will gaining critical accolades, literary prizes and substantial sales in the bookshops. This was not, however, a story of instant success. Almost thirty years and more than twenty other books stood between that first publication and *The Amber Spyglass*. The story of Pullman's rise to fame, therefore, is not one of instant acclaim but rather one of a much slower development and a more gradual realisation and public recognition of his talents. Nonetheless, Pullman had already received a certain level of recognition for his publications prior to *His Dark Materials*, at least in the children's book world. *The Firework-Maker's Daughter* (1995) won the Smarties Prize Gold Award, and his book of the following year, *Clockwork: Or All Wound Up* (1996), won the Smarties Prize Silver Award. It is undeniable, though, that it was the three *His Dark Materials* books that sealed Pullman's success as a writer and expanded his audience beyond children and those involved in the children's book world.

In numerous interviews, Pullman mentions the initial discussion of his plans for the trilogy that would make his name with his publisher, David Fickling. The inspiration had been one of Pullman's A-level set texts (the examinations taken by English schoolchildren at the age of eighteen): John Milton's epic poem *Paradise Lost* (1667). Pullman describes his aim in writing the trilogy as '"*Paradise Lost* for teenagers in three volumes"', and although this intent may initially have been half in jest, the ambition began to be realised through the publication of the successive volumes of the trilogy (Parsons and Nicholson 1999: 126). Indeed, the trilogy went on to achieve remarkable international success, acquiring fame and in some circles infamy for its author, as this book later explores. Yet *Northern Lights*, the first volume in the trilogy, was not an overnight hit upon publication in 1995; rather, as is more typical in the world of children's books, the popularity of the series developed steadily over the months and years with the publication of *The Subtle Knife* in 1997 and *The Amber Spyglass* in 2000. Nonetheless, *Northern Lights* itself was acclaimed, and reviews indicated a mounting sense of expectation for the rest of the trilogy. The *Scotsman*, in a roundup of children's books, said *Northern Lights* was 'one of those books which one can hardly bear to close; an astonishingly gripping and convincing story for readers aged 11 years upwards' (Fraser 1995). Pullman's fellow children's writer Nina Bawden reviewed *Northern Lights* in the London *Evening Standard* in an article presciently entitled 'It's Not Just Kids' Stuff'. In this article, she said the book 'should . . . please all ages—well, from eight to 80'. She went on to describe the first in the trilogy as 'an impressively realised fantasy set in a solid and convincing universe', which leaves its readers 'dangling in terror at the end', making it 'hard to wait' for the sequel (Bawden 1995). With the award of two major prizes for children's books—the *Guardian* Children's Fiction Award and the Carnegie Medal—it was clear that Pullman had achieved recognition as a leading writer of children's fiction.

Joanna Carey, commenting on her newspaper's award to Pullman, wrote in the *Guardian* that the writer 'enjoys the freedom . . . as a children's author to move at will from historical novels to comic stories, fairytales to contemporary thrillers—he has written successfully in all fields—but those books seem like literary foothills before the craggy heights of *His Dark Materials*' (Carey 1996). Nevertheless, commentary on *Northern Lights* in the UK was for the most part limited to the small sections of the books pages devoted to children's books. In the US, however, *Northern Lights* was published and promoted as both a children's *and* an adults' book, a marketing strategy which gratified Pullman. In an interview in the *Guardian*, he commented that 'the structure of reviewing and distribution [in the UK] makes it difficult for adults to be aware of books that may appeal beyond the children's/young adult market', and that the US decision to sell to both the adults' and children's markets was a shrewd one (Carey 1996).

The publication of *The Golden Compass* (the title under which *Northern Lights* was published in the US) was greeted with prominent and largely enthusiastic reviews in major American newspapers, and the book's 'crossover' status was documented in numerous articles, including one by Julie Boehning (1996). In the emotional range of Pullman's creation of Lyra, Michael Dirda in the *Washington*

Post drew comparisons to earlier great characters of children's literature who are also much loved by adults: 'Alice or Dorothy, Wart or Bilbo' (he is referring to characters from books and series by Lewis Carroll, L Frank Baum, T H White and J R R Tolkien). Dirda concluded his review with the comment that if the sequel to *The Golden Compass* is as good, 'we'll be two thirds of the way to the completion of a modern fantasy classic' (Dirda 1996). In the *New York Times*, *The Golden Compass* was again compared to classics of children's literature, although in a more measured way: '"The Golden Compass" doesn't quite achieve the majestic poetry of Tolkien's powerful sagas, or the sinewy gravity of Ursula K Le Guin's "Wizard of Earthsea," or the wit of Russell Hoban's fable "The Mouse and his Child." But it is still very grand indeed' (Langton 1996).

When Pullman was short-listed for the Carnegie Medal for *Northern Lights* in 1996, comparisons to earlier classics were drawn once again. However, Christina Hardyment, writing in the UK *Independent*, displayed anxiety about the extent to which Pullman's work would be noticed by those outside of the children's book world:

> Rarely if ever have children been offered such a rich casket of wonders. *Northern Lights* stands up to comparison with both *The Once and Future King*, T H White's tribute to Malory's *Morte d'Arthur*, and Tolkien's Norse-derived *Lord of the Rings*. It is, moreover, as well-suited to an intelligent eight-year-old as to an 18-year-old . . . but if Pullman wins the Carnegie, a great many people will ignore the book because they will think of it as 'just a children's book'. (Hardyment 1996)

Northern Lights did indeed go on to win the Carnegie. In his acceptance speech, Pullman courted controversy on the very subject of the divide between children's and adults' books. He premised his speech on the theme of storytelling and made the provocative claim that 'there are some themes, some subjects, too large for adult fiction; they can only be dealt with adequately in a children's book' (Pullman 1996b). He went on to lambast—without specifically naming—a recent 'highly praised adult novel' he was 'about to stop reading'. The speech decried the tendency of 'adult literary fiction' to prioritise style over story. Children's authors, on the other hand,

> know how important stories are, and they know, too, that if you start telling a story you've got to carry on till you get to the end . . . In a book for children you can't put the plot on hold while you cut artistic capers for the amusement of your sophisticated readers, because, thank God, your readers are not sophisticated. They've got more important things in mind than your dazzling skill with wordplay. They want to know what happens next. (Pullman 1996b)

Pullman's celebration of the power of story and of the children's writers who create it caused an explosion of media comment. The novelist and critic Malcolm Bradbury defended Britain's contemporary adult writers against Pullman's attack in the pages of the *Evening Standard* (Bradbury 1996). In a call to arms for children's literature, an editorial in the *Independent* backed Pullman, saying, 'Such words come like rain after drought for everyone who has struggled in vain with the "literary" writers of our age' (*Independent* 1996).

The point of Pullman's speech was perhaps not so much to decry contemporary adult writers as to promote the wealth of writing for children—and indeed of genre writing—overlooked and even ghettoised by the literary establishment. Despite the classic status of much writing for children, including Lewis Carroll's *Alice* books (1865–71), C S Lewis's *The Chronicles of Narnia* (1950–56) and J R R Tolkien's *The Hobbit* (1937) and *The Lord of the Rings* series (1954–55), children's literature occupies a secondary place in the literary hierarchy. As David Lister reported in the *Independent*, Pullman's win 'highlights the problem many British authors feel, of books being pigeonholed into the children's market, and then being ignored by adults' (Lister 1996).

The award of the Carnegie medal, and the controversy Pullman's speech provoked, did much to extend the knowledge of Pullman to adult readers. Indeed, it is arguably Pullman's canny media sensibility that granted his book this extended reach and thrust the issue of children's writers and their lack of visibility into a spotlight which was further strengthened by a growing interest in children's literature with the publication of J K Rowling's phenomenally successful *Harry Potter* series (1997–). This interest is discussed further in chapter 6 of this book.

Through the reviews of *Northern Lights*, the award of two high-profile children's prizes and Pullman's capacity to attract media attention in his public utterances, a growing sense of expectation was thus created for the remaining two novels in the trilogy. This expectation would eventually be fulfilled and, indeed, surpassed by the reception of *The Subtle Knife* in 1997 and *The Amber Spyglass* in 2000.

Critics on both sides of the Atlantic were overwhelmingly positive in their reception of the trilogy and the individual books within it. In a review of *The Subtle Knife*, Terence Blacker in the UK *Mail on Sunday* referred to *Northern Lights* as 'mesmerising, spectacular' and went on to describe the second novel as 'a genuine masterpiece of intelligent, imaginative storytelling, a multi-layered quest and adventure story' (Blacker 1997). Peter Kemp in the UK *Sunday Times* wrote of *The Subtle Knife* that 'marvels and monsters, tragedies and triumphs are unrolled with a lavishness typical of this prodigiously gifted author' (Kemp 1997). For Claire Dederer, writing in the US *Newsday*, *Northern Lights* was 'a ripping yarn with diabolical cleverness and angelic clarity', while *The Amber Spyglass* 'brilliantly completes the preceding books and casts a reflected glory upon them' (Dederer 2000). Michael Dirda, one of Pullman's biggest advocates in the US, wrote in his review of *The Amber Spyglass* in the *Washington Post* that 'Pullman's sheer storytelling power [is] sinfully irresistible . . . a novel of electrifying power and splendor, deserving celebration, as violent as a fairy tale and as shocking as art must be' (Dirda 2000).

As the reviews here quoted indicate, Pullman's trilogy began to be marked out for classic status from the beginning. Dirda, who prophesied the completion of a 'modern fantasy classic' in 1995, felt his predictions to have been justified by the publication of *The Subtle Knife*. He affirmed that *Northern Lights* 'can be mentioned in the same breath as such classics as Madeleine L'Engle's *A Wrinkle in Time*, Philippa Pearce's *Tom's Midnight Garden*, and Alan Garner's *The Owl Service*' and concluded that 'actually, Pullman's book is more breathtakingly, all-stops-out thrilling than any of them' and that its sequel is 'just as quick-moving and unputdownable as its predecessor' (Dirda 1997). The *New York Times* recommended that the reader 'put Philip Pullman on the shelf with Ursula K Le Guin, Susan Cooper, Lloyd Alexander, at least until we get to *See* Volume 3' (Maguire 1998). Sarah Johnson, in *The Times* (UK), believed that the trilogy 'promises to live alongside the works of Tolkien and C S Lewis as an icon of imaginative writing for children. It's a claim made for many books but it is to be taken seriously in Philip Pullman's case, because of the depth of his vision' (Johnson 1997).

By the time of the publication of *The Amber Spyglass*, then, the pattern was set for the nomination of the trilogy for a place in posterity. Matt Berman, writing in the New Orleans *Times-Picayune*, said that *The Amber Spyglass* 'completes the finest and most original fantasy series since The Lord of the Rings' (Berman 2000). Boyd Tonkin in the UK *Independent* also referred to Tolkien and C S Lewis in his assessment of *His Dark Materials*, declaring, 'These books deserve a place alongside . . . The Lord of the Rings and . . . The Chronicles of Narnia as classic attempts to restore debate about the meaning of life to a culture that often drowns in trivia' (Tonkin 2002a). Andrew Marr in the UK *Daily Telegraph* judged the trilogy to be 'one of the greatest adventure stories I've ever read', leading to his assertion that it 'will be bought, and pulled, dog-eared from family bookshelves, in 100 years' time' (Marr 2002). Opinions about the trilogy's potential for being read years into the future are summed up by Carla Mckay in the UK *Daily Mail*: 'It tells an incredible story—one that will harness the imaginations of children and adults now and in future generations' (Mckay 2000).

The reception of the trilogy did also include criticism—of plotting, characterisation, and subject matter, particularly with regard to Pullman's treatment of religion and the death of god. These critiques are addressed later in this book. Nonetheless, amid the mass of positive commentary on the individual books and on the trilogy as a whole, the negative voices were meagre. The critical consensus on Pullman in the media is that *His Dark Materials* indicates the presence of a consummate storyteller whose work has the potential to join the greats of children's writing and fantasy literature.

Like the first volume in the trilogy, the concluding book also received recognition in the form of literary awards. When, for the first time in 2000, a long-list of that year's Booker Prize for Fiction was officially published, *The Amber Spyglass* was on the list. Although it did not proceed any further in the judging process, it was notable that a novel ostensibly published as a children's book in the UK was taken sufficiently seriously to be at least in the running for Britain's highest profile literary award, which had previously been granted to writers including Salman Rushdie, J M Coetzee, Pat Barker and Ian McEwan.

This preliminary incursion onto adult prize lists would soon be repeated in more spectacular fashion with the Whitbread Awards. These prizes are composed of several category awards (for best novel, poetry collection, biography, first novel and children's book). The winners of each category are then judged against each other for the title of the Whitbread Book of the Year. *The Amber Spyglass* was judged to be the 2001 Whitbread Children's Book of the Year by its category panel. It then went on to win the overall prize, an unprecedented act in the face of competition from work written for adults. The award of the Whitbread Book of the Year to Pullman cemented his reputation as a writer with an appeal to children *and* to adults, but also achieved what Pullman has long claimed that writing for children is capable of—appealing to a multi-generational audience through storytelling virtuosity and the urgency of its themes. For any doubters, the Whitbread Award was a sign that Pullman—and children's literature more generally—should be taken seriously. When Pullman was granted the Eleanor Farjeon Award at the end of 2002, an honour given not for a particular book but to an individual for his or her distinguished contribution to the world of children's literature, it was very suitably in recognition of his achievement in altering adult perceptions of children's books. In 2005, Pullman received similar recognition on an international stage, in the shape of the Astrid Lindgren Memorial Award, which has as its aim strengthening and increasing interest in children's and youth literature around the world.

In terms of the global reach of *His Dark Materials*, the trilogy has now been published throughout the world in English-language editions and also has been translated into numerous languages and appeared in foreign-language editions in countries ranging from Brazil to Croatia, Iceland to Japan. The trilogy also has been adapted into a variety of formats. As well as an audio version of the book, a BBC Radio dramatisation was aired in January 2003. The National Theatre in London staged a sell-out stage version of *His Dark Materials*, which ran over two seasons in 2003–4 and 2004–5. The trilogy was adapted for the stage by Nicholas Wright (Wright 2003) and was directed by Nicholas Hytner. The staging of the trilogy was documented in Robert Butler's book *The Art of Darkness* (2003). Further adaptations of the trilogy are planned in the medium of film by New Line, the production company which made the very successful *Lord of the Rings* adaptations in the 2000s, buying the rights. All of these adaptations, and their implications for the interpretation of the worlds of *His Dark Materials*, are explored in more detail in chapter 7.

Philip Pullman's *His Dark Materials*, then, has been a phenomenal success in the literary marketplace, in both critical and commercial terms. Its success has also extended beyond the world of books to embrace other media forms. But what are the prevailing themes of the trilogy, and what are the elements of the individual books that have contributed to this recognition of Pullman's work?

An adventure story set in multiple worlds with two young protagonists, *His Dark Materials* carries weighty themes. The passage from innocence to experience is central to the narrative, as is the importance of growing up and human sexuality. An anti-religious sentiment prevails throughout the three books. Issues of good and evil are addressed, as are questions of faith and morality. Predestination and free will are also crucial to the story, and as such, Pullman directly addresses the text that inspired the trilogy, Milton's *Paradise Lost*. The ongoing critical debate surrounding *Paradise Lost*—whether it succeeds in its stated aim in Book One to 'justify the ways of God to men' or rather depicts God and Christianity as essentially cruel, free will as a trap for humankind and the human desire for knowledge as wrong—becomes a key theme in *His Dark Materials* (Milton 2000: 4). Yet Pullman's rewriting of the Bible and of *Paradise Lost* is consciously anti-God and pro-temptation, with the Fall as 'completely essential . . . the best thing, the most important thing that ever happened to us' (Parsons and Nicholson 1999: 119). William Blake, another writer whom Pullman specifically acknowledges in his creation of the trilogy, famously commented of *Paradise Lost* in his *The Marriage of Heaven and Hell* (1790) that 'the reason Milton wrote in fetters when he wrote of angels and God, and at liberty when of devils and Hell, is because he was a true poet, and of the Devil's party without knowing it' (Blake 1998: 75). In his inversion of the morality of the Fall, and also in his exploration of the rich imaginative possibilities afforded by devils, Hell, and the multiple worlds travelled through by Satan and the angels in *Paradise Lost*, Pullman is both a profoundly intertextual writer, as chapter 5 explores, and a provocative one. As Andrew Marr put it in the *Daily Telegraph*, 'Pullman does for atheism what C S Lewis did for God' (Marr 2002). Pullman has created a new, anti-religious myth with *His Dark Materials*. It should come as no surprise, then, that the trilogy has provoked much controversy.

Pullman is a writer who is very interested in science and in a scientific approach to understanding the world, which has been affirmed by the publication of Mary and John Gribbin's book *The Science of Philip Pullman's* His Dark Materials, to which Pullman contributed the introduction. This book explores the scientific concepts the trilogy has drawn upon, including quantum physics and string theory, consciousness and dark matter. In creating 'Dust' Pullman develops an idea of consciousness that is connected to human evolution and the development of the human body during the course of adolescence, revisiting and rewriting philosophical ideas of the split between the material body and the soul. There is also an underlying theme of environmentalism in *His Dark Materials*, one which has largely been undervalued by the critics of the trilogy thus far, and which this present volume explores in more detail in chapter 3.

The weighty themes addressed by the trilogy might seem to suggest that *His Dark Materials* would be a ponderous read, stuffed as it is with theological debate and intellectual engagement with previous literary texts. Yet Pullman weaves his big themes into the trilogy by means of a fast-paced plot that pulls the reader breathlessly through multiple worlds at the heels of his child protagonists, Lyra and Will. For before and beyond the weighty themes of *His Dark Materials* is a compelling adventure story, and one which, moreover, has storytelling as a central theme, as chapter 4 in this book discusses.

Philip Pullman, Master Storyteller engages with *His Dark Materials* over the ensuing chapters in a number of different ways. The next chapter spends some time thinking about Philip Pullman himself—his background, his upbringing and his route to writing the *His Dark Materials* trilogy—and is thus biographical in orientation. It is then followed by a series of chapters that examines different facets of the trilogy, from a lengthy description of *His Dark Materials'* major characters and plots in chapter 2, 'Stories of Multiple Worlds', via chapter 3, entitled 'Politics and Morality', which concentrates on the various themes of the stories, including those of religion, science and belief, gender, innocence and experience, and environmentalism. In chapter 4, 'Telling Stories', the central theme of storytelling is assessed for the way it functions as a form of morality. Chapter 5 examines the intertextual nature of Pullman's writing in the trilogy, whereas chapter 6 takes up the question, what type of story is *His Dark Materials*? and considers aspects of genre in the trilogy. This includes a discussion of the trilogy as 'crossover' writing, for audiences of both children and adults.

This current critical volume concentrates on *His Dark Materials*, but Pullman's other writing is not neglected. Chapter 7 provides a consideration of other work by Pullman, including his early adult novels, the range of other children's writing he has published, his further creative interventions in the worlds of *His Dark Materials*, and adaptations of those worlds for other media. Finally, this book provides a collected bibliography of materials by and about Pullman, including major Internet resources.

≪◎ 1 ◎≫

Pullman the Man

'EVERYTHING ABOUT PULLMAN'S CHILDHOOD contributed to the making of a master storyteller,' an *Observer* profile of the writer has stated (McCrum 2002). On the other hand, Parkin and Jones warn against biographical readings of Pullman's writing, claiming that these can stray 'too far into the territory of mythologizing or pop psychology' (Parkin and Jones 2005: 8). This chapter provides a biographical account of Pullman's life, one which gives details of his childhood as well as his later life. It also portrays in detail Pullman's development as a writer and discusses the way in which the success of the *His Dark Materials* trilogy has allowed Pullman to occupy a public position from which he has made a number of statements about a variety of issues going beyond literature to education, religion, science and morality. In so doing, the chapter inevitably demonstrates some of the similarities between Pullman's own life and that of his principal characters in *His Dark Materials*, but—both to avoid the pop psychology trap and to assess more properly his literary development—concentrates on his path to writing which has culminated in the trilogy. Pullman has provided much useful information on his coming-to-writing in interviews and articles and particularly through an extended autobiographical piece entitled 'I Have a Feeling All This Belongs to Me', which is reproduced on his website.

Philip Pullman was born on 19 October 1946 in Norwich, England, to Alfred Outram Pullman and Audrey Evelyn Pullman (née Merrifield). His father was a fighter pilot in the RAF (Royal Air Force), and the Pullman family, including Philip and his younger brother, Francis, followed him in his career to Southern Rhodesia (now Zimbabwe). During the family's stationing in Africa, there occurred the event that has led to many of the mythologizing accounts of Pullman's upbringing: the death of his father. Pullman's father died in action at the age of thirty-eight while flying a sortie against the Mau Mau in Kenya. Alfred Pullman was decorated for his 'gallantry in operations' with the posthumous award of the Distinguished Flying Cross (Tucker 2003: 3–4). His widow and children were received by the Queen at Buckingham Palace in 1954, when Philip was just seven years old.

Yet despite the high-level honour bestowed on Pullman's father, his death retained an air of mystery. Nicholas Tucker, who provides an account of this episode in *Darkness Visible*, reports, 'Pullman still feels certain that there was something not right about the reasons given for his father's fatal accident', and many years later he in fact discovered that his parents were in the process of divorcing at the time of his father's death (Tucker 2003: 5, 3). In 'I Have a Feeling All This Belongs to Me', Pullman has written in some detail about this mystery:

> It was only when I was a grown man that I found out more of the truth about my father, and I don't suppose I shall ever know the whole of it. He hadn't been shot down in battle; he had been drinking, and he'd crashed while practising for an air display. That was the first thing I found out, and the second was even more of a shock: I learned that it was generally known among his friends that he'd crashed his plane on purpose. He'd committed suicide. That had been covered up so that he could be awarded the medal and so that my mother could receive a widow's pension. Apparently he had been in all sorts of trouble: he'd borrowed money without being able to repay it, his affairs with other women were beginning to get

out of control, and he had had to agree to a separation from my mother. (www.philip-pullman.com: a)

Tucker mentions that even though Pullman was not aware of these circumstances at the time, the events of his early childhood would eventually lead to a preoccupation in his writing with dead or missing fathers (Tucker 2003: 5). This is a key element of Pullman's history upon which autobiographical readings of both *His Dark Materials* and earlier books by numerous critics of Pullman's writing have been based. Tucker, for example, writes that 'it is not surprising that Pullman often creates young characters in his fiction who have problems with their parents, sometimes stretching far back into the past' (Tucker 2003: 5). In another example, an interview with Pullman in the *Sunday Express* came to the same conclusion, that 'lost or orphaned children play a significant role in his books' (Stanistreet 2002). Certainly, both of the young protagonists of *His Dark Materials* are in an orphaned or near-orphaned state. At the beginning of the trilogy, Lyra thinks she is an orphan, and even when it becomes apparent that both of her parents are alive, her relationship with Lord Asriel and Mrs Coulter is such that she still functions without parental care and protection. Will's father is missing, presumed dead, and his mother suffers psychological problems which mean that Will becomes her carer. For much of the time, he is in charge of the household.

The trope of the orphaned child or the child with absent parents is, however, a recurrent one throughout children's literature: Frances Hodgson Burnett's Mary in *The Secret Garden* (1911) and Roald Dahl's James in *James and the Giant Peach* (1967) are only two classic examples, while Harry Potter is a more recent orphan (*See* Kimball 1999). As Parkin and Jones comment, 'It's almost a necessary part of the story, as it allows the young heroes and heroines to have adventures' (Parkin and Jones 2005: 7). It is this aspect that leads Parkin and Jones to warn against too-narrowly conceived biographical readings, which would deny, or at least put into the background, the substantial influences of the traditions of children's literature on Pullman's writing.

Nonetheless, Pullman has written at some length about the impact that the death of his father had upon himself and his literary development, and so to introduce biographical readings into the analysis of that development is a legitimate critical activity. It is perhaps fair to say, though, that it was not so much Pullman's father's death that made the strongest impression upon the boy, but rather the life that he and his family then led as a result of that death. As Pullman himself narrates, the death of his father actually occurred when he, his mother and his brother were in England, staying with their grandparents in Norfolk. Pullman writes, 'I suppose that my brother and I cried, though I didn't really feel sad. The fact was that we hadn't seen my father for a long time, and apart from the glamour that surrounded him, he was a figure who hadn't played much part in our lives' (www.philip-pullman.com: a). In an interview in the *Independent*, Pullman expands on his feelings towards his father's death: '"I knew him so little and saw him so seldom that I didn't feel a connection. I felt surprise more than anything, and then I was self-aggrandising: 'Hey, look at me, I'm half an orphan!'"' (Ross 2002).

How quickly in reality Pullman made this psychological transition is unclear, although in Pullman's depiction of himself, he knowingly sets up the 'self-aggrandising' child as the precursor to the writer, the storyteller who has perhaps not a little in common with the Lyra of *His Dark Materials* who rejoices in telling sometimes fictional stories about her background. In terms of the impact on Pullman's writing career, rather than the psychological effect on him as an individual, it is this self-narration that is most interesting, alongside his perception of the lives of his parents. To the young Pullman, these lives were intensely glamorous. He recalls that

> there were two kinds of glamour: my mother's, which consisted of a scent called Blue Grass by Elizabeth Arden, and my father's, which was more complicated. There were cigarettes in it, and beer, and leather armchairs. The smell of my father's glamour was very strong in the Club, which we children were sometimes allowed in, but not to run around. (www.philip-pullman.com: a)

After the death of his father, his mother's life as a working woman in London had a similar allure, which he and his brother only occasionally witnessed:

> She had lots of friends, and they were all young and pretty or handsome; the women wore hats and gloves to go to work, their dresses were long and flowery, and the men drove sports cars and smoked pipes, and there was always laughter, and the sun shone every day. (www.philip-pullman.com: a)

The memory of his parents is based strongly on the senses, and particularly on sight and smell and touch. Without doubt, these sensual memories of glamorous parents, their friends and environments, would eventually ignite his imagination in the creation of *His Dark Materials'* Lord Asriel and Mrs Coulter. His father is surrounded by a clubbish male aura reminiscent of *His Dark Materials'* Retiring Room at Jordan College. His mother, like Mrs Coulter, has a retinue of chic London friends and the well-dressed mystique of an attractive woman at the centre of attention of a smart London set. It is perhaps these evocative personal memories of people, rather than the fate of his father, that Pullman drew upon in the creation of characters and their environments in *His Dark Materials*.

Both before and after his father's death, much of Pullman's childhood was spent with his maternal grandparents. His grandfather was the vicar in Drayton, a small Norfolk village, where he lived in the rectory with his wife and his wife's sister. For Pullman and his family, 'Grandpa [was] the centre of the world. There was no one stronger than he was, or wiser, or kinder' (www.philip-pullman.com: a). Pullman's grandfather was a formative figure in the young boy's life. His profession meant that Pullman attended church regularly and that from early childhood he was surrounded by biblical language and stories. Pullman would eventually turn away from God and his religious upbringing, but this grounding in Christianity meant that he had a theological background to draw upon in the creation of *His Dark Materials*. Of this religious upbringing and its relationship to his subsequent lack of belief, Pullman comments,

'"Although I call myself an atheist, I am a Church of England atheist, and a 1662 Book of Common Prayer atheist, because that's the tradition I was brought up in and I cannot escape those early influences"' (Miller 2005/2006). Moreover, Pullman's grandfather had a talent that undoubtedly inspired the young Pullman: 'He told stories . . .'; he was a 'wonderful storyteller' (www.philip-pullman.com: a; Pullman 1999b: 181).

Eventually, however, Pullman's mother remarried another RAF man, and so the family once more left England for Australia via a long sea voyage. Pullman's own description of his travel to, and time spent in, Australia marks this period as one of imagination and wonder, from the ever-changing vistas of the ocean journey itself to the excitement on arrival of discovering the Australian and American media to which he then had access. The young Pullman was already a keen reader, but during the years he was in Australia, he was introduced to comic books, becoming an avid fan of Superman, Superboy, Captain America and Batman. His interest in comics and graphic novels has continued into his adult life, manifested both in his own creative work, including *Spring-Heeled Jack* (1989a), a book in which text and image unite to narrate the story, and in critical essays on the use of pictures in storytelling (Pullman 1989b; 1998b). In an interview with *The Times*, Pullman talked about the creative impulse his youthful consumption of comics provoked in him:

> Even at this early age, Pullman took an unusually analytical approach to reading. 'I don't know what other children like about those comics—maybe they like pretending to be Superman or Batman, but what I enjoyed most was the sense of the storyteller, of this eye that zoomed in and chose this bit of action and then moved out to a panoramic picture of Metropolis late at night. I loved that sense of a directing, story-telling consciousness.' (Dickson 2001)

The development of the storytelling consciousness came early to Pullman and, as he describes it, with a strong sense of awareness of his preferences: not to '*be* Batman, but write about him', as he has put it elsewhere (www.philip-pullman.com: a). Australian radio also inspired Pullman to creativity. As well as the further adventures of comic-book heroes in a different medium, home-grown stories were transmitted over the airwaves: Clancy of the Outback and a story featuring a kangaroo. The radio was a fertile resource in the coming-to-being of Pullman's 'story-telling consciousness':

> I shared a bedroom with my brother then, and every night when the lights went out I used to tell him a story that I made up as I went along. I don't know whether he enjoyed it, or whether he even listened, but it wasn't for his benefit; it was for mine. I remember vividly the sense of diving into the dark as I began the story, with no idea at all what was going to hap-pen or whether the story would 'come out' as I called it, by which I mean make sense or come to a neat end. I remember the exhilaration of the risk: Would I find something to say? Would I dry up? And I remember the thrill, the bliss, when, a minute ahead of getting there, I saw a twist I could give to the end, a clever way of bringing back that character who'd come into it earlier and vanished inconclusively, a neat phrase to tie it all up with. (www.philip-pullman.com: a)

This is what Pullman has elsewhere termed the 'vertiginous delight of storytelling' and what he reflexively draws fictional pictures of repeatedly in his creative work (Pullman 1999b: 187). *His Dark Materials'* Lyra is obviously one example and Fritz the story-teller in *Clockwork* is another. Oral storytelling, then, is where Pullman began on his route to *His Dark Materials*, and it would again play an important role at a later stage of his adult life as a schoolteacher.

In 1957, Pullman moved back from Australia to the UK, initially to London, but later to North Wales when his stepfather got a job as a civil aviator there. Life in the Welsh village of Llanbedr was good: children were given the freedom to roam the countryside without being protected or impeded by adults, and Pullman and his friends inhabited an adventurous world now largely lost to British children of today. One of Pullman's favourite classic writers for children, Arthur Ransome, wrote of this world in his *Swallows and Amazons* series (1930–47). The precept of childhood adventure unfettered by adult intervention, and the consequent emphasis on the early learning of responsibility, is a theme that Pullman would eventually carry through to his characters in *His Dark Materials*.

It was also in Wales that Pullman encountered a schoolteacher who would foster his love of literature and inspire his early writing. Pullman attended Ysgol Ardudwy, a secondary school in Harlech. His English teacher there, a woman called Enid Jones, is credited in the acknowledgements at the end of *The Amber Spyglass* as 'the teacher who introduced me so long ago to *Paradise Lost*'. Pullman also wrote that it was to her that he owed 'the best that education can give, the notion that responsibility and delight can co-exist' (AS 550). He has kept in close touch with his teacher, sending her copies of his books and featuring in a *Guardian* article with her about their relationship and the importance and value of education (Moore 1996).

Through Jones, Pullman was introduced to some of the canonical writers of English literature. He also began writing his own poetry. Influenced particularly by Dylan Thomas and the Metaphysical poets, Pullman nominates this poetry-writing period as formative, even though he now concentrates on prose. 'Rhythm is profoundly important,' he wrote, and in his eyes it is through the formal discipline of poetic structure that his 'command of prose' developed (Pullman 1999b: 181–82). Throughout his years at university and beyond, he continued to write poetry and learnt much about the sound and rhythm of language that he would use in his prose writing.

The obvious degree for Pullman to study at university was English, although he has mentioned his later regret that he did not have the opportunity to go to art school (Carey 1996). He won a scholarship to study at Oxford and was an undergraduate at Exeter College from 1965 to 1968. From all accounts, his education at Oxford was a disappointment after the inspiration offered by Enid

Jones in North Wales. He found the tutorial system limiting and at the end of his three years discovered that he actually knew very little about the practicalities of the creation of literature, which was, by that time, what he had decided he wanted to do. Nonetheless, Oxford still offered rich imaginative possibilities to Pullman. In an article about the influence of the city's architecture upon *His Dark Materials*, the genesis of Lyra's daredevil exploits becomes evident, as does the name of one of the central characters in Pullman's *Sally Lockhart* series of books, Jim:

> When she's not exploring underground, Lyra spends a good deal of time on the college roof, spitting plum-stones on the heads of passing scholars or hooting like an owl outside a window where a tutorial is going on. That, too, is based on something I remember from Exeter. In my second year I occupied the rooms at the top of staircase 8, next to the lodge tower, and a friend, Jim Taylor, discovered that you could get out of the window and crawl along a very useful gutter behind the parapet. From there you could climb in through another window further along. I gave Lyra a better head for heights than I have, but I did the gutter crawl a number of times, usually when there was a party on the next staircase. (Pullman 2002a: 28)

On the conclusion of his studies, Pullman received a third-class honours degree, which is not a high accolade. But on the morning following his final examination for the course, he had resolved to begin writing a novel, and so he did.

Eventually, Pullman's literary ambition would lead to his being able to work full-time as a writer. But this would not happen for more than two decades, and after he had turned to writing for children. Initially, Pullman's aim was to write for adults, and in the 1970s, he did in fact publish two novels for an older audience. For the first, he won a £2,500 prize and the right to be published by NEL (New English Library). Pullman now claims that this, his first novel, *The Haunted Storm* (1972), was 'a terrible piece of rubbish', and his youthful efforts clearly embarrass him (Pullman 1999b: 182). Indeed, the book, which is a weird narrative concerning murder and incest, featuring among its characters a Gnostic cleric and a twenty-three-year-old ridden by existential angst, would hardly recommend itself to a child fan of the *His Dark Materials* trilogy. Its portrayal of perverted sexuality is a very adult topic, but nonetheless its quest for religious knowledge is a theme also central to *Northern Lights, The Subtle Knife* and *The Amber Spyglass*.

Pullman's second novel was *Galatea* (1978), and although the book is now out of print, he clearly has more affection for this work than *The Haunted Storm*, saying publicly, 'I'm still proud of it' (www.philip-pullman.com: a). *Galatea* is a picaresque, magic realist tale, similar in structure and style to fantastical work of the same period, such as Angela Carter's *The Infernal Desire Machines of Doctor Hoffman* (1972). Pullman has said that it is a book 'I can't categorise, because it isn't really fantasy or science-fiction, but it certainly isn't realistic. Nobody else was sure about it either; most reviewers were puzzled or indifferent, though some found things to praise' (www.philip-pullman.com: a). Both of these novels are discussed in greater detail in the final chapter of this book.

While writing and publishing these adult novels, Pullman took on a variety of jobs: he moved to London and worked for a while in Moss Bros, a company that sells and hires men's formal wear. Later, he worked as a librarian. Influenced by his wife, Jude, whom he had married in 1970, however, he decided to train as a schoolteacher, and so he attended Weymouth College of Education. Once qualified, he then applied for and gained a teaching job in Oxford, and with his young family—he had a first son, Jamie, by this time and would later have a second son, Tom—moved back to his old university city.

Between 1973 and 1986 Pullman taught at a number of middle schools in Oxford, teaching children aged nine to thirteen. This was another highly formative period for him. At the time, the school curriculum was very open, allowing him to concentrate on teaching what he liked best and discovered he was best at: storytelling. He recounted Greek myths to his classes, with Homer's *The Iliad* and *The Odyssey* being particular favourites for his retellings. This freedom in the school curriculum was one he cherished, allowing his teaching to be 'passionate, if not formal', as Eccleshare put it (Eccleshare 2002a: 124). More than anything, Pullman sees his time as a school-teacher as one in which he refined his oral storytelling skills, in a tradition stretching all the way back to 'Homer and the bards' (Pullman 1999b: 183). Pullman refers to his storytelling at this time as a 'set of exercises . . .', like practising musical scales or studying perspective in the visual arts: 'the same stories, over and over, but not from the same words, always fresh, always speaking them—without a book or any props' (Pullman 1999b: 182–83).

He also began to write plays for his pupils to perform, which later became novels in their own right. The books *Count Karlstein* (1982), *The Ruby in the Smoke* (1985) and *The Firework-Maker's Daughter* (1995) were all initially conceived in this way. In writing for a dual audience for these plays—for the child performers and audience, and for their parents—he began to experiment with the incorporation of various levels of narration and meaning in his texts.

Pullman went on to publish a wide variety of books for children of different ages after his initial publication of *Count Karlstein*. Early among Pullman's publications are books which might be thought of as social realist in nature and aimed at an older, teenage audience: *The Broken Bridge* (1990) and *The White Mercedes* (1992; reissued under the title *The Butterfly Tattoo* in 1998). At the same time, however, Pullman was publishing a series of adventure stories set in Victorian London, the *Sally Lockhart Quartet* (as it would eventually be named): *The Ruby in the Smoke* (1985), *The Shadow in the Plate* (1987; later renamed *The Shadow in the North*), *The Tiger in the Well* (1991) and *The Tin Princess* (1994). Another version of *Count Karlstein* was published in 1991, in which the story is partly told through comic strip sections. A similar blend of visual and textual technique is used in *Spring-Heeled Jack* (1989), and illustrations are also important in *Clockwork: Or All Wound Up* (1996) and *I Was a Rat!* (1999). Pullman has also published a number of shorter books and retellings of traditional folk and fairy tales, including his versions of *The Wonderful Story of Aladdin and the Enchanted Lamp* (1993) and *Puss in Boots* (2000). These texts are examined in more detail in chapter 7.

Pullman began to be feted for his writing among the children's book world early in his career. *The Ruby in the Smoke*, only his second children's publication, was granted the Children's Book Award from the International Reading Association. *The Firework-Maker's Daughter* was given the Smarties Gold Award, and *Clockwork* a Smarties Silver Award. But it was with the publication of the three volumes of *His Dark Materials* that Pullman really began to achieve recognition. *Northern Lights*, the first volume, was granted the Carnegie Medal as well as a British Book Award for Children's Book of the Year. The final volume of the trilogy also won the British Book Award for Children's Book of the Year, but more notably, as the introduction discussed, it was named as Whitbread Book of the Year against competition from books written for and entered in the adult categories of the Award. Pullman also achieved some general accolades, but it can be assumed that their award is associated with the success of *His Dark Materials*. These include the Booksellers Association Author of the Year in both 2000 and 2001, the Eleanor Farjeon Award in 2003, in recognition of a distinguished contribution to the world of children's books, and the Astrid Lindgren Memorial Award in 2005, an international prize awarded for lifelong work rather than a single publication. In 2003, the *His Dark Materials* trilogy was voted by the British public as its third favourite title in the BBC's *The Big Read*, defeated only by Tolkien's *The Lord of the Rings* series (which was currently enjoying a renaissance due to the release of films based on it) and Jane Austen's *Pride and Prejudice* (1813).

While a schoolteacher, Pullman was seconded to Westminster College in Oxford to set up a centre to co-ordinate language teaching in the region. He was subsequently made a lecturer at the college, teaching courses in both adults' and children's literature, including the Victorian novel, folktales and creative writing, as well as training future teachers. Pullman later gave up this work in 1996 to write full-time after the success of *Northern Lights*, but this experience has made him an outspoken critic of more recent UK government education policy. He has passed frequent comment in the media on what he perceives to be the malign effect of the National Curriculum and the literacy strategy—which has had the function of directing much more closely what is taught in classrooms and how—on children's reading and creativity. Commenting on the literacy strategy in his speech accepting an honorary degree at Oxford Brookes University, which later became home to Westminster College, he remarked that

> [it] seems to force children to read and write in a particular way that is inimical to the development of true understanding. Teachers should rise up in revolt and throw off the shackles. It's as if they were under the spell of a wicked fairy who's cast a spell on the whole education system. (Whitehouse 2003: 2)

In 2003, Pullman was invited with several other children's writers, including Bernard Ashley and Anne Fine, to meet with the British Secretary of State for Education, Charles Clarke. Under discussion was the writers' belief that 'the national literacy strategy and literacy hour are killing children's enjoyment of reading and writing' (Katbamna 2003). Enjoyment is a key term for Pullman, who explains, 'what I do as a writer is to delight. I hope that the children who read me will do so because they enjoy it' (Pullman 2003d). The results of the writers' thoughts were published in a collective volume, *Meetings with the Minister* (2003c).

Pullman's contributions to this debate reveal his profound desire to bring his love of literature and storytelling to children and also to decry any political interventions which he perceives as thwarting that desire. Undoubtedly, his status as a best-selling and critically acclaimed writer for children has granted him a platform from which to make such contributions, although on his own website Pullman has downplayed them, saying, 'I have maintained a passionate interest in education, which leads me occasionally to make foolish and ill-considered remarks alleging that not everything is well in our schools.' He goes on to comment, however, 'My main concern is that an over-emphasis on testing and league tables has led to a lack of time and freedom for a true, imaginative and humane engagement with literature' (www.philip-pullman.com: b).

Pullman's commitment to the cause is clearly heartfelt and borne of his own rich experience. However, it is also clear, despite his disavowals, that Pullman enjoys the position of a public spokesman and has relished the opportunities his fame has given him. As well as speaking out in public forums on the subject of education and current government policy, he has variously commented on morality in fiction, children's and adults' literature, the responsibility of the storyteller, the political climate and Conservative Party ideology, environmentalism and even the Australian soap opera *Neighbours*, of which he is a big fan, on BBC Radio 4's flagship news programme, *Today*.

To a greater or lesser degree, all of these interventions relate to his central role as a writer and storyteller, and there is also undoubtedly something of the old-fashioned didact in the role Pullman has taken on subsequent to the success of *His Dark Materials*. But in addition to these teacherly qualities, there is also an element of publicity generation in his public comments. Pullman candidly admits that he was 'deliberately provocative' in his Carnegie Medal acceptance speech, and his decision to intervene in many public debates has both been made possible by his public profile and increased that public profile (Parsons and Nicholson 1999: 123). Ironically, however, Pullman has commented that the hours available to him for writing are reduced by the demands made on his time resulting from his fame and that he has decided to put all other invitations and commitments to one side to concentrate on further writing. It is clear, though, that he has relished the opportunities to make his voice heard on a broad range of issues.

In addition to public statements on a variety of issues in the media, Pullman has also provided much additional material around his own books in the form of interviews and commentary. In addition to the microsites run by his various publishers, he has his own website—www.philip-pullman.com—which provides the long autobiographical essay that this chapter draws upon, a question and answer section about his writing processes, an area about his books, and links to further articles and interviews. Pullman has been interviewed and profiled prominently and regularly in print, broadcast, and electronic media. He had a *South Bank Show* TV programme devoted to him in 2003, and a BBC film, *The World of Philip Pullman*, in 2002. He was a guest on the BBC Radio 4 institution, *Desert Island Discs* in 2002. He has also made countless appearances at bookshops, on the literary festival circuit and through lectures and panel discussions.

Throughout these public utterances, Pullman has provided a wealth of material concerning his writing. Much of this material is autobiographical, but some also signals Pullman's intentions and interpretation of his own work. His comment, for example, that *His Dark Materials* is '"*Paradise Lost* for teenagers in three volumes"' provides an interpretive framework to the trilogy that a reader may or may not otherwise pick up on. In other words, because of his public presence, Pullman has availed himself of the opportunity to direct interpretive approaches to his own work, although he cannot dictate them. This is in contrast to some of contemporary writing's more invisible authors, 'author-recluses' such as J D Salinger and Thomas Pynchon (Moran 2000). The subject of the author as a public persona, intrinsically involved in the promotional circuit, has been studied in some detail in recent years. Contrary to the comments of theorists in the 1960s and 1970s, who argued against the place of the author in critical interpretation, this has meant that the author is increasingly present in the public debate about his or her own work, and in some cases provides a wealth of extra-textual material to that debate. Critics including Andrew Wernick (1993), Joe Moran (2000) and Juliet Gardiner (2000a; 2000b) have argued that authors are now playing a major part in the marketing and promotion of their books, thus moving their role from one of production to one of influencing reception and consumption. It is this last point that is most pertinent here: Pullman has been a canny player of the promotional game through an often-controversial staging of his authorial presence. This has meant that there is much information and commentary about and by Pullman available in the public sphere, in addition to the texts of his creative works. The question is then to what extent this material should be drawn upon or indeed privileged in interpretations of his writing.

The perspective this volume takes is that the additional material created by Pullman is extremely useful in analysis of the trilogy itself, particularly in terms of exploring its wider contexts and its impact. As such, this material is drawn upon extensively in the following pages. However, this volume also steers away from a dogmatic biographical reading and also, in some parts, questions Pullman's own analysis of his writing. The author should not be the final authority on his or her own work; the contributions of critics and general readers—both children and adults, professional and non-professional—should also be strongly audible. The aim here has been to strike a balance between Pullman's own very articulate assessments of his writing and the interpretations of a range of other readers of his work. The next two chapters looks in detail at the nature of that work.

⁽⁰ 2 ⁰⁾

Stories of Multiple Worlds

THREE BOOKS—*Northern Lights*, *The Subtle Knife* and *The Amber Spyglass*—make up *His Dark Materials*. The trilogy is considered by Pullman to be 'one story in three books', despite the three separate publication dates, a concept with which his publisher concurs (Parsons and Nicholson 1999: 124; Fickling 2006). The trilogy as a whole is a richly complex work, with a fast-paced plot featuring a wealth of characters and interwoven with ideas of religion, science and philosophy. This chapter explores the characterisation and plotting of *His Dark Materials* and looks closely at the multiple worlds of the trilogy.

The protagonists of *His Dark Materials* traverse multiple worlds of adventure, encountering friends and enemies in both human and other forms. As Pullman's note at the beginning of *Northern Lights* has it:

> This first volume is set in a universe like ours, but different in many ways. The second volume, *The Subtle Knife*, moves between three universes: the universe of *Northern Lights*; the universe we know; and a third universe, which differs from ours in many ways again. The final volume of the trilogy, *The Amber Spyglass*, moves between several universes. (NL x)

Then, from its very first sentence, *Northern Lights* conjures up a sense of these various worlds as, in a place called Oxford, the reader is introduced to 'Lyra and her dæmon' (NL 3). These two are sneaking through the Hall towards the forbidden Retiring Room and the great adventure on which, unknowingly, they are soon to embark.

With these opening words, a sense of familiarity and strangeness is induced. Lyra is immediately situated as the heroine of the adventure, already intruding into a place where she shouldn't be. In plot terms, Lyra is recognisable as an inquisitive, plucky heroine, familiar to readers of children's books. Yet Lyra is accompanied by a thing—her 'dæmon'—that is unknown to the reader. As the first page continues, more information is given about this strange thing. It can talk, and it tells Lyra to '"Behave yourself"' (NL 3). It seems to have its own consciousness, or at least one that conflicts with Lyra's more impudent nature. Next, the reader is told of the name of this dæmon—Pantalaimon—and that its current form is that of a dark brown moth.

The Hall of the Oxford college into which the girl and her dæmon are venturing is an environment both real and fantastic, modelled closely on real-life Oxford colleges: places of ritual, tradition and, frequently, struggles for power. As the reader of *His Dark Materials* discovers, although Lyra grows up in a place called Oxford, there are significant differences between this Oxford and the Oxford in which Pullman studied and continues to live. Jordan College, for example, is an invention of Lyra's world and will not be found in the University of Oxford prospectus. Lyra's Oxford, moreover, is to be found in a place called Brytain rather than Britain, a parallel place 'like ours, but different in many ways', as Pullman puts it in his prefatory note. This alternative reality is clearly signalled when Lyra ventures into the Oxford of Will's world, the world that is, as Pullman's note phrases it, 'the universe we know'. She sees 'people of every sort, women dressed like men, Africans, even a group of Tartars meekly following their leader, all neatly dressed and hung about with little black cases'—Japanese tourists, it may be assumed. She is amazed by her visit to the cinema, but is nearly caught out in 'this mock-Oxford' by asking for a bar of 'chocolatl' rather than chocolate (SK 78).

Such a pattern of recognition and defamiliarisation continues throughout the trilogy, with its introduction of strange characters and new worlds and its depiction of the 'universe we know'. The adventures that are to come for Lyra and Pantalaimon, for Will and Iorek and for Lord Asriel and Mrs Coulter oscillate between Pullman's rich invention and readers' recognition. This chapter explores some of those inventions, particularly through the characters of the trilogy, and tracks their incorporation into the world-traversing plots of *His Dark Materials*.

Dæmons

In Lyra's world, each human being has a constant companion in his or her 'dæmon', which takes the form of an animal. This invention of Pullman's is one of the most striking features of the trilogy, which he has described in various interviews as being one of the best ideas he ever had (*See* MacPherson 2000). Over the course of the opening chapters of the trilogy, certain rules and patterns begin to emerge about humans and their dæmons. A dæmon is nearly always the opposite sex to its human, though there are exceptions, including the gyptians' pastry-cook spy at Jordan, Bernie Johansen (NL 125). Adults' dæmons remain in a fixed animal form, while children's dæmons change from one animal to another. Pantalaimon appears first as a moth but later in 'sleeping-form as an ermine' and then as a variety of creatures (NL 28). Servants' dæmons are almost invariably dogs.

Just as humans talk to and touch each other, so do their dæmons, but there is a 'prohibition against human-dæmon contact . . . so deep that even in battle no warrior would touch an enemy's dæmon' (NL 143). A wound inflicted on either human or dæmon is felt by the second in the pair, and if humans die, so do their dæmons. For a human to be separated from his or her dæmon causes immense physical pain and mental anguish. Lyra feels it as 'a strange tormenting feeling when your dæmon was pulling at the link between you; part physical pain deep in the chest, part intense sadness and love' (NL 194).

When Lyra first meets the second protagonist of the trilogy, Will, in *The Subtle Knife*, each is equally surprised. Will, who comes from our world, a world of no dæmons, finds Pantalaimon's shape-shifting 'extraordinary' (SK 21). Lyra, on the other hand, is shocked to find a properly living person with no visible dæmon: she resorts to thinking that Will's dæmon must be inside him. Lyra's dual nature—human and dæmon—is apparent in her attempt to explain to Will what he is lacking, an explanation that makes Will feel 'profoundly alone': '"Me and Pantalaimon. Us. Your dæmon en't *separate* from you. It's you. You're part of each other. En't there *anyone* in your world like us? Are they all like you, with their dæmons all hidden away?"' (SK 26).

Dæmons, then, are much more than companions, as Will discovers when he eventually sees his own dæmon, Kirjava. Rather, they are intrinsically part of their humans, though taking on separate physical forms. As such, they reflect the character of their humans but also, as with the opening scenes of *Northern Lights*, can act as restraints, setting up an externalised internal dialogue. When Lyra and Pantalaimon *See* the Master of the College put poison in wine destined for her uncle, Lord Asriel, they argue about what to do. Pantalaimon advocates minding their own business. Lyra disagrees completely, stating that they don't have 'any choice' and are now involved in the murder plot (NL 9). At this point she goads Pantalaimon with words that suggest one possible explanation for the concept of the dæmon. She says, '"You're supposed to know about conscience, aren't you?"' (NL 9), and indeed one interpretation of dæmons might be that they are the expression of their humans' consciences. Yet, as Lyra's thoughts go on to reveal, it is she who is the moral being in the dual relationship at this point, and she who has to make increasingly difficult decisions as they both set off on their adventures through multiple worlds: 'Lyra felt a mixture of thoughts contending in her head, and she would have liked nothing better than to share them with her dæmon, but she was proud too. Perhaps she should try to clear them up without his help' (NL 9).

It is clear, then, that human and dæmon, although physically and emotionally linked, do not share the same consciousness, and it is the human who is the controlling party in the relationship. Pantalaimon cannot decide where they will go or what they will do.

Lyra leads their relationship, as all the other humans lead their relationships with their dæmons.

Other beings from Lyra's world have slightly different relationships to their dæmons than those of the humans of her world. Or, like the humans from Will's world, some do not have dæmons at all. The witches of Lyra's world have dæmons, which are invariably birds. However, the witches can be separated from their dæmons by a much greater physical distance than a human could possibly withstand. The armoured bears of the North do not have dæmons, but rather, as Lyra's accomplice Iorek Byrnison explains to her, '"a bear's armour is his soul, just as your dæmon is your soul"' (NL 196).

Iorek's explanation of his armour as his 'soul' provides another theory for what the dæmon is: a personification (or rather, an animalification) of the soul. Marina Warner, in the epilogue to *Fantastic Metamorphoses, Other Worlds: Ways of Telling the Self* (2002), sees Pullman's invention as a direct response to the closing words of Plato's *Republic*, written more than two thousand years earlier. The souls of dead Homeric heroes take on new incarnations in the form of demons. Warner interprets Pullman's trilogy as developing 'the relation between metamorphosis as truth-telling about people, through an extraordinary dramatic device, a personal dæmon accompanying every character, a kind of external soul' (Warner 2002: 206). Yet the division between human and dæmon is certainly not one of body and soul, as both have a physical form and both have their own consciousness.

Dæmons do not function in *His Dark Materials* solely as a philosophical idea, nor as an attractively rich creation whose appeal to children will draw on their own strong relationships to pets, or frequently invented imaginary friends, as constant and biddable companions. Pullman has asserted that he did not want dæmons to be 'a picturesque detail' but rather wanted them to be fully integrated into the themes and plotting of the trilogy. As he goes on to explain, dæmons 'symbolise the difference between the infinite plasticity, the infinite potentiality and mutability of childhood and the fixed nature of adulthood' (Pullman 1999b: 190). This relates to the 'settling' of dæmons as children pass through adolescence into adulthood. In a key passage in *Northern Lights*, Lyra discusses this with the Able-Seaman during her voyage to the North:

> 'Why do dæmons have to settle?' Lyra said. 'I want Pantalaimon to be able to change for ever. So does he.'
>
> 'Ah, they always have settled, and they always will. That's part of growing up. There'll come a time when you'll be tired of his changing about, and you'll want a settled kind of form for him.'
>
> 'I never will!'
>
> 'Oh, you will. You'll want to grow up like all the other girls. Anyway, there's compensations for a settled form.'
>
> 'What are they?'
>
> 'Knowing what kind of person you are. Take old Belisaria. She's a seagull, and that means I'm a kind of seagull too. I'm not grand and splendid and beautiful, but I'm a tough old thing and I can survive anywhere and always find a bit of food and company. That's worth knowing, that is. And when your dæmon settles, you'll know the sort of person you are.' (NL 167)

Dæmons are intimately connected to the process of character development, the journey from innocence to experience, and thus to questions of choice and morality, as Lyra's conversation with the Able-Seaman demonstrates. The General Oblation Board's project to sever children from their dæmons in the Experimental Station in Bolvangar before the settling—and oncoming sexual maturity—of adolescence is linked to *His Dark Materials'* rewriting of the story of Adam and Eve and the Fall, as the next chapter explores in more detail. As the protagonist of *His Dark Materials*, Lyra finds herself inextricably caught up in these plot developments. In Bolvangar, she is saved only at the last minute from being severed from Pantalaimon. Then, at the moment of her sexual awakening with Will, as they break the interdiction on touching another human's dæmon:

> Will put his hand on hers. A new mood had taken hold of him, and he felt resolute and peaceful. Knowing exactly what he

was doing and exactly what it would mean, he moved his hand from Lyra's wrist and stroked the red-gold fur of her dæmon.

Lyra gasped. But her surprise was mixed with a pleasure so like the joy that flooded through her when she had put the fruit to his lips that she couldn't protest, because she was breathless. With a racing heart she responded in the same way: she put her hand on the silky warmth of Will's dæmon, and as her fingers tightened in the fur she knew that Will was feeling exactly what she was.

And she knew too that neither dæmon would change now, having felt a lover's hands on them. These were their shapes for life: they would want no other. (AS 527–28)

Dæmons are thus, as Pullman hoped for, fully integrated into the thematics of the trilogy, as well as providing a richly imaginative creation.

Lyra

In *The Amber Spyglass*, as Lyra walks through the land of the dead, the Chevalier Tialys looks down to *See* all the dead following 'that bright and living spark Lyra Silvertongue' (AS 318). The gloom of the underworld accentuates Lyra as one of the most vivid heroines of children's literature, one who has attracted many readers to her story and who has received the plaudits of the critics.

Lyra Belacqua—as she is called before her friend Iorek nicknames her Silvertongue—spent her early years in Oxford. She is left in the care of the Master and Scholars of Jordan College to live a 'half-wild' life among its 'grandeur and ritual' (NL 37). She is told that she is an orphan, the child of the Count and Countess Belacqua who were killed in an accident in the North. Lord Asriel, whom she believes to be her uncle, leaves her upbringing to the Master and Scholars of the College. Lyra's early education is haphazard, following the Scholars' often esoteric interests and hampered by her own 'fidgeting' nature (NL 32). Much of her childhood is spent in other parts of Oxford, however: on the roofs and in the cellars of the colleges with her good friend Roger the kitchen boy (exploits inspired by Pullman's undergraduate experiences); in the streets of Oxford, fighting pitched battles with the children of other colleges and the 'townies'; and in the rougher districts of Jericho, among the brick-burners' children and the gyptians (NL 36). Despite her aristocratic lineage, Lyra's unusual guardians do not prevent her excursions into the outside world, thus allowing her friendships to cross class boundaries. Lyra revels in the 'rich seething stew of alliances and enmities and feuds and treaties which was a child's life in Oxford' and is described as 'a coarse and greedy little savage', a 'barbarian' (NL 36, 37, 35).

Lyra realises, however, that her childhood Oxford is not all there is and that her life is also connected to 'the high world of politics' of which Lord Asriel is part (NL 37). It is this connection that *His Dark Materials* chronicles, as Lyra is swept into danger, intrigue, betrayal and an involvement with that 'high world of politics'. In the course of the plot, it is revealed that Lyra is not, after all, an orphan but the illegitimate child of the great adversaries and former lovers Lord Asriel and Mrs Coulter. As a baby, she was entrusted to the care of the gyptian Ma Costa, and later to Jordan College. So although she is not, after all, an orphan, Lord Asriel and Mrs Coulter offer no parental safety for her, and their treachery and occasional uneasy alliances force their daughter to rely on her own capacity for friend-ship rather than these lately acquired parents.

Lyra has a great destiny within the stories that unfold in *His Dark Materials*, which is whispered and hinted at throughout the three volumes. The first intimation of her role is spoken by the Master of Jordan College. She has a 'major' part to play and will commit a 'great betrayal', but 'must do it all without realizing what she's doing' (NL 32, 33, 32). The witches, according to their Consul, have spoken of this great destiny for centuries, and in *The Subtle Knife*, a captured witch is tortured in order to discover the nature of this destiny (NL 175; SK 39–41). Yet Lyra is unaware of her destiny and is, according to Farder Coram, the wise old gyptian, '"a strange, innocent creature"' (NL 175). Her destiny as '"Eve! Mother of all! Eve, again! Mother Eve!"' is explored in the following chapter (SK 328).

As Lyra moves towards her destiny in *The Amber Spyglass*, her character is revealed as resourceful, brave and loyal. She also, however, can be haughty and self-righteous, and she is an inveterate liar. She makes deep alliances with Iorek, Will and Lee Scoresby but also commits two great betrayals: first of her friend Roger at the end of *Northern Lights*, whom she unwittingly leads to his death at the hands of Lord Asriel, and then—the betrayal of which the Master prophesises—of her own Pantalaimon, from whom she must separate on the riverbank in order to reach the land of the dead.

Towards the end of *Northern Lights*, as a consequence of her storytelling talents, Iorek renames his friend Lyra Silvertongue. These talents prove vital in winning many of the battles of *His Dark Materials*, and particularly in extricating Lyra from difficult situations. The events that lead Iorek to dub her 'Silvertongue' are those in which Lyra helps Iorek win back the bear kingdom from Iofur Raknison. The latter is a bear who has erred from his nature by desiring a dæmon. Lyra realises Iofur's weakness and through her verbal skill sets a trap and thus arranges the fight that Iorek will eventually win. Lyra manages to convince Iofur that she is Iorek's dæmon but that she is willing to become his if he defeats Iorek in battle. Iorek, however, wins the battle and regains his kingdom from Iofur with Lyra's aid. In other situations of danger and uncertainty, Lyra frequently lies, parading a series of alternate identities: 'Lizzie Brooks' when she is captured and taken to the Experimental Station at Bolvangar; the child of a duke and duchess when she is on the banks of land of the dead; and 'Alice' when a suspicious man in a top hat attempts to put brandy in her coffee after she runs away from Mrs Coulter's London house. She lies for self-protection, but also, sometimes, for the sheer love of invention, as the account of her narration of the false story of her duke and duchess parents demonstrates:

'I'll tell you all about it,' said Lyra.

As she said that, as she took charge, part of her felt a little stream of pleasure rising upwards in her breast like the bubbles in champagne. And she knew Will was watching, and she was happy that he could *See* her doing what she was best at, doing it for him and for all of them. (AS 276)

The morality of storytelling and the lessons that Lyra learns in the land of the dead are examined later in this book.

Lyra has a form of control in addition to the one of having a captive audience. That control relates to her readings of the alethiometer. The alethiometer is a truth-telling device given to Lyra by the Master of Jordan just before she leaves the College with Mrs Coulter for London. She quickly learns how to read this golden compass by carefully watching the movements of its hands from symbol to symbol in response to her questions. The alethiometer becomes one of Lyra's principle weapons in the battles of *His Dark Materials*, inferring upon her the qualities of a seer, able to communicate with a consciousness that people of her own world name 'Dust'. It means she can also communicate with the 'Shadows' in Mary Malone's world via the computer Mary calls the Cave.

Lyra's relationship to the alethiometer, however, also signals a change in her own relationships and a development of her character. When, in *The Subtle Knife*, she enters the parallel world of Will's Oxford, the compass tells her, '*You must concern yourself with the boy. Your task is to help him find his father. Put your mind to that*' (SK 83). This Oxford is a place where Lyra is 'a lost little girl in a strange world, belonging nowhere' (SK 73). For a while, her quest becomes secondary to Will's, or at least can be accomplished only through following Will. In fact, from the second volume of the trilogy onwards, after meeting Will, Lyra must unlearn some of her independence. This submission goes alongside Lyra's growing feelings for Will as the two pass from childhood into adolescence. Lyra's character softens as the trilogy proceeds and—as chapter 7 considers—is altered yet further in *Lyra's Oxford*. As an illustration of this, *The Amber Spyglass* opens with Lyra imprisoned, fairy-tale-like, in a drugged sleep, waiting to be rescued by Will. At this point she has lost her own volition—her own will—and must rely on those external to her. Lyra's mission becomes secondary to, and dependent on, Will's, and her credentials as a feminist protagonist are arguably undermined. She must learn humility, dependence, trust and love, virtues that make her realise that, counter to her earlier wishes, she does want things to change, and she does want to grow up. Lyra's softening is thus represented as part of the inevitable process of adolescence, whereby the individual becomes increasingly socialised. Nonetheless, a case could clearly be made that this process shifts her character away from the feisty attractiveness of the young girl. And yet, eventually, it is Lyra's destiny as the new Eve that impels the plot of *His Dark Materials*, and Pullman's rewriting of this role makes a different feminist claim than that of character analysis.

Will

Will Parry does not make an appearance in *His Dark Materials* until the second volume of the trilogy, but he is nonetheless its second protagonist. *The Subtle Knife* opens with Will leading his frightened mother down the street to entrust her to the care of his piano teacher. He then goes back to his home to search for a leather case of letters and to discover more about the Arctic expedition during which his father, John Parry, mysteriously disappeared many years earlier.

With an absent father and a mother troubled by the enemies in her own confused mind, Will is, like Lyra, a child cast adrift of adult supervision. He has to fend for himself, care for his mother and face his responsibilities. When he returns home, he is woken in the night by men who have broken into the house, also looking for the case of letters. In the struggle that ensues, one of the men, tripped by Will's cat, falls down the stairs and is killed. The guilt that Will feels for this, and for the further violence he is drawn into when he meets Lyra, is one expression of his character, which is more reflective and thoughtful than Lyra's. In one scene, he 'wrestled with the horror of what he'd done'; in another, when he kills for the second time, 'his body revolted at what his instinct had made him do, and the result was a dry, sour, agonizing spell of kneeling and vomiting until his stomach and his heart were empty' (SK 104; AS 171). Will's revulsion is quite different from Lyra's blithe acceptance of Will as 'a murderer', which the alethiometer tells her he is (SK 29).

Pullman depicts the male child protagonist of *His Dark Materials*, therefore, as a more sensitive and troubled being than the female. He is quieter, more introspective, 'good at not being noticed', while Lyra likes nothing more than to be the centre of attention (SK 13). His difficult childhood, with his odd mother, means he also has knowledge of the cruelty of children, which he recognises when he and Lyra are confronted by an angry mob in Cittàgazze (SK 237–42). Will thinks, when faced by them, that 'he had seen children in this mood before' (SK 237): 'They weren't individual children: they were a single mass, like a tide. They surged below him and leaped up in a fury, snatching, threatening, screaming, spitting . . .' (SK 241).

Nonetheless, Will proves himself to be a fierce and determined fighter, with the same bravery and loyalty displayed by Lyra. When he becomes the bearer of the 'subtle knife', he also acquires a destiny, but one about which he is very equivocal. The knife has special powers: not only is it a weapon that can cut Iorek's armour like 'butter', but it also can open windows between the various worlds in *His Dark Materials* (AS 112). Moreover, as the dying man whom Will meets at the end of *The Subtle Knife* tells him, the bearer of the knife will have immense power in the '"greatest war there ever was"':

'We've had nothing but lies and propaganda and cruelty and deceit for all the thousands of years of human history. It's time we started again, but properly this time . . .'

He stopped to take in several rattling breaths.

'The knife,' he went on after a minute; 'they never knew what they were making, those old philosophers. They invented a device that could split open the very smallest particles of matter, and they used it to steal candy. They had no idea that they'd made the one weapon in all the universes that could defeat the tyrant. The Authority. God. The rebel angels fell because they didn't have anything like the knife; but now . . .' (SK 334)

Will tries to refuse this weighty destiny, but by becoming the bearer of 'Æsahættr', his nature as a 'warrior' shows itself, and so he must accept his destiny by choosing to fight on the side of Lord Asriel (SK 335). By choosing this path, he must endure pain and suffering, but also, alongside Lyra, he will make powerful and redemptive choices that contribute to their building of the republic of heaven and to changing the universes of *His Dark Materials* forever.

The dying man at the end of *The Subtle Knife* who confronts Will with these choices is in fact his father, John Parry. During his Arctic expedition twelve years earlier, Parry and two companions go through a window between their world and another but cannot find their way back. Parry investigates the multiplicity of worlds he then finds, and eventually, under the name of Dr Stanislaus Grumman, becomes a member of the Berlin Academy in Lyra's world. It is therefore his head that Lord Asriel pretends to show to the Master and Scholars of Jordan at the beginning of *Northern Lights*, although Grumman is in fact still alive and living as the shaman 'Jopari' with a tribe of Siberian Tartars.

When Will eventually meets his father, the two recognise their relationship only seconds before John Parry dies. At first it seems that Will is orphaned once more and is left alone again, but with an even greater knowledge of the task that lies before him. Yet due to his own and Lyra's bravery, he will have another opportunity to encounter his father in the land of the dead in *The Amber Spyglass*. Will thus has a second chance and develops his relationship more fully with his father during this strange, ghostly phase of the elder man's existence.

At the end of the trilogy, Will—with Lyra—faces an agonising choice, the answer to which means that he will have to stay apart for ever from Lyra, back in his own world. Will's future—which *The Amber Spyglass* dwells on much less than Lyra's—does not seem an enticing prospect, and not simply because he is cast back into our own more prosaic world, one which does not have armoured bears and witches and dæmons. As Mary Malone, who is also from Will's world, explains:

'Tomorrow we'll go and find out where his mother is, and *See* what we can do to help her get better. There are so many rules and regulations in my world . . . ; you have to satisfy the authorities and answer a thousand questions; I'll help him with all the legal side of things and the social services and housing and all that, and let him concentrate on his mother.' (AS 533–34)

Will's adventuring days seem to be over, and his only connections to his recent past are Mary Malone and a promise to 'meet' Lyra in the Botanic Garden once a year to, as Lyra says, '"pretend we [are] close again"' (AS 537). Will's character changes much less than Lyra's in the course of *His Dark Materials*, but he experiences great adventure in the multiple worlds he travels through. His return to 'the universe we know' is a return to parochial everyday life, away from adventure and excitement. For Will, the nature of growing up seems a disappointing return to the troubled life he had, for a brief period, left behind.

Lord Asriel

Lord Asriel first appears early in *Northern Lights* while Lyra is hidden in the Retiring Room. From the safety of a wardrobe, she observes the man she believes at this point in the story to be her uncle:

Lord Asriel was a tall man with powerful shoulders, a fierce dark face, and eyes that seemed to flash and glitter with savage laughter. It was a face to be dominated by, or to fight: never a face to patronize or pity. All his movements were large and perfectly balanced, like those of a wild animal, and when he appeared in a room like this, he seemed a wild animal held in a cage too small for it. (NL 13)

Asriel is described as a Byronic hero, muscling with power and energy, and with a 'savage', 'wild', and dangerous edge. Elsewhere he is described as '"a passionate man"' (NL 122). For Lyra, he is a figure of whom to be simultaneously proud and frightened, and one whom, when she reveals herself, threatens to break her arm for her impudence in entering the Retiring Room. By recounting the plot to murder him, however, she saves Asriel's life, for which he begrudgingly allows her to watch and listen from the wardrobe to his explanation of his findings about Dust and the 'Grumman expedition' in the North.

As Lyra eventually discovers, Asriel is not her uncle at all, but her father. His love affair with the married Mrs Coulter resulted in her birth. Mrs Coulter attempted to keep secret her infidelity from her husband by hiding Lyra away under the care of a gyptian woman, Ma Costa. The vengeful husband finds the hiding place and attempts to kill Lyra, but Asriel arrives in time to save his child and kill the husband. In the resulting lawsuit, Asriel is not imprisoned, but all his vast wealth is confiscated.

Asriel is far from a loving father. When Lyra confronts him at the end of *Northern Lights* with her new knowledge of her parentage, his response is a dismissive '"Yes. So what?"' (NL 367). To him, family ties are secondary to his great utopian mission, a visionary project that requires the building of '"a bridge between this world and the world beyond the Aurora"'—the Northern Lights of the title of the first volume (NL 188). This project is to create the 'republic of heaven'. The '"free citizens"' of this republic, according to Asriel, will be released from the shackles imposed by the '"kingdom of heaven"'. It will be a world, as his ally Ogunwe puts it, with '"no kings, no bishops, no priests"' (AS 222). Asriel plans to bring to an end centuries of oppressive control by the Church and by its godhead, the 'Authority'. In *The Amber Spyglass*, he amasses a mighty army to achieve his aim. His passionate conviction of the physicality of the human body fuels his mission:

> Lord Asriel turned and gripped his arm with fingers that all but bruised him to the bone.
> 'They haven't got *this!*' he said, and shook Ogunwe's arm violently. 'They haven't got *flesh!*'
> He laid his hand against his friend's rough cheek.
> 'Few as we are,' he went on, 'and short-lived as we are, and weak-sighted as we are—in comparison with them, we're still

stronger. They *envy* us, Ogunwe! That's what fuels their hatred, I'm sure of it. They long to have our precious bodies, so solid and powerful, so well adapted to the good earth!' (AS 394)

Asriel, then, is a leader of men but fighting for equality, and a fervent believer in the primacy of flesh. Yet his ambitions make him ruthless, as Lyra discovers at the end of *Northern Lights*. The alethiometer tells her that she has something to take to Asriel in order for him to accomplish his plan to bridge the worlds. She wrongly assumes that it is the alethiometer itself that he needs '"for this experiment"' (NL 360). Her consequent arrival at Svalbard is greeted with horror by her father. Lyra has mistaken what it is she is bringing for him, because he needs a child for his experiment— a child who will be sacrificed in order for the Aurora to be torn apart. Until Asriel sees that Lyra is accompanied by another child, Roger, his shocked reaction shows that despite his horror, he would consider using Lyra, his own child, for the experiment.

Asriel is estranged from Mrs Coulter, but in erotically charged moments at the end of *Northern Lights* which confuse the watching Lyra, he asks his lover to join him on his mission. Mrs Coulter's refusal separates them for another two volumes, but they are reunited towards the end of *The Amber Spyglass*. Asriel's grand vision is not accomplished, and yet his dramatic fall into the abyss with Mrs Coulter, as they unite to battle against the Authority's representative, Metatron, is their great sacrifice which allows Lyra to accomplish her destiny.

Mrs Coulter

At the beginning of *Northern Lights*, all over Brytain, children are disappearing. One of these disappearances—or 'bewitchings'— introduces Mrs Coulter (NL 45). She is 'a beautiful young lady' accompanied by a golden monkey dæmon (NL 42). After tempting a group of children into a London cellar with promises of chocolatl, she tells them they are going on a voyage to the North. She offers to have letters delivered from the children to their families, but in a stroke of evil timing, she puts the children on the boat, 'turn[s] back inside . . . and [throws] the little bundle of letters into the furnace before leaving the way she had come' (NL 45). In the opening few chapters of *Northern Lights*, Mrs Coulter's character is established as mysterious, glamorous and dangerous.

When Mrs Coulter encounters Metatron in *The Amber Spyglass*, he delivers a scathing verdict on her life. He sees

> 'corruption and envy and lust for power. Cruelty and coldness. A vicious probing curiosity. Pure, poisonous, toxic malice. You have never from your earliest years shown a shred of compassion or sympathy or kindness without calculating how it would return to your advantage. You have tortured and killed without regret or hesitation; you have betrayed and intrigued and gloried in your treachery. You are a cess-pit of moral filth.' (AS 419)

This litany of accusation shakes her self-assurance, and yet she still manages to turn the situation to her advantage, using her own knowledge of human—and angel—sexuality to ensnare Metatron by persuading him of her capacity to do the same to Lord Asriel. Her behaviour is equally treacherous towards her lover Lord Boreal, whom she kills in *The Subtle Knife*.

Mrs Coulter, then, is a seducer of both children and men, an archetype of a certain kind of dangerous yet glamorous femininity. She comes to claim her daughter, Lyra, from Jordan while Lord Asriel is held captive by the armoured bears in the North, and hence cannot protest. To Lyra, Mrs Coulter represents a new kind of womanhood that her early life in Jordan has not prepared her for, 'one with dangerous powers and qualities such as elegance, charm and grace' (NL 82). Pantalaimon is uncertain about Mrs Coulter, despite being as fascinated by her as Lyra is. When Mrs Coulter washes Lyra's hair, Pantalaimon watches 'with powerful curiosity until Mrs Coulter looked at him, and he knew what she meant and turned away, averting his eyes modestly from these feminine mysteries as the golden monkey was doing. He had never had to look away from Lyra before' (NL 78).

The division that 'feminine mysteries' enforce between Lyra and her dæmon is a development of the disagreements the two have in the opening scenes, but also foretells the great separation they will undergo in *The Amber Spyglass*. Yet before that parting, Lyra is exposed to another process of separation that Mrs Coulter is involved with in her work as the head of the 'General Oblation Board', or the 'Gobblers', as the children call it. Rumours are rife about the work of the General Oblation Board, and Lyra, with her own capacity for storytelling and duplicity, tricks Lord Boreal into telling her more about it. What she and Pantalaimon learn about Mrs Coulter's work precipitates their flight from her house.

When Lyra and Mrs Coulter meet again at the Experimental Station in Bolvangar, Lyra is to learn much more about the terrifying process of 'severing' or 'intercision', in which captured children are forcibly separated from their dæmons with a silver guillotine. Mrs Coulter surrounds herself with a bodyguard of adults who have undergone the same process. More will be said about the process itself, and its implications for Dust and for notions of sexuality, in the chapter that follows this one. The rationale for Mrs Coulter's involvement with the General Oblation Board, however, is defined by Lord Asriel as a result of her gender and her lust for power. He explains to Lyra:

'You see, your mother's always been ambitious for power. At first she tried to get it in the normal way, through marriage, but that didn't work, as I think you've heard. So she had to turn to the Church. Naturally she couldn't take the route a man could have taken—priesthood and so on—it had to be unorthodox; she had to set up her own order, her own channels of influence, and work through that. It was a good move to specialize in Dust. Everyone was frightened of it; no one knew what to do; and when she offered to direct an investigation, the Magisterium was so relieved that they backed her with money and resources of all kinds.' (NL 374)

Mrs Coulter's manipulation, ingenuity and independence are largely used to evil purpose, but they nonetheless mark her similarity in character to her daughter. Will realises this when, despite their enmity, 'he found himself liking her, because she was brave, and because she seemed like a more complicated and richer and deeper Lyra' (AS 150).

From her characteristics, Mrs Coulter would seem to be as illfitted to be a mother figure as Lord Asriel is to his fatherhood. Indeed, Lyra's very early years are overseen by the maternal Ma Costa, who presents a very different model of womanhood. For the sake of power, Mrs Coulter even seems prepared, like Asriel, to kill her own daughter to prevent Lyra's destiny as a new Eve. Yet when she captures Lyra and holds her prisoner in a cave at the beginning of *The Amber Spyglass*, she undergoes an unexpected transformation and begins to have maternal feelings towards her daughter, wishing to protect her from the Magisterium, who want her killed. However, it is a difficult and sometimes dubious path to motherhood. She shields Lyra from the dangers of the world by keeping her drugged and imprisoned. Her subsequent motivations in *The Amber Spyglass*, when she joins Asriel's forces, are also suspicious. Her justification of her switch from the Church to the fighters for the republic of heaven is met with scepticism by Asriel himself, who sees her as 'shameless' and lying 'in the very marrow of her bones' (AS 218). It is only later, when she treacherously leads Metatron to Asriel, that he accepts her love for Lyra, a love which she herself does not understand, a love which, as she says, '"came to me like a thief in the night"' (AS 426–27). The ultimate vindication of Mrs Coulter is not in her words, however, but in her final action alongside Asriel in the battle with Metatron. As Asriel calls out to her, she makes the ultimate sacrifice:

> The cry was torn from Lord Asriel, and with the snow leopard beside her, with a roaring in her ears, Lyra's mother stood and found her footing and leapt with all her heart, to hurl herself against the angel and her dæmon and her dying lover, and seize those beating wings, and bear them all down together into the abyss. (AS 430)

Mary Malone

Mary Malone appears in many fewer scenes than Lyra, Will, Asriel and Mrs Coulter in *His Dark Materials*, and yet her role is pivotal. She is a scientist based in a research laboratory, the 'Dark Matter Research Unit', in Will's Oxford (SK 87). The experiments she has been conducting are into what she calls '"Shadows"' and describes as '"particles of consciousness"' (SK 92). This is the Dust of Lyra's world (SK 92). When Lyra reaches her, guided by the alethiometer, her lab is about to be closed down, and so the appearance of an unusual young girl is greeted by Mary with more attention than it might otherwise have been given.

The intervention made by Lyra into Mary's life leads her on a voyage through 'the multiple worlds predicted by quantum theory'; to play anthropologist to the mulefas, a strange group of wheeled beasts; to discover the purpose of Dust, which she observes through her invention of the amber spyglass; and to fulfil her part in Lyra's destiny (AS 90). Although she does not know what form this role will take, the Shadows, through her computer, order her to 'find the girl and the boy. Waste no more time. You must play the serpent' (SK 261). Thus, Mary is cast in the role of the tempter of Lyra's Eve.

Before Mary can tempt Lyra at the end of *The Amber Spyglass*, however, she must learn the lesson that Lyra has taught to the dead earlier in the book. The mulefas take her to the place where the dead, thanks to Lyra, escape out of the darkness of the underworld. One of the joyful dead speaks to Mary, telling her of the 'injunction to *tell them stories*' (AS 456). The phrase plays in Mary's mind, and the following chapter of *The Amber Spyglass*, 'Marzipan', sees her carrying out its bidding.

The story that Mary tells in 'Marzipan' is in response to Lyra's question about why she stopped being a nun. The story is to do with her loss of faith, but more importantly reveals her experiences of sex and love, first as a twelve-year-old at a party, and later with an Italian man she met during a scientific conference in Portugal. Mary's portrayal of her adolescent kisses and her renunciation of the Church on a balmy summer night opens Lyra's eyes to a world of sexuality and excites her consciousness:

> [Lyra] felt a stirring at the roots of her hair: she found herself breathing faster. She had never been on a roller-coaster, or anything like one, but if she had, she would have recognized the sensations in her breast: they were exciting and frightening at the same time, and she had not the slightest idea why. The sensation continued, and deepened, and changed, as more parts of her body found themselves affected too. She felt as if she had been handed the key to a great house she hadn't known was there, a house that was somehow inside her, and as she turned the key, deep in the darkness of the building she felt other doors opening too, and lights coming on. She sat trembling, hugging her knees, hardly daring to breathe (AS 467–68)

Lyra's nascent feelings for Will, and her adolescent sexuality, culminate in a scene in a 'little wood of silver-barked trees', where Lyra offers, and Will takes, the fruit that Mary packed for them earlier (AS 489), in a rewriting of the scene in which Eve encourages Adam to eat an apple in the Garden of Eden.

Friends, Allies, Enemies and Multiple Worlds

In their journeys through the multiple worlds of *His Dark Materials*, Lyra, Will, Lord Asriel, Mrs Coulter and Mary Malone encounter a vast range of other characters and creatures. Some of these become friends and allies: notably Iorek Byrnison, the armoured bear; Lee Scoresby, the Texan aëronaut and Iorek's comrade-in-arms; the gyptians, including Farder Coram, John Faa and Ma Costa; and the witch Serafina Pekkala. Others are enemies, or at the very least present challenges to the protagonists: the harpies of the land of the dead; the cliff-ghasts; and the clerics of the Magisterium, including the menacing figure of Father Gomez, the eager young priest detailed to follow Mary Malone and thence to kill Lyra before she has a chance to fulfil her destiny. Some of these characters are human in form, others draw on traditional figures such as angels and witches, and yet others, such as the Gallivespians, are more original creations. The teeming populations of *His Dark Materials* are nowhere more fully displayed than in the two opposing forces in *The Amber Spyglass*. On Lord Asriel's side are the Africans led by King Ogunwe; the Gallivespians, Chevalier Tialys and the Lady Salmakia, and their dragonfly steeds; and the rebel angels, including Balthamos and Baruch. On the side of the Magisterium and the Consistorial Court is the Swiss Guard; some of the witch clans; and the angels of the Authority, headed by Metatron. Both sides utilise a wealth of inventions in their struggle for supremacy, which in their inventiveness ally Pullman's trilogy to science fiction writing: the alethiometers (held by both Lyra and the Magisterium); a demonic clockwork bug unleashed by Mrs Coulter; the 'intention craft', which is controlled by the processes of the mind alone; and the lodestone resonator, which the Gallivespians use to communicate with one another.

All these characters, and their armoury and gadgetry, indicate the rich creativity of *His Dark Materials* and its fully conceived universes. As the notes to each of the volumes quoted at the beginning of this chapter describe, in *His Dark Materials* there are several universes. These include 'the universe we know', which is where Will and Mary Malone come from, and where Lord Boreal disguises himself as Sir Charles Latrom and steals the alethiometer from Lyra. They also include the place where Lyra comes from, which is 'like ours, but different in many ways'. There is a recognisable Oxford in this universe, but one which nevertheless differs in important respects from that of Will's world. There is also a recognisable world geography, but one which is inhabited by fantastical beasts including witches and armoured bears. At the beginning of *The Subtle Knife*, Lyra and Will first meet each other in another world, where Cittàgazze is located, and which is overrun by the fearsome Spectres. Mary Malone travels through this world on her way to the land of the mulefas, which she discovers in *The Amber Spyglass*, and to which

Lyra, Will and Serafina Pekkala also travel in the final volume. In *The Amber Spyglass*, several more universes are mentioned or hinted at, including the land of the dead and the world into which Will places strands of Lyra's hair a split second before the detonation of a bomb directed towards her through a matching lock of hair. These universes present a richly imagined setting for Lyra and Will's adventures, as well as giving Pullman the opportunity to experiment with the invention of different creatures, to dramatise dæmons and Dust and to establish different moral and physical rules.

In other words, in the creation of multiple worlds, Pullman attempts to do much more than provide the canvas against which Lyra and Will's epic adventures are set. In his lecture 'Let's Write It in Red', Pullman discusses the scientific notion of 'phase space', which provides a prevailing metaphor for the trilogy (Pullman 1998c). As he explains it, 'Phase space is a term from dynamics, and it refers to the untrackable complexity of changing systems. It's the notional space which contains not just the actual consequences of the present moment, but all the possible consequences' (Pullman 1998c: 47).

Pullman illustrates this by quoting the poem 'The Road Not Taken' (1916) by Robert Frost:

Two roads diverged in a wood, and I—
I took the one less travelled by,
And that has made all the difference.

The multiple universes of *His Dark Materials* are drawn, then, to demonstrate this scientific principle as a literary metaphor, and also as a description of the process of writing itself. As Pullman elaborates, 'I am surely not the only writer who has the distinct sense that every sentence I write is surrounded by the ghosts of the sentences I could have written at that point, but didn't' (Pullman 1998c: 47). Yet Pullman's use of the concept of 'phase space' is neither solely an illustration of a scientific principle nor only a metaphor for the process of creating a story, but also a means by which to articulate the necessity of choice. At the beginning of *The Amber Spyglass*, Will finds himself desolate. The witches he was travelling with at the end of *The Subtle Knife* are slain, Lyra and Serafina Pekkala are missing and his only companions are the invisible and, to Will, incomprehensible angels Balthamos and Baruch:

> Will considered what to do. When you choose one way out of many, all the ways you don't take are snuffed out like candles, as if they'd never existed. At the moment all Will's choices existed at once. But to keep them all in existence meant doing nothing. He had to choose, after all. (AS 14–15)

The insistence on Will's choice constitutes a form of morality at this point in the story. Will chooses to go on—to rescue Lyra, and thence the dead, and also to join forces with Asriel.

The future of the armoured bears, with Iorek and Iofur battling for their leadership in *Northern Lights*, is similarly discussed, with 'two kinds of beardom opposed here, two futures, two destinies. Iofur had begun to take them in one direction, and Iorek would take them in another, and in the same moment, one future would close for ever as the other began to unfold' (NL 349–50). The final settling of a child's dæmon as he or she reaches adulthood is yet another example of this: character is constituted by the choices made earlier on and the rejection of other paths. Phase space then becomes a politicised metaphor, one in which choices are indicative of morality. The agonising choice that Lyra and Will are forced to make at the end of the trilogy—whether to See each other occasionally but close the window through which the dead escape, or to say goodbye for all time—is the greatest example of the principle Pullman incorporates into *His Dark Materials*. When Lyra and Will decide they must stay apart for ever, they make one promise, at Lyra's suggestion:

> 'What I thought was that if you—maybe just once a year—if we could come here at the same time, just for an hour or something, then we could pretend we were close again— because we *would* be close, if you sat here and I sat just *here* in my world—' (AS 537)

The two Oxfords are laid over one another as a palimpsest, and the bench in the Botanic Garden in Oxford is the symbol of their choice, a heartrending image of the two young lovers' sacrifice, of all they have given up for the sake of saving their universes. Their decision to separate and remain in their own worlds reflects favourably on their characters and provides a form of morality analysed in the next chapter. The question that remains is whether this great sacrifice is yet another denial or instead an act of realism that will enable their attempt to build the republic of heaven on earth.

⟪ 3 ⟫

Politics and Morality

'SOMEWHERE IN HER LIFE,' Pullman writes of Lyra early on in *Northern Lights*, 'there was a connection with the high world of politics represented by Lord Asriel' (NL 37). For the worlds of adventure traversed by Will and Lyra are not, as the politicised metaphor of phase space suggests, merely the brightly illustrated backdrop for a richly inventive narrative. Rather, the imaginative adventures are suffused with political intrigue and, in *The Amber Spyglass*, all-out war. These power struggles inform much of the thematic nature of the trilogy, and so this central chapter explores the themes of *His Dark Materials* from the perspective of politics and morality. It begins by looking at the 'high world of politics' and then considers the trilogy's treatment of religion, belief and the church; its representations of science, sexuality and gender; the religious and literary theme of the Fall; and the passage from innocence to experience. The chapter then moves on to a consideration of the morality of the trilogy and the themes of free will and predestination, choice and responsibility. Finally, it touches on how storytelling as a theme intersects with the political aspects of the trilogy, leading to the subsequent chapter, 'Telling Stories.'

Politics

"'I *know* there's something going on—something political"', Lyra says to Pan at the beginning of the trilogy (NL 8). The political nature of *His Dark Materials* is apparent from the opening pages, as Lyra invades the male space of Jordan College's Retiring Room and discovers the treachery and power games of the adult world. This space is explicitly gendered, as 'only Scholars and their guests were allowed in . . . , and never females' (NL 4). When Lyra is trapped in there at the opening of *Northern Lights*, she overhears that Asriel is arriving that evening. Asriel is 'a man whom she admired and feared greatly. He was said to be involved in high politics, in secret exploration, in distant warfare' (NL 6). The very next moment, however, Lyra finds herself in a position from which she will make a crucial intervention in this world of high politics. From her hiding place, she sees the Master of the College stir white powder into a decanter of wine destined to be drunk by Asriel. Asriel is bound up with the political life of the country: Lyra knows that he—with the Master of the College—is a member of the Cabinet Council, the Prime Minister's special advisory body (NL 10). There are rumours of war in Lyra's world: Tartars are seeking to dominate western Europe through violent invasion (NL 10). Yet the threat to Asriel is more imminent—the Master is attempting to poison him. Lyra prevents Asriel from drinking the wine, and despite his anger that she has intruded into the male space of the Retiring Room, he allows her to stay in hiding to watch the Master's reaction. Thus, Lyra also hears what Asriel has to say to the assembled Scholars, and so is sucked into the political intrigue herself. In fact, Lyra, excited by Asriel's talk of '"Northern Lights and bears and icebergs and everything"', claims that she is now complicit in the intrigue: '"If you wanted me to be a spy in the wardrobe you ought to tell me what I'm spying about"' (NL 29).

Asriel refuses to tell Lyra any more, and so she is left unenlightened about the nature of Dust, the importance of the North, and the location of the city in the air that Asriel photographed. Asriel considers that for a child, and a female child at that who should concentrate on being a '"good girl"', '"the times are too dangerous"' to know any more about what is going on (NL 29).

Others also have the intent of protecting Lyra from the wider world of politics and war. In the next scene, out of Lyra's hearing, the Master and the Librarian discuss the foiled murder attempt, a deed the Master was very reluctant to pursue and yet felt to be necessary. They also discuss a heady brew of theology, science and politics, and a world subject to power struggles between various branches of the Church (NL 31). They refer to the Barnard-Stokes heresy, a theory put forward by two '"*renegade* theologians who postulated the existence of numerous other worlds like this one, neither heaven nor hell, but material and sinful"' (NL 31–32). Asriel appears to have taken a photograph in the North of one of these other worlds, and so potentially has evidence to contradict Church orthodoxy and to confront the Church's leaders. He has come back to Jordan to appeal to the College for more funds to conduct his research, and after some argument, they agree to give him the money.

The Master and the Librarian also discuss Lyra's place in this, as the Master has warning from the truth-telling alethiometer that she will be drawn into the '"appalling consequences"' of Asriel's research in the North (NL 30). It is for this reason that the Master attempts to poison Asriel, in order to safeguard Lyra as long as possible from her destiny. As the Master states, '"Lyra has a part to play in all this, and a major one"' (NL 32). Within a very few pages of the beginning of *Northern Lights*, then, political struggle, religious heresy and murderous intrigue are made central elements of the trilogy's plotting.

Lyra is swept into this grown-up world through her intrusion into the Retiring Room but is soon introduced to another form of political life when Mrs Coulter takes her to live with her in London. While staying for several weeks in Mrs Coulter's London home, Lyra undergoes a round of shopping and theatre trips but also meetings at the Royal Arctic Institute in preparation for the promised trip to the North, along with lunches with politicians or clerics, as Mrs Coulter exerts her sphere of influence. This politicking culminates in a cocktail party, during which Lyra hears rumours about Dust,

Mrs Coulter's work in the North and Asriel's imprisonment, all of which lead to her escape from Mrs Coulter's house.

For much of the trilogy, the political world inhabited by Lord Asriel and Mrs Coulter provides a context for Lyra's and, later, Will's adventures. Scientific and religious domains also underpin the story. In *The Amber Spyglass*, however, the political world moves centre stage, and—combined with religion and science—becomes a crucial element of the narrative as cosmic war breaks out between opposing parties. This is tied to Asriel's political ambitions, and principally his aim to create a 'republic of heaven' as opposed to the oppressive 'kingdom of heaven' that Asriel's right-hand man, Ogunwe, describes to Mrs Coulter:

> 'We're not going to invade the kingdom [of heaven], . . . but if the kingdom invades us, they had better be ready for war, because we are prepared. Mrs Coulter, I am a king, but it's my proudest task to join Lord Asriel in setting up a world where there are no kingdoms at all. No kings, no bishops, no priests. The kingdom of heaven has been known by that name since the Authority first set himself above the rest of the angels. And we want no part of it. This world is different. We intend to be free citizens of the republic of heaven.' (AS 222)

Asriel's vision is utopian and democratic, his central tenet being the idea of a 'republic' which resists the authority of kings, bishops and priests, as well as the Authority of God himself. Pullman thus aligns Asriel with a series of radical and anti-authoritarian thinkers, notably William Blake, whom Pullman credits in his acknowledgements to the trilogy (AS 550).

Asriel's vision is clearly one that Pullman also espouses. Asriel's affirmative attitude towards human physicality and comradeship, as evidenced by his impassioned speech to Ogunwe about the primacy of the human body, is one of the prevailing messages of the trilogy. The trilogy celebrates adolescent love and sexuality, but more generally it is very evocative in its representations of the sensation of existing in the material world. Asriel's allies are depicted favourably, whereas his opponents are very negatively portrayed. And yet in the figure of Asriel himself, the desire for political power—even if it is sought for a cause which would seem commendable—is shown to be a dubious, even dangerous attribute. It is unclear throughout the majority of the trilogy whether Asriel is in fact a force for good or for evil. His first appearance is very soon marked by his twisting Lyra's arm so hard she sinks to the floor in pain, while he dominates her with a look of 'restrained fury' (NL 14). At the end of *Northern Lights*, Asriel causes the death of Lyra's best friend, Roger, in order to achieve his political and scientific aims, thus proving himself to be ruthless in the pursuit of his cause. In their discussion of Dust at this point, Lyra and Pantalaimon decide that it must be good, because Asriel wants to destroy it, as do '"the Oblation Board and the Church and Bolvangar and Mrs Coulter and all"' (NL 397). Pantalaimon's logic is that '"if *they* all think Dust is bad, it must be good"' (NL 397). It is only later in the trilogy that it becomes clear that Asriel, in battling against the Magisterium and the Authority, is fighting a good cause.

Asriel is largely depicted at a remove. He does not appear in person in *The Subtle Knife* at all, and in this volume his political activity is reported rather than directly narrated. Ogunwe, Ruta Skadi and Asriel's servant Thorold all speak on his behalf in *The Subtle Knife* and *The Amber Spyglass*. His narrative, and some of its direct political import, is therefore distanced from Lyra and Will's adventures, and yet it continues to provide a backdrop throughout the trilogy. In the later stages of *The Amber Spyglass*, however, it comes to the fore during the pitched battles between the assembled forces. During these battles, Lyra, Will, the subtle knife and various of their allies, including Iorek and Lee Scoresby, are conscripted to Asriel's cause.

The trilogy's narrative does not dwell too long on Asriel as a figure, nor on his cause, although the brief depictions of them are vivid. This is perhaps because Asriel and his politics do not bear too much inspection. Asriel himself is ruthless and violent, and whether, once he had achieved power, he would exercise it benevolently is open to debate. He has a stated aim of creating a 'republic of heaven', but how this would operate in pragmatic political terms is unclear. When his political ambitions are sacrificed in his tumble into the abyss with the angel Metatron and Mrs Coulter, Lyra and Will are given the freedom to create their own 'republic of heaven', as Lyra says to Pantalaimon in the very final sentence of the trilogy (AS 548). Yet Lyra's version is a very different entity from Asriel's grand political vision. Asriel's politics are not realised, and the political vision that *His Dark Materials* represents through the medium of Asriel is only partially explained and explored. There is a narrative gap here, a loose end of the sort referred to in the introduction to this book, a space in which the ideology underpinning the trilogy is left open.

In an essay which gives a thought-provoking critique of the trilogy, Daniel P Moloney suggests that there may have been some confusion in Pullman's mind in his creation of Asriel, with particular regard to the rewriting of *Paradise Lost* and *His Dark Materials'* stance towards Christianity (Moloney 2005: 179–80). This is explored in the next section of this chapter, which deals with the specific politics of religion and the Church. Much of the 'high politics' of the trilogy is bound up with the power play of the Church and its detractors in Lyra's world. The struggle for control is religious as well as political.

Religion and Science

Religion in Lyra's world—like much else in her Oxford and Brytain—has similarities to the Christianity of 'our own universe' but also crucial differences. It is run by the Magisterium, a set of male priests whose appearance and structural organisation are reminiscent of the Catholic Church. The Magisterium is based not in the Catholic centre of Rome, however, but in Geneva, Switzerland, where the centre of religious power, narrates Pullman, moved in the Middle Ages under the aegis of John Calvin. This historical back story to *His Dark Materials* is an example of the phase space of alternate worlds in the trilogy. Calvin was a real-life theologian and a leader of the Protestant Reformation who founded a 'Consistorial Court of Discipline'—a phrase that Pullman picks up and uses in *His Dark Materials*—in Geneva in the sixteenth century. Calvin also established a theocracy which attempted to direct all the business and life of the city through a code of moral severity and systematic doctrine. Pullman imagines a world in which the ecclesiastical rule founded by Calvin in Geneva has extended throughout Europe and dominates religious thinking and moral behaviour:

> Ever since Pope John Calvin had moved the seat of the Papacy to Geneva and set up the Consistorial Court of Discipline, the Church's power over every aspect of life had been absolute. The Papacy itself had been abolished after Calvin's death, and a tangle of courts, colleges, and councils, collectively known as the Magisterium, had grown up in its place. These agencies were not always united; sometimes a bitter rivalry grew up between them. For a large part of the previous century, the most powerful had been the College of Bishops, but in recent years the Consistorial Court of Discipline had taken its place as the most active and the most feared of all the Church's bodies. (NL 31)

In Lyra's day, the Consistorial Court of Discipline remains '"the most powerful and effective arm of the Holy Church"', although its dominance is challenged by Mrs Coulter and her activities at Bolvangar with the General Oblation Board (AS 73). The President of the Consistorial Court is the ascetic Father MacPhail:

> a dark-featured man, tall and imposing, with a shock of wiry grey hair, and he would have been fat were it not for the brutal discipline he imposed on his body: he drank only water and ate only bread and fruit, and he exercised for an hour daily under the supervision of a trainer of champion athletes. As a result, he was gaunt and lined and restless. His dæmon was a lizard. (AS 73)

The religion of Lyra's world has also—in variance to ours—developed a strain of scientific philosophy called 'experimental theology'. Jordan College, as Lyra is aware, is the world's leading centre of the subject. She is much less clear, however, about what experimental theology actually is: 'She had formed the notion that it was concerned with magic, with the movements of the stars and planets, with tiny particles of matter, but that was guesswork, really' (NL 35). Later, Lyra's patchy education reveals that she does know something about this subject, and of 'atoms and elementary particles, and anbaromagnetic charges and the four fundamental forces and other bits and pieces of experimental theology' (NL 83).

The image Lyra sees of Asriel's experiments in the North while hiding in the Retiring Room wardrobe further suggests that this is a practical science as much as an abstract enterprise: 'Beside the hut stood an array of philosophical instruments, which looked to Lyra's eye like something from the Anbaric Park on the road to Yarnton: aerials, wires, porcelain insulators, all glittering in the moonlight and thickly covered in frost' (NL 21). From Lyra's haphazard knowledge, experimental theology seems to be a fusion of astronomy and quantum physics, and yet it clearly also has a religious dimension to it. Experimental theology is controlled by the Church, and heresy is firmly dealt with. Asriel's photograms of another world in the Aurora remind the Scholars of the '"Barnard-Stokes business"', as the Master of the College explains to the Librarian later in private:

As I understand it, the Holy Church teaches that there are two worlds: the world of everything we can *See* and hear and touch, and another world, the spiritual world of heaven and hell. Barnard and Stokes were two—how shall I put it—*renegade* theologians who postulated the existence of numerous other worlds like this one, neither heaven nor hell, but material and sinful. They are there, close by, but invisible and unreachable. The Holy Church naturally disapproved of this abominable heresy, and Barnard and Stokes were silenced. (NL 31–32)

In this speech, delivered very early on in the trilogy, Pullman introduces into the narrative theological debate, astronomical enquiry, the concept of phase space, the idea of sin and the chilling notion that those who disagree with the orthodoxy are '"silenced"'.

This is a heady mix of science and religion, carefully monitored by the controlling power of the Holy Church. Asriel's scientific explorations and political machinations are entangled in this mix and bring him into direct conflict with the Magisterium and, later, the God figure and second-in-command themselves, the Authority and Metatron.

Central to the religious and scientific thematics of *His Dark Materials* is Pullman's second inspired creation after the dæmons, that of 'Dust'. To the fundamentalist Consistorial Court of Discipline, Dust is the root of all evil and the justification for their plot to assassinate Lyra. Moreover, the Court would accept even its own destruction for the sake of ridding the world of Dust:

> 'If in order to destroy Dust we also have to destroy the Oblation Board, the College of Bishops, every single agency by which the Holy Church does the work of the Authority—then so be it. It may be, gentlemen, that the Holy Church itself was brought into being to perform this very task and to perish in the doing of it. But better a world with no church and no Dust than a world where every day we have to struggle under the hideous burden of sin. Better a world purged of all that!' (AS 74)

The President's avowal has a destructive logic that would prefer nothingness to an existence with '"the hideous burden of sin"'. This is an extreme denial and is an important factor in the image Pullman builds up of the Holy Church. The Church in *His Dark Materials* is populated with life-denying clerics like Father McPhail, whose lust for power is eclipsed only by his fervent desire to eradicate Dust— and its correlatives of human knowledge and sexuality, as the next section of this chapter examines—from the world. According to Pantalaimon's reasoning at the end of *Northern Lights*, Asriel also seems to want to destroy Dust, and it is this rationale that persuades Lyra to follow Asriel out of her world and 'into the sky' (NL 399). Yet Asriel's attitudes towards Dust and the Church are complex. After her conversation with him at the end of *Northern Lights*, Lyra is left confused. Asriel explains his paradoxical mission to her:

'Somewhere out there is the origin of all the Dust, all the
death, the sin, the misery, the destructiveness in the world.
Human beings can't *See* anything without wanting to destroy
it, Lyra. *That's* original sin. And I'm going to destroy it. Death
is going to die.' (NL 377)

Asriel equates Dust with death, sin, misery and destructiveness
and thus states that he wants to kill death. After Asriel crosses to the
next world in pursuit of his mission, Lyra debates with Pantalaimon
whether Dust is a good or bad thing. Pantalaimon says that Asriel is
'"going to find the source of Dust and destroy it"' (NL 397), whereas
in fact what Asriel actually says is that he will destroy *death* and
eradicate the concept of 'original sin'. It is perhaps Pantalaimon's
confusion that leads the critic Moloney to interrogate Asriel's mission and to conclude that Pullman changes his mind about its purpose in the course of writing the trilogy. Moloney comments on
Asriel's explanation to Lyra:

This is clearly an allusion to the fall of man, the topic of the
later books of Milton's epic poem. But . . . in *The Subtle Knife*
Pullman goes out of his way to tell us that Asriel wants to con-
quer heaven and overthrow the Authority—a clear allusion to
the *opening* books of *Paradise Lost*. The reader finds out, and
Asriel is supposed to know, that destroying the Authority will
not affect Dust at all, that these are two different tasks. So it
seems Pullman has changed his mind about Asriel's intentions.
He tries to patch up this significant amendment to the plot by
having Asriel explain away one of his speeches from [*Northern
Lights*]—at the end of *The Amber Spyglass*, Asriel admits to Mrs
Coulter that he lied to her about destroying Dust during their
passionate embrace at Svalbard. But Pullman never explains
away Asriel's much more powerful speech to Lyra arguing for
the same thing. (Moloney 2005: 179–80)

Moloney's reading of Asriel's apparent change of direction, then,
is based on Pantalaimon's misapprehension of Asriel's task, and also,

perhaps, by Asriel's own powerful rhetoric. Asriel's position is more consistent than Moloney suggests, although there is a considerable amount of ambiguity in his character. It is overwhelmingly clear that in him Pullman has created a character through whom to voice strong anti-Church ideology. The purpose of Dust, on the other hand, remains unconfirmed until the final volume of the trilogy, by which time Asriel's mission has solidified into a wholesale war against the forces of the Church. The witch Ruta Skadi reports to Lyra, Will and the witch clans on her conversations with Asriel about this forthcoming battle against the Authority:

> 'He showed me that to rebel was right and just, when you con-
> sidered what the agents of the Authority did in his name . . .
> And I thought of the Bolvangar children, and the other terri-
> ble mutilations I have seen done in our own south-lands;
> and he told me of many more hideous cruelties dealt out in the
> Authority's name—of how they capture witches, in some worlds,
> and burn them alive, sisters, yes, witches like ourselves . . .
>   'He opened my eyes. He showed me things I never had
> seen, cruelties and horrors all committed in the name of the
> Authority, all designed to destroy the joys and the truthful-
> ness of life.' (SK 283)

Through Ruta Skadi, Pullman voices some of his own criticisms of the Church and organised religion: that it has been responsible in our world for burning witches alive and, as he hints, for 'terrible mutilations' in the form, perhaps, of circumcision and genital muti-lation. Within the realms of the narrative of *His Dark Materials*, the mutilations refer specifically to the General Oblation Board's work of intercision at Bolvangar. Yet Ruta Skadi's speech makes it clear that Pullman's argument with organised religion extends beyond the fictional frame of his narrative, as many of his comments in the media have emphasised, and at least part of the didactic role of the trilogy is to convey this very negative message about organised reli-gion. As Pullman clarifies on his website, although he finds 'the reli-gious impulse' an understandable and necessary part of humankind, *organised* religion has led to 'terrible damage'. 'In the name of their god', churches and priesthoods 'have burned, hanged, tortured, maimed, robbed, violated, and enslaved millions of their fellow-creatures, and done so with the happy conviction that they were doing the will of God, and they would go to Heaven for it' (www.philip-pullman.com: g). Pullman's words are emphatic in their condemnation of the Church.

Returning to the frame of *His Dark Materials*, Asriel's passionate campaign against the crimes committed in the name of the Authority convinces Ruta Skadi and several other witch clans to join his forces. Asriel makes it his mission to battle not just against the forces of the Church but against the Authority—or the God figure—himself. As his servant Thorold reports, Asriel is attempting a second rebellion against the Authority, after the failure of the rebel angels that is narrated in *Paradise Lost* (SK 47–49). Asriel's mission, then, is to institute his republic of heaven.

When the Authority eventually appears in *The Amber Spyglass*, he proves a poor comparison to the dynamic Asriel: he is old and terrified, 'crying like a baby and cowering away into the lowest corner', 'demented and powerless' (AS 431). This is the depiction of the Authority that would prove so contentious to Christian critics of the trilogy. John Houghton, in his very critical Christian approach to Pullman in *A Closer Look at* His Dark Materials, comments that 'the Authority, as he calls him, appears to be in character very much like . . . a rather nasty and fallible Old Testament god' (Houghton 2004: 115). Moreover, Pullman describes the Authority not as the creator but as the 'deceiving first angel', who, when he is found by Lyra and Will, 'is deserving only of pity and hardly worth the bother; he is too pathetic to waste your life on—a total irrelevancy' (Houghton 2004: 115, 118). Houghton sees this depiction as a gross parody of the god of the Christian Church. The alternate vision of the Christian Church and of god that Pullman presents through his rewriting of the Fall, original sin, sexuality and Lyra as the new Eve inevitably proved controversial.

Yet Pullman is not only creating a revised religion in the trilogy but also inserting a scientific fabric into his narrative. Experimental theology has as much to do with science as religion, and the city in the sky which Asriel photographs recalls the alternate-worlds theory of quantum physics. Pullman's interest in science suffuses the trilogy, and this has been recognised by the dedication of an entire book and several essays to the investigation of the science that inspired *His Dark Materials* (Gribbin and Gribbin 2003; Metzger 2005; Markham 2005). In Pullman's introduction to the book by Mary and John Gribbin, he claims, 'Although I did try to get a bit of science in, and to get it right, it was very much there as a background, as a sort of stage set for the story to take place in front of' (Pullman 2003b: xvii). Pullman is being disingenuous here, for although he is prioritising his plotting and characterisation in the trilogy, it is clear that science, and a scientific rather than a religious perspective, is the prevailing ethos of the story. The Gribbins offer chapters on dark matter, the northern lights, the unconscious mind, quantum physics, string theory, choice and possibility, and Gaia. Indeed, another scientific and political strand of the trilogy, and one largely overlooked by its critics, is its environmentalism. On his website, Pullman has pronounced his own personal commitment to the environmental cause of the real world and warned of the dangers of irresponsible stewardship of the earth's resources and the consequent impact of climate change (www.philip-pullman.com: c). His political concern is carried into the narrative of *His Dark Materials*, linking the dangers of ecological catastrophe to the political and moral aspects of the trilogy.

In the mulefas' world of *The Amber Spyglass*, Dust is drifting out to sea, the seed-pod trees are dying and the mutually interdependent relationship of the trees and the mulefas is unravelling. The mulefas tell Mary of the many years of living with their trees 'in perpetual joy' (AS 139). Their communion with nature is symbiotic, and their lifestyle almost hippy-like in its gentle but enriching existence. The threat posed to this lifestyle is from the disruptions caused to the boundaries between the worlds three hundred years earlier, when the subtle knife was invented and used to make windows from one world to the next. This is profoundly exacerbated by Lord Asriel's blowing apart of the boundaries at the end of *Northern*

Lights. The mulefas, and their close relationship to the land, are a fascinating invention not least because they are clearly a metaphor for humanity: they are sentient beings with language, history and culture, who have their own founding myth that occurred around thirty-three thousand years ago—the time at which humans are commonly believed to have developed in evolutionary theory, and the point at which Mary and her research team calculate that Dust started to cluster on the human skulls housed in the museum. In narrating the 'make-like', or metaphor, of their acquisition of 'memory and wakefulness' to Mary, the mulefas are also used to express a belief in evolutionary science rather than creationism. This is a developmental pattern rather than a god-given one, which is consistent with Pullman's anti-Church stance and his belief in scientific explanations over religious ones (AS 236).

The vision of a disrupted ecosystem is supplemented by other warnings of environmental damage, which form an understated and yet insistent theme in both *The Subtle Knife* and *The Amber Spyglass*. At the end of *Northern Lights*, when Asriel harnesses the energy produced by splitting Roger from his dæmon in order to open his way to the next world, he unleashes upon his own world the hazards of climate change. Its effects are similar to the implications of real-world global warming. Will mentions these to Lyra, saying that '"people have been interfering with the atmosphere by putting chemicals in it and the weather's going out of control"' (SK 322). In the North of Lyra's world, there are thaws and floods and rivers flowing in the opposite direction than usual. The migration patterns of animals are disturbed. Serafina Pekkala, viewing the damage from her vantage point flying above the earth, feels 'heartsick' as 'the whole of nature [is] overturned' (AS 39).

On his travels in *The Amber Spyglass*, when he is separated from Lyra, Will meets a priest with an apocalyptic vision. He tells Will this environmental change is foretold in the Bible as 'a convulsion in the earth', a turning of rivers:

'All the way from the mountains of central Asia it flowed north for thousands and thousands of years, ever since the

Authority of God the Almighty Father created the earth. But
when the earth shook and the fog and the floods came, everything changed . . . The world is turned upside down.' (AS 103)

In his mission to defeat the Authority, Asriel splits the Aurora,
with the effect of changing the face of the world that others believe
the Authority to have created. Asriel thus casts himself in the role of
a new creator, defiantly 'controlling' the northern lights (NL 392). In
so doing, Asriel's intentions are highly contentious. He may aspire to
create a republic of heaven, but he quite literally risks the earth itself.
Asriel's enterprise is therefore a very equivocal one, as is his political
mission generally.

In comparison to Asriel's scientific actions, which result in a
series of ethical dilemmas, Mary Malone is a much more responsible scientist. In *The Subtle Knife*, she is very resistant to the idea of
her investigation into dark matter being controlled by a funding
body, represented to her by Sir Charles Latrom, which might use her
findings for military purposes. In *The Amber Spyglass*, she turns into
a participant anthropologist, observing and interacting with the
mulefas. Then, through her careful observation and hard graft in the
construction of the spyglass, she discovers why the seed-pod trees
are dying and sets out to solve the problem, although it is Lyra and
Will's act which actually reverses the flow of Dust.

As Will's father explains to Will and Lyra, Asriel's scientific and
political mission is doomed to failure because a dæmon can live a
full life only in the world in which it was born—a rule that will have
serious implications for Will and Lyra at the end of the trilogy. This
ruling, as John Parry explains, dooms Asriel's ambitions, as '"we
have to build the republic of heaven where we are, because for us
there is no elsewhere"' (AS 382). Pullman's affirmation of the here
and now in *His Dark Materials* is one of the strongest messages of
the trilogy. Human morality is not invested in another world or in
an afterlife. It is firmly rooted in the physical being, the material
body and the present time. As Lyra says to Pantalaimon in the very
final section of *The Amber Spyglass*, '"He meant the kingdom was
over, the kingdom of heaven, it was all finished. We shouldn't live as

if it mattered more than life in this world, because where we are is always the most important place"' (AS 548).

Lyra's emancipation of the dead from the underworld also connects, then, to the environmental morality of *His Dark Materials*, thus (ironically) fulfilling the Bible's myth of Dust that Asriel reads to Lyra. As Lyra explains to the fearful dead:

> 'When you go out of here, all the particles that make you up will loosen and float apart, just like your dæmons did . . . But your dæmons en't just *nothing* now; they're part of everything. All the atoms that were them, they've gone into the air and the wind and the trees and the earth and all the living things. They'll never vanish. They're just part of everything. And that's exactly what'll happen to you, I swear to you, I promise on my honour. You'll drift apart, it's true, but you'll be out in the open, part of everything alive again.' (AS 335)

Lyra's explanation of their future as once more part of the living world is achieved, and people are indeed connected to the 'air and the wind and the trees and the earth' at an atomic level. Ironically, this destiny of Dust returning to dust is the language of the traditional Christian burial service, and in some ways, this pantheistic myth of atoms dispersing into the environment to rejoin nature is as much of a consolatory myth as that of an afterlife in heaven. Nevertheless, the impact of how these two different afterlives might affect people's actions during their lives is perhaps different. One myth implies a judgement by the Church and by the Authority, whereas the other does not. In having to tell stories to the harpies before they are released, the dead nevertheless have to make some sort of account for their lives, although the harpies do not have a judgemental role. There are, however, some paradoxes in Pullman's alternate vision of an afterlife. Some characters are allowed an existence beyond their lifetime and their time in the land of the dead, thus allowing for moments of catharsis and reconciliation. As such, Lyra is able to atone for her unintentional betrayal of her friend Roger, which resulted in his death at the hands of Lord Asriel at the end of *Northern Lights*. Moreover, Will is granted precious further moments to speak with his father's ghost after his premature death at the end of *The Subtle Knife*. Lee Scoresby, who is also killed at the end of *The Subtle Knife* in an act of heroic defence, is also granted further life in death in *The Amber Spyglass*, and with John Parry joins Lord Asriel's forces as a ghost. For the child protagonists of *His Dark Materials*, this allows them to regain past time, recapture relationships they thought were lost for ever and make good past mistakes and oversights. This lack of consistency in Pullman's narrative, and its consequent disruption of his ideological intent, is one of the loose ends of the trilogy.

Science, politics and religion are thus bound together in *His Dark Materials*, even if their treatment is occasionally self-contradictory. The experiments that Lord Asriel is conducting in the North, and Mrs Coulter's activities in the Experimental Station at Bolvangar, are both explorations of the relationship between Dust and human activity. This scientific dimension to the trilogy is also part of its moral dimension, and so is connected to *His Dark Materials*' emphasis on choice and the concept of phase space, and Pullman's inscription of human—and particularly adolescent—sexuality, to which this chapter turns next.

Sexuality

At the end of *Northern Lights*, Lord Asriel explains to Lyra about Dust and the way it connects to his mission and the version of the Creation story by which their universe abides. In Asriel's explanation of Eve's temptation and Adam and Eve's consequent banishment from the garden in Genesis, Pullman's text is a rewriting of both *Paradise Lost* and its source text, the Bible. Lord Asriel reads to Lyra from Pullman's subtly altered version of the Bible, adding words about dæmons to the tempter's speech: '*For God doth know that in the day ye eat thereof, then your eyes shall be opened, and your dæmons shall assume their true forms, and ye shall be as gods, knowing good and evil*' (NL 372). The consequences of Adam and Eve's eating the forbidden tree's fruit are extreme:

'And the eyes of them both were opened, and they saw the true
form of their dæmons, and spoke with them.

'But when the man and the woman knew their own
dæmons, they knew that a great change had come upon them,
for until that moment it had seemed that they were at one with
all the creatures of the earth and the air, and there was no difference between them:

'And they saw the difference, and they knew good and evil;
and they were ashamed, and they sewed fig leaves together to
cover their nakedness . . .' (NL 372)

For the Church, this Fall is the source of 'original sin' (NL 371),
of the transition of innocence to experience and also, in Pullman's
version, of the fixing of the dæmon in its '"*true form*"'. The recent
scientific discoveries in Lyra's world provide '"a physical proof that
something happened when innocence changed into experience"'
(NL 373). The Russian scientist Rusakov discovered what Asriel
terms '"a new kind of elementary particle"' which clusters around
human beings, and particularly adults (NL 370). Through reference
to another biblical passage, the elementary particles come to be
called 'Dust' (NL 373): '"*In the sweat of thy face shalt thou eat bread,
till thou return unto the ground; for out of it wast thou taken: for dust
thou art, and unto dust shalt thou return . . .*"' (NL 373). Lyra's emancipation of the dead thus ironically fulfils the Bible's myth of Dust
when their atoms disperse into the environment.

Mrs Coulter's route to power was '"to specialize in Dust"', directing an investigation into it on behalf of the Church. Her work at the
Experimental Station in Bolvangar, in which the children she has
bewitched away from their homes are forcibly separated from their
dæmons, is concerned with the transition from innocence to experience a child makes when passing through adolescence to adulthood. Dust, as the '"physical proof"' of this transition, is closely
connected to the terrifying process the children undergo at the
Experimental Station. Rumours of this circulate through Lyra's
world. Dr Lanselius, the witches' consul, says to Lyra and the gyptians that he has '"heard the phrase *the Maystadt Process*"', and also

'"*intercision*"', in connection with the General Oblation Board's mission (NL 171). Earlier, at Mrs Coulter's cocktail party, one of the guests explains to Lyra the origin of the name of the General Oblation Board. Based on the mediaeval tradition of parents giving their children to the Church as monks or nuns, '"the unfortunate brats were known as oblates"', a word that means '"a sacrifice, an offering, something of that sort"' (NL 91).

Lyra soon finds out the terrible truth of these euphemisms. She meets her old friend Tony Makarios, who has undergone the process and lives a half-life without his dæmon. Later, when she is captured and taken to Bolvangar herself, she discovers glass cases full of dæmons that have been severed from human children. When she is discovered spying on the scientists at the Station, she almost undergoes severing herself. She and Pantalaimon are forced into separate compartments of a mesh cage, and the silver blade of the guillotine is already descending when Mrs Coulter arrives and saves them. This, incidentally, is the first moment when Mrs Coulter seems to show some maternal feeling for Lyra—she is 'in a moment haggard and horror-struck' as she realises the implications of what was just about to happen to her daughter (NL 279).

Mrs Coulter recovers from her shock and justifies the severing process to Lyra:

'All that happens is a little cut, and then everything's peaceful. For ever! You see, your dæmon's a wonderful friend and companion when you're young, but at the age we call puberty, the age you're coming to very soon, darling, dæmons bring all sort of troublesome thoughts and feelings, and that's what lets Dust in. A quick little operation before that, and you're never troubled again. And your dæmon stays with you, only . . . just not connected. Like a . . . like a wonderful pet, if you like. The best pet in the world! Wouldn't you like that?' (NL 284–85)

Lyra is repelled by Mrs Coulter's light-hearted explanation of the work of the Oblation Board, though for the time being she keeps her thoughts to herself, waiting for her moment to free the children from the Station. Lyra escapes a future as a severed adult, like the nurses in the Station with 'their strange blank incuriosity, the way their little trotting dæmons seemed to be sleepwalking' (NL 284).

Mrs Coulter's repudiation of Dust as '"something bad, something wrong, something evil and wicked"' is part of her attempt to win Lyra over through her mention of the '"troublesome thoughts and feelings"' that begin to occur at puberty (NL 284). Sexuality and Dust are connected, and it is the Church's fear of and distaste for the onset of sexual maturity that legitimates Mrs Coulter's experiments in the eyes of the Magisterium. As Lord Asriel later explains to Lyra, this fear and distaste extends back to the founding story of Adam and Eve's Fall, through Eve's desire for knowledge and to be, as the serpent puts it, '"*as gods, knowing good and evil*"'. Yet Mrs Coulter's motives in leading the Church's investigations into Dust—as with many of her actions—are profoundly dubious: she is a very sexual being and repeatedly uses her powers of seduction to achieve her own ends.

The contradiction inherent in Mrs Coulter's actions derives from and contributes to the gender politics of the trilogy. The Church, the politics of Brytain and Jordan College are all male-dominated institutions. To make her way in this patriarchal society, as Asriel explains to Lyra, Mrs Coulter turns first to marriage and seeks power by association. Later, despite being a woman and hence not able to achieve power via the priesthood, she convinces the Church to let her head the General Oblation Board. Through this position, she employs all her feminine guile and seductiveness in order to gain influence and to provide the Experimental Station with a ready supply of young victims. Her character is an archetype of a certain dangerous yet glamorous type of femininity: the femme fatale. It is evident that Mrs Coulter takes on this role in response to the limited options available to her in a male-dominated society.

Yet Mrs Coulter's is not the only model of femininity and female sexuality depicted in *His Dark Materials*. Lyra's gyptian foster parent, Ma Costa, has maternal attributes which are in stark contrast to Mrs Coulter's. In the witch clans, *His Dark Materials* represents an all-female society. The witches' relations with humans are on an equal footing, although the difficult nature of female witch and human male sexual relations is evident—because of the longevity of the witches, the objects of their love are doomed to die centuries before them. Back in Oxford, Lyra initially dismisses the Female Scholars as 'serious elderly ladies' of no interest to her (NL 67). By the end of *The Amber Spyglass*, however, Lyra shows herself more willing to accept the life of the mind as well as that of the body and agrees to join the girls' boarding school connected to one of the women's colleges, which is run by a headmistress who is 'clever, young . . . , energetic, imaginative, kindly' (AS 545). Mary Malone, the nun-turned-scientist, further extends the depiction of feminine types in her renunciation of faith for sexuality. Finally, Lyra's own transition from girl to adolescent, as the previous chapter discussed, calls into question the characterisation of women, both in her trajectory towards love and womanhood and the possible softening of her feminist credentials and in her primary role as the new Eve. In both of these manifestations of her character, gender politics are central and are part of the thematics of *His Dark Materials*.

This paradox of Mrs Coulter's behaviour, in which she uses her sexuality in order to fulfil the Church's denial of sexuality—is one of many in *His Dark Materials*. Dualistic thoughts—of the opposition between innocence and experience, for example, or between good and evil—are contested and confused by Pullman, as William Blake did before him. Mary's explanation of good and evil gives a truer representation of Pullman's belief in the combination of opposites:

'When you stopped believing in God,' [Will] went on, 'did you stop believing in good and evil?'

'No. But I stopped believing there was a power of good and a power of evil that were outside us. And I came to believe that good and evil are names for what people do, not for what they are. All we can say is that this is a good deed, because it helps someone, or that's an evil one, because it hurts them. People are too complicated to have simple labels.' (AS 470–71)

Mary's loss of faith, but not of morality, is an indication of the attitudes towards religion which *His Dark Materials* conveys and which Pullman's rewriting of the myth of Adam and Eve promotes. Morality is possible without religion. In fact, in Pullman's version, morality is much more emphatically personalised without religion. In *His Dark Materials*, there are three versions of the story of the Fall. These versions are created in Pullman's grand project of rewriting *Paradise Lost* and the story of Adam and Eve in Genesis. The first version is the one that Asriel reads to Lyra from the Bible of their universe, a version closely adapted from the real-world Old Testament of Judaism and Christianity. The second is a story narrated to Mary Malone by the mulefas. In this story, the mulefas gain knowledge—'*memory and wakefulness*'—through their use of the seed-pods and the creation of 'sraf', as the mulefas term Dust (AS 236). The relationship of happy mutuality between the mulefas and the seed-pod trees is a very different one from the harsh banishment of Adam and Eve by God. When Mary meets the mulefas, however, this symbiotic relationship is in jeopardy: the seed-pod trees are dying, and Dust, as Mary discovers by looking through the amber spyglass, is drifting out to sea rather than falling on the trees and fertilising them. Environmental jeopardy spurs her involvement in the reversal of the traditional morality associated with the Fall. Her understanding of Dust leads her towards her own role as tempter in the third version of the story, in which Lyra plays Eve and Will is Adam.

Mary's narration of her sexual experience is the spur to Lyra's fulfilling her destiny as Eve. Lyra's growing feelings for Will become apparent as she listens to Mary's story. On the morning in which Lyra and Will set off to find their dæmons, they walk together as if they were 'the only people in the world', a clear reference to their re-enactment of the biblical myth of the first two people on earth (AS 483). Their pursuit of their dæmons leads them into the 'little wood of silver-barked trees', to their declaration of their love for one another and to a physical manifestation of that love. For Father Gomez, commissioned by the Church to follow and stop them, this adolescent sexuality is 'mortal sin' (AS 489). For Lyra and Will it is a mixture of confusion and happiness and adoration. Pullman's third version of the Fall is a celebration of love and adolescent sexuality and a vindication of a very different morality from that espoused by the Church. In this scene, Pullman counters the Church of *His Dark Materials*, but also the real-world Christian Church, and its tortured and frequently repressive stance towards sex, as Pullman would view it.

The implications of Lyra and Will's venture into the wood, and into adulthood, are observed, and welcomed, by Mary and the mulefas. The drift of Dust is reversed, and the seed-pod trees once more are 'drinking in this golden rain' after being 'starved for so long' (AS 496). Ecological catastrophe is averted. Mary sees Lyra and Will returning to the mulefa village:

> There was no need for the glass; she knew what she would see; they would seem to be made of living gold. They would seem the true image of what human beings always could be, once they had come into their inheritance.
>
> The Dust pouring down from the stars had found a living home again, and these children-no-longer-children, saturated with love, were the cause of it all. (AS 497)

Lyra and Will's transition, then, from children to young adults is portrayed with extreme favour, and their intervention in the history of Dust is crucial in the reorientation of morality in Pullman's revision of the Fall. The vision of young love and a new moral order at the end of *The Amber Spyglass* is in contradiction to the repressive morality of the Church of *His Dark Materials* and is a crucial element of the trilogy's alternative morality.

Morality

His Dark Materials depicts two child protagonists in adult worlds, who, by the end of the trilogy, are themselves entering adulthood, both through their moral decisions and their sexual activity. As the introduction discussed, Pullman conceived the trilogy as a version of *Paradise Lost* for teenagers. In the UK, the books were published by Scholastic, a children's publisher. David Fickling, the UK editor of the trilogy and the publisher of *Lyra's Oxford*, describes his eponymous publishing house as 'ostensibly for children' (Fickling 2005). Despite his early adult novels *The Haunted Storm* and *Galatea*, Pullman was known as a children's writer before the publication of *Northern Lights*, *The Subtle Knife* and *The Amber Spyglass*.

Yet many of the themes discussed in this chapter—religion, politics, sexuality—might be ones traditionally thought of as the domain of serious adult literature. In chapter 6, which looks at the question, what type of story is *His Dark Materials*?, this issue is explored in more detail with regard to the trilogy's publishing, literary and genre contexts. This section investigates the positioning and potential controversy of the trilogy as a children's story, thinks about how this relates to Pullman's rewriting of the Fall and his sense of morality within the trilogy, and considers how issues of free will, choice and predestination fit into this morality.

The narrative of *His Dark Materials*, then, is centrally concerned with the transition from childhood to adulthood. At the beginning of *Northern Lights*, despite her connections to the adult worlds of politics and religion, Lyra's life is lived as a child. While her early childhood friendships and activities are not dismissed, she follows a trajectory through the trilogy via adolescence towards adult responsibility. As such, she becomes enmeshed in the political worlds of her father and her mother and develops a sexual relationship with Will. Yet the narration of Lyra's experience of politics and sex is different from her father's and mother's, and the republic of heaven envisioned by Asriel is an entity very different from the one Lyra settles for at the end of *The Amber Spyglass*. Asriel's republic is an intensely political one, one which, it could be assumed, would necessarily involve political structures and organisations to replace those of the Magisterium. Whether the utopian ideals of Asriel's republic could be sustained, and how such a political entity might operate, is unanswered. These questions remain unanswered because Asriel dies, and the political shape of Lyra's world is left undetermined. A brief paragraph at the end of *The Amber Spyglass* suggests that some good has come to her world and that at least some of the oppressive power of the Church has been undermined. The General Oblation Board has been dissolved, and 'upheavals in the Magisterium . . . toppled the zealots and brought more liberal factions into power' (AS 541). Nevertheless, Asriel's mission is unaccomplished and the hold of the Church over Lyra's world endures. College life returns to 'the calm of scholarship and ritual', and despite the cataclysmic nature of Asriel's quest, political life and social organisation seem to have changed little in Lyra's world (AS 541).

Lyra's republic of heaven, on the other hand, is a different entity. It is not so much a method of political organisation as a moral code. It is a path first articulated to her and Will by the angel Xaphania, in her explanation of the creation of Dust and its loss through the windows cut into other worlds by the subtle knife:

> 'Conscious beings makes Dust—they renew it all the time, by thinking and feeling and reflecting, by gaining wisdom and passing it on.
>
> 'And if you help everyone else in your worlds to do that, by helping them to learn and understand about themselves and each other and the way everything works, and by showing them how to be kind instead of cruel, and patient instead of surly, and above all how to keep their minds open and free and curious . . . Then they will renew enough to replace what is lost through one window. So there could be one left open.' (AS 520)

At the end of her speech, Xaphania refers to the choice that Lyra and Will make at the end of the trilogy, to spend the rest of their lives apart, restricted to their separate worlds. This decision is part of the narrative and moral substance of the trilogy, and it is bound up with Pullman's concept of the republic of heaven, which Lyra reiterates at the very end of *The Amber Spyglass*: '"We have to be all those difficult things like cheerful and kind and curious and brave and patient, and we've got to study and think, and work hard, all of us, in all our different worlds"' (AS 548). The result of such activity will be, according to Lyra, '"the republic of heaven"' (AS 548). This projected republic, then, is established from the individual's own sense of morality and responsibility and builds on liberal values that are also, arguably, traditional to children's literature in its instructional tendency rather than the structures of the adult world of politics.

Less traditional to children's literature—though certainly not a stranger to more recent teen and young adult books—is the narration of Lyra's sexual awakening. However, as with the political activity of her parents, Lyra's sexual activity is less overt than that of her parents. Particularly in comparison to her mother, who explicitly uses sex for political purposes, Lyra's sexuality, although central to the plot, is both subtler and more subtly described. Lyra and Will's first sexual encounter, the one that reverses the flow of Dust out of the mulefas' world and makes Lyra the new Eve, is depicted with due regard for their innocence and inexperience: 'Like two moths clumsily bumping together, with no more weight than that, their lips touched. Then before they knew how it happened, they were clinging together, blindly pressing their faces towards each other' (AS 492).

This is an act which makes them 'children-no-longer-children' (AS 497). And yet the description of their later sexual encounter, which is cited in chapter 2, is written with a certain coyness about what they are actually doing. It is not entirely clear whether Lyra and Will have had sex or are fumbling around each other's bodies. As a metaphor of sexual union, the moment in which Will reaches out for Lyra's dæmon is entirely in keeping with the laws Pullman has set up regarding dæmons. The two children are depicted as lovers, and their dæmons' settling marks their ultimate transition to adulthood. The structure of metaphor means that a sexual act is not directly described, however, and so readers must make their own interpretation. This could be thought of as prudishness—the trilogy is, after all, ostensibly written for children and perhaps a veil of modesty is being drawn over the sexual act. Instead, rather than slavishly celebrating human sexuality via explicit description, metaphor and the poetics of the trilogy intervene. This is an instance of Pullman's leaving the narrative open to interpretation, to readerly intervention and to a more poetic description of the trilogy's themes. Pullman depicts their union glancingly rather than explicitly, turning it into one of the loose ends of the trilogy.

Yet for Pullman, despite the openness and interpretability of these scenes, the narrative is also a device through which he delivers moral messages via the medium of story. Lyra and Will's first sexual encounter is the one which casts Lyra as the new Eve, and their act as a second, positively constructed, Fall. It is the point at which the trilogy fulfils Pullman's ambition of rewriting *Paradise Lost*, and indeed the Bible, in its depiction of a woman offering fruit to a man, as Lyra does to Will. Pullman has articulated his argument with the biblical Fall story and sets about in *His Dark Materials* to rewrite it, via the previous writings of Milton in *Paradise Lost*, Heinrich von Kleist in 'On the Marionette Theatre' (1810; sometimes translated as 'The Puppet Theatre') and C S Lewis's *Voyage to Venus* (1943; alternatively titled *Perelandra*). With particular reference to the latter, Pullman describes in an interview the different perspective he is trying to create in his trilogy. In Lewis's novel,

> there is a new Paradise on the planet Venus. There's an Eve and there's an Adam, and there's a wicked person just like Satan setting off to tempt Eve in the Garden of Eden. There's a wicked scientist from earth who's going to go there and cause her Fall, and we, the good guys, must go there and get to her before he does . . . Only mine is precisely the reverse. Eve must fall. Lyra must be tempted. It is the Church, the ostensibly good guys, who are trying to protect her, and we are with Satan this time, as it were. But this time Satan is understood to be good rather than evil. (Parsons and Nicholson 1999: 119)

Pullman goes on to say that in his view the Fall is 'completely essential. It's the best thing, the most important thing that ever happened to us, and if we had our heads straight on this issue, we would have churches dedicated to Eve instead of the Virgin Mary' (Parsons and Nicholson 1999: 119).

For Pullman, then, the Fall narrative is a necessary precursor to consciousness, knowledge and experience. For the child protagonists of his trilogy, it is also the beginning of their adult lives. Yet the trilogy concentrates on their childhood and adolescence, and as such, the Fall scene is placed towards the end of the narrative rather than at the beginning, as it is in the Bible. However, Pullman's Fall is woven into his story in an additional way. When Lyra offers the fruit to Will, and they kiss, the moment may seem personal, but it has other, broader ramifications. Mary Malone is aware of these ramifications because of her scientific study with the amber spyglass. Previously, Dust had being flooding into the sky, away from the seed-pod trees. After the Fall scene, though, the flow of Dust is reversed, and it falls down, into the flowers of the trees. Mary sees Lyra and Will's return but knows without the aid of the amber spyglass that she will *See* Dust 'pouring down from the stars', finding 'a living home again' (AS 497).

Environmental catastrophe is averted, human sexuality is celebrated, and consciousness, knowledge and experience are cast as positive virtues. Here, rather than just breaking down the Fall myth and rejecting Christian morality, Pullman is attempting to construct an alternate morality. It is one that is not religious but is nonetheless deeply grounded in the Christian narrative. Pullman does not espouse an amoral universe but rather one with a strong sense of purpose, value and responsibility. *His Dark Materials* is a profoundly moral work, and Lyra's closing description to Pantalaimon of the task that faces them at the end of *The Amber Spyglass*—to build the republic of heaven on earth—is an emphatic articulation of that morality.

A central tenet of the replacement morality posited in the trilogy is that of responsibility and the consequences of choice. These moral values are incorporated into the plotting of the trilogy, determining the shape of the story. Towards the end of *The Amber Spyglass*, Lyra and Will are confronted with a major choice, one which has profound implications for their own lives and those of everyone around them. Xaphania explains to them that the windows made between various worlds by the subtle knife are leaking Dust and must be closed. If Lyra and Will teach people the morality that they have learnt, the angel tells them that there will be enough Dust to leave open one window. The awful choice that Lyra and Will are then faced with is whether they will leave open one window between their two respective worlds so that they can continue to *See* each other or whether they will choose to leave open the window through which the dead can escape into 'the world of grass and air and silver light', a place where 'their faces [transform . . .] with joy' as they 'h[o]ld out their arms as if they were embracing the whole universe' before they 'simply [drift . . .] away, becoming part of the earth and the dew and the night breeze' (AS 455). In other words, Lyra and Will face the choice of whether to put their own new-found happiness above that of all of the dead. This places on their young shoulders an immediate and weighty moral burden, which they face up to with bravery and resilience. They decide to live in their separate worlds, without an open window through which they can be reunited.

Before arriving at this moment of major choice, though, the children face a series of choices throughout the trilogy, all of which test their ingenuity, bravery and morality. Early on, Lyra decides she will intervene in the plot to assassinate Lord Asriel despite Pantalaimon's attempt to dissuade her. Later, a most painful choice for Lyra is the moment at which, in order to enter the world of the dead and rescue her friend, she must separate from her dæmon, leaving him behind on the riverbank. Pullman articulates Lyra's thoughts explicitly as a moral struggle between what she knows she should do, but which will cause her to endure great pain, and selfish self-preservation:

> She *could* turn back.
> She could say no, this is a bad idea, we mustn't do it.
> She could be true to the heart-deep, life-deep bond linking her to Pantalaimon, she could put that first, she could push the rest out of her mind—
> But she couldn't. (AS 298)

Choice is therefore integrally bound up with morality, and in the trilogy it is also linked to the process whereby children's dæmons settle as they become adults. This is the process by which, as the Able-Seaman explains to Lyra, humans come to know '"what kind of person you are"', marking their transition from innocence to experience (NL 167). Humans cannot choose the forms of their dæmons, as the Able-Seaman makes very explicit. But the form in which a dæmon settles depends on the character of its human, which has been informed by his or her previous acts and decisions. This narrative articulation of the concept of phase space therefore demonstrates how decision-making is morality. Choice, then, is a key component of the alternative morality posited by Pullman in *His Dark Materials*. However, it is worth considering what informs the choices of his characters and how that morality of choice can be accounted for, as such an analysis uncovers some paradoxical elements.

For Lyra, one of the great guiding forces throughout the trilogy is the alethiometer. Given to her by the Master of Jordan College, he explains it as a truth-telling device, which she should keep '"private"', at least from Mrs Coulter (NL 74). As Lyra learns how to read the golden compass, she discovers that it will guide her on her quest. In *The Subtle Knife*, for example, it instructs her to help Will search for his father (SK 83). Later, she asks the alethiometer about how to accomplish her quest into the land of the dead. The compass replies:

Go down. Follow the knife. Go onwards. Follow the knife.
    And finally she asked hesitantly, half-ashamed: *Is this the right thing to do?*
    Yes, said the alethiometer instantly. *Yes*. (AS 251)

It could be argued that Lyra already knows what she should do and asks the alethiometer only for reassurance. It is evident from this passage, however, that the alethiometer at the very least influences a decision which she is finding hard to make, and possibly directly causes that decision. Conscience and morality are easier to accomplish if the right decision is indicated by an external agency, even if the individual has to undergo the consequences of that decision. In a sense, a decision directed by the alethiometer is no different than a moral code laid down by a God figure or the Church. Although it could be argued that the process by which Lyra reads the alethiometer is a form of divination into her own conscience, the compass is actually controlled by Dust, a force external to Lyra. Dust, as the trilogy establishes, is created by human consciousness but then takes on an external existence which holds together the environmental and moral fabric of the multiple worlds of the trilogy. Although it is very different from a God figure and certainly bears no similarity to the Authority of the trilogy, it is both an external form of morality and an expression of it. It is an invented theology, a representation of human consciousness and its impact, but expressed in terms which mean that there remains—even after the death of god in the trilogy—an external moral force to which Lyra has access. In the creation of an alternate morality in *His Dark Materials*, then, the props of external moral systems are not entirely eradicated. As the critic Karen Traviss argues, what child—or adult—would not want an alethiometer to help him or her make decisions (2005)? In the absence of God, it is reassuring to invent alternative systems through which moral decisions can be made.

There are other ways in which the morality of choice is complicated and compromised by the narrative. The opening scene of Lyra in the Retiring Room hints at this. When Lyra debates with Pantalaimon what they should do about the assassination plot, she says:

> 'But now I've seen what the Master did, I haven't got any choice. You're supposed to know about conscience, aren't you? How can I just go and sit in the Library or somewhere and twiddle my thumbs, knowing what's going to happen? I don't intend to do *that*, I promise you.' (NL 9)

For Lyra, having seen what has happened, she cannot do anything but intervene: she has no '"choice"'. Lyra's statement conjures up a puzzling moral paradox. Being who she is, with her already strongly developed sense of morality, she does not *See* the question of intervention as a choice at all. She is bound to do it because of her character. Morality, then, is posited as a question of character. Within the narrative frame of *His Dark Materials*, character, perhaps unexpectedly, is destiny.

Lyra's act at the beginning of the trilogy—the choice that is no choice at all—foreshadows the choice that she and Will must make at the very end: whether selfishly to stay together, or selflessly to stay apart. For the young protagonists, who have only just discovered their love for one another, this seems a terrible choice. However, within the framework of the narrative, it is once more not a choice at all. Given the characters of Lyra and Will, and the way in which they have developed over the course of the trilogy, there is no doubt that they will make the 'right' choice, which is to stay apart for the sake of the dead. It is inconceivable that they would make the 'wrong' choice—to stay together—and so although the scene in which their 'decision' is made is one of great pathos, that pathos is derived from the inevitability of their choice rather than a profound sense of their responsibility and morality. Predestination figures large in the narrative, as Will realises when faced with his separation from Lyra:

> And at the word *alone*, Will felt a great wave of rage and despair moving outwards from a place deep within him, as if his mind were an ocean that some profound convulsion had disturbed. All his life he'd been alone, and now he must be alone again, and this infinitely precious blessing that had come to him must be taken away almost at once. He felt the wave build higher and steeper to darken the sky, he felt the crest tremble and begin to spill, he felt the great mass crashing down with the whole weight of the ocean behind it against the iron-bound coast of what had to be. And he found himself gasping and shaking and crying aloud with more anger and pain than he had ever felt in his life, and he found Lyra just as helpless in his arms. But as the wave expended its force and the waters withdrew, the bleak rocks remained;

there was no arguing with fate; neither his despair nor Lyra's had moved them a single inch. (AS 522)

Will and Lyra experience their 'fate' as an extreme physical force that cannot be resisted. They are forced apart by their own good natures and the logic of the narrative, which—very paradoxically in a trilogy which seems to embrace free expression and the material body—ends with an act of sacrifice and denial. Paradoxically, the act of growing up and gaining experience seems to enforce pain and renunciation. Acts of morality, choice and responsibility are, then, dictated by the way in which characters have been constructed as well as by the narrative drive of the trilogy.

When interrogated on this issue and its relationship to the settling of the dæmon that the Able-Seaman explains to Lyra, Pullman denied that character is destiny in the trilogy:

> All the important questions remain with us still. Am I going to work hard, or am I going to laze about and waste my life? Am I going to cleave to what I think is good, or am I going to slump towards what I know is bad? Am I going to be courageous?
>
> The concept doesn't determine outcomes, it suggests a nature. But then that's just a picture of what we're all like ... there's nothing we can do about those characteristics. But the things we *can* do something about still remain within our path ... I don't think it's deterministic. (Parsons and Nicholson 1999: 129)

Pullman argues that despite his protagonists' defining characteristics, they still must make a choice. However, both Lyra and Will have defining characteristics of being good, brave and loyal. Although both may make mistakes, they learn from them, and neither—unlike Lord Asriel and Mrs Coulter—is a morally ambiguous character. It is inconceivable that Lyra would make the wrong choice—her previous 'bad' acts were done either unintentionally (leading Roger to his death) or for a greater good (separating from her dæmon). For Mrs Coulter to make the decision to leap into the abyss with Lord

Asriel is a much greater choice, and a much stronger moral act as a consequence. It is entirely conceivable that she could have left her former lover to die alone in his struggle with Metatron, but she chooses not to. For Lyra, her defining characteristics are such that her seeming choices are hardly that at all, although they may seem so to her at the time. She is destined to be the new Eve and to make the right choices. She is actually a slave to her character as it is constructed in *His Dark Materials*, and hence to the demands of the trilogy's plot.

Will's father also explains to his son his paradoxical choice with regard to the subtle knife. He has to '"choose"', but John Parry also says that Will does not have '"any choice: you're the bearer: it's picked you out"' (AS 335, 334). John also tells Will that he can '"argue with anything else, but don't argue with your own nature"' (AS 335). Will's father is then killed by the vengeful witch, and his son promises to his dead body that he will fight. For both Will and Lyra, then, the narrative is a brute force, a controlling agency and an authority more powerful than any of the other political or religious agencies within the trilogy. The source of this authority is the trilogy's omniscient narrator, and behind that, the storytelling powers of the author himself. Storytelling is thus a didactic strategy, one through which Pullman can communicate a range of opinions on issues such as religion, power, childhood, adulthood and sexuality. Storytelling is central to the thematics of the trilogy, and it is to this topic that the next chapter turns.

⟪ 4 ⟫

Telling Stories

TOWARDS THE END OF *Northern Lights*, Lyra convinces Iofur Raknison, the leader of the armoured bears, that she is Iorek Byrnison's dæmon. Iofur wants his own dæmon and so agrees to fight Iorek for possession of her. When Lyra reports this to Iorek, he is amazed that Lyra has managed to trick an armoured bear and confers on her a new surname to reflect her skills of verbal mastery: Lyra Silvertongue (NL 348).

Throughout the trilogy, Lyra's love of storytelling is evident, as is narrative's utility and power: she escapes the clutches of a lascivious man after her flight from Mrs Coulter's house with a story about a murderer-father; she invents a new identity for herself at Bolvangar so her presence is not immediately reported to Mrs Coulter. She experiences her own storytelling as 'a little stream of pleasure rising upwards in her breast like the bubbles in champagne' (AS 276). For Lyra's creator, Philip Pullman, storytelling is also a great joy, but at the same time a great risk. He describes his experience as 'both the exhilaration of telling a story and the sense that every step you take is actually on the edge of a yawning pit that you might suddenly fall into by getting the story wrong or by failing to find something. It's that vertiginous delight of storytelling' (Pullman 1999b: 187).

This chapter examines storytelling, both as a theme within *His Dark Materials* and in terms of Pullman's craft. As such, it considers

Lyra's role as a storyteller and the responsibilities that she learns about her skill as the trilogy progresses. It also explores the ways in which the act of telling stories in *His Dark Materials* works to propel the narrative, driving it towards the ending and Lyra's destiny. This destiny then leads on to questions of the controlling role of the narrator and authorial didacticism, before coming to rest on the numerous loose ends of the trilogy and the spaces they leave for readerly interventions.

The Morality of Storytelling

Lyra's storytelling skill, and her pleasure in it, is evident throughout the trilogy, whether in an incidental moment to amuse her friends, a clever ruse to evade danger, or a scene integral to the plotting. An important discussion of the act of storytelling occurs when Lyra and Will enter the land of the dead in *The Amber Spyglass*. Here they encounter harpies: 'repulsive' creatures, with 'the cruelty and misery' of 'thousands of years' forming 'hateful' expressions on their features, and trailing 'a drift of putrescent stink' (AS 304). Lyra and Will face up to the leader of these repellent beings, who is negatively named No-Name. When this harpy demands to know what they can give her, Lyra offers the thing she knows she is best at—narrative: '"We could tell you where we've been, and maybe you'd be interested, I don't know. We saw all kinds of strange things on the way here"' (AS 307). At first, No-Name sounds as though she is extremely unimpressed by this suggestion, but then nonetheless tells Lyra to try. Despite her fear, Lyra sees hope, feeling that 'she'd just been dealt the ace of trumps', as she has learnt during her adventures that narrative is the most effective weapon she has (AS 307).

Yet during this interlude, Lyra learns that there is an added dimension to narrative, a morality of storytelling that she had not previously understood. For when she attempts to tell the harpy another of her grand fictitious tales of '*parents dead; family treasure; shipwreck; escape . . .*', No-Name flies at her in anger, screaming, '"Liar!"', 'so that *Lyra* and *liar* were one and the same thing' (AS 307, 308). The act of storytelling is here identified as verbal trickery rather than verbal mastery. It is a deceiving art. In this sequence of the trilogy, Lyra must learn to tell the truth, the virtues of narrating simple descriptions of the Oxford landscape where she grew up, 'the smells around the place: the smoke from the kilns, the rotten-leaf-mould smell of the river when the wind was in the south-west, the warm smell of the baking potatoes the clay-burners used to eat; and the sound of the water slipping slickly over the sluices' (AS 330). Far from her colourful tales of high adventure and fabricated noble origins, the stories that draw the dead in, and that please the harpy, are of a more mundane but more truthful nature. As No-Name explains, it is this quality that saves Lyra and the dead:

> 'Because it was true,' said No-Name. 'Because she spoke the truth. Because it was nourishing. Because it was feeding us. Because we couldn't help it. Because it was true. Because we had no idea that there was anything but wickedness. Because it brought us news of the world and the sun and the wind and the rain. Because it was true.' (AS 332–33)

The injunction to *tell them stories* then reverberates throughout the trilogy (AS 456). Tialys and Salmakia, the Gallivespian spies who accompany Lyra and Will into the underworld, strike a deal with the harpies that, in return for being told the ghosts' stories, '"the truth of what they've seen and touched and heard and loved and known in the world"', the harpies will lead the dead to '"the new opening out into the world"' (AS 333, 334). It is thus the emancipation this truth-telling offers to the dead, and not Asriel's high-minded ideals, which will defeat the powers of the Church. As Tialys realises, '"This will undo everything. It's the greatest blow you could strike. The Authority will be powerless after this."' (AS 326). The implication is that without the dread of the land of the dead awaiting humankind, the Church's power over it will be loosened. In *His Dark Materials*, storytelling therefore acquires its own morality.

It is also from this scene that a chain of stories propels the narrative line of the trilogy. Lyra teaches the dead to tell stories, who then teach Mary Malone, who in turn tells her story of 'Marzipan' to Lyra, through which Lyra realises her destiny as the new Eve. Storytelling is incorporated into the narrative of *His Dark Materials* as an integral part of the plotting, as well as one of its central themes. Pullman writes self-reflexively about the power of storytelling, making narrative itself both the medium and the subject of his work. *His Dark Materials*, then, is a story about stories: a meta-story. Pullman's incorporation of meta-story into the trilogy is a pattern he has repeated in numerous places in his other works, as chapter 7 explores. In the trilogy itself, the theme and morality of storytelling are connected to the subjects of consciousness and knowledge. The experiences accrued by the characters as their lives progress contribute to their character formation, to the decisions they make and, once more, to the ways in which they live their lives. This circular morality is articulated through the process of storytelling, indicated by the life stories the dead will come to tell the harpies. It is much more than a form of entertainment: it is the process of truth-telling itself.

Yet the morality of storytelling that develops during Lyra's quest into the land of the dead might well be perceived as contradictory to *His Dark Materials*' own narrative line, which, like Lyra's favoured tales, is brimming with high adventure, fantastical creatures, and world-crossing feats. There is therefore a tension within the trilogy between the excitement of the plotting, the sheer inventiveness of the writing and a simpler, calmer life and narrative style. This calmer life is advocated through the harpies' demand to the dead to tell the truth, through the ending of the trilogy, in which Lyra and Will are separated, and Lyra decides she will go to school, and also through the peaceful existence of the mulefas. Although these patterns of existence have psychological realism and emotional truth, their appeal to the reader is arguably less than that of the world-traversing excitements of other parts of the work. It is telling that for the purposes of shortening the story for the stage version, the mulefas were completely excised from Nicholas Wright's play text (Wright 2003). In addition to the process of creating a narrative line that would be effective on the stage, the producers had the added difficulty of creating fantastical beasts such as the mulefas as real stage presences. The excision, however, was made by the adapter rather than the director. Wright discussed the process of abridgement as one in which the story still had to make sense, and 'to meld all the seams together so that the whole story ... seemed to be moving forward at the same time' (Haill 2004: 73). These comments about the need to keep the various elements of the narrative moving forward consistently would seem to suggest that in Wright's eyes, the quieter, more reflective elements of the narrative set in the mulefas' world slow the pace down considerably.

The reading experience of the trilogy itself, rather than the stage adaptation, is similar. Much of the scenes in the mulefas' world is either explanatory dialogue or descriptive prose, and is in strong contrast to some of the more active elements of the rest of the trilogy. Yet even the forceful narrative drive of the trilogy moves towards calmness and towards the ending in which Lyra and Will are separated at the dawn of their adult lives. Excitement and high adventure lead towards quiet and acceptance, and these two quite different, even paradoxical narrative modes are combined in the trilogy.

In a largely appreciative review of *The Amber Spyglass* in the *Sunday Times*, Nicolette Jones nonetheless provided a very perceptive critique of the paradox of Pullman's virtuoso storytelling and the seeming message of the trilogy:

> The book's message is that we have only one life and it is on earth ... But this sits awkwardly with a creation that has made us believe in several parallel universes, and which can imagine so comprehensively the land of the dead. The theme of the book suddenly seems at odds with its method. (Jones 2000)

The drive towards the conclusion, and the implications of what happens as Lyra and Will grow up and separate, insists on a particular form of morality and on the quieter form of storytelling that the harpies value. But what arguably remains in the mind are the worlds of high adventure. Through the tension generated between different modes of storytelling, and the emphasis on the meta-story, the narrative therefore comes to hold itself hostage.

Didacticism and the Storyteller

At numerous points in the narrative, Lyra uses storytelling as a weapon, a way out or a way to achieve something. Her own verbal dexterity is foregrounded. Behind each of Lyra's utterances, though, are Pullman's own. The verbal dexterity of his characters reflects directly back on his *own* storytelling technique. Each time Pullman, as the author of the trilogy, refers to the power of storytelling and the responsibilities of the narrator and their morality, he also, inevitably, refers to his own narration. Lyra is thus a storytelling avatar for Pullman himself, a personification of the authorial role in *His Dark Materials*. Such figures are not unusual in novels and are commonplace in postmodern narratives and also frequently occur in literature for children. In any metanarrative, attention is drawn to the art and artifice of the plot, and so Pullman raises the stakes in his storytelling enterprise.

In much of the commentary made by Pullman outside the trilogy itself, he also prioritises storytelling. In his Carnegie Medal acceptance speech for *Northern Lights*, for example, he said that 'stories are vital . . . There's a hunger for stories in all of us, adults too. We need stories so much that we're even willing to read bad books to get them, if the good books won't supply them' (Pullman 1996b). Pullman's argument here is largely one concerned with the primacy of storytelling in literature for children, and hence the superiority, in his view, of children's literature over much contemporary literature for adults. Yet the claim he makes is above all to do with the importance of storytelling in literature, be it directed at adults or children. So then, the question arises of the extent to which Pullman can be seen to be fulfilling his own stated mission as a storyteller.

Much of the review coverage of the trilogy, both of its individual novels and of the story as a whole, bear testament to Pullman's storytelling mastery. *Newsday* in the US, for example, referred to *Northern Lights* as 'a ripping yarn with diabolical cleverness and angelic clarity' (Dederer 2000). The UK *Mail on Sunday* wrote of *The Subtle Knife* as 'a genuine masterpiece of intelligent, imaginative storytelling, a multi-layered quest and adventure story' (Blacker 1997). Michael Dirda wrote in the *Washington Post* of *The Amber Spyglass* that 'Pullman's sheer storytelling power [is] sinfully irre-sistible [. . . it is] a novel of electrifying power and splendour, deserv-ing celebration, as violent as a fairy tale and as shocking as art must be' (Dirda 2000). Further praise came from the UK *Financial Times*, which defined Pullman as 'a charismatic storyteller'; from the *New York Times*, which described the entire trilogy as 'a narrative of tremendous pace'; and from the *Boston Globe*, which termed it 'a roller-coaster of an adventure story' (Rustin 2000; Jefferson 2002; Loer 2000). These are only a sample of some of the plaudits for Pullman's storytelling in high-profile newspapers, all of which undoubtedly increased his reputation as one of the foremost con-temporary storytellers.

Not all of the commentary on Pullman's storytelling, however, was completely affirmative. Some dissenting voices should be added to the ones mentioned above, particularly as the grounds of their dissent gives pause for interesting thought. Much of the criticism is directed not at the first two volumes of the trilogy but at the long-anticipated *The Amber Spyglass*. The UK *Daily Telegraph* called it 'a great baggy mess of a book. Threads left lying about in the two pre-vious volumes of the trilogy are picked up and re-examined but there's not a lot of tying up' (Fitzherbert 2002). In a different review in the same newspaper, S F Said thought *The Amber Spyglass* 'per-haps the weakest of the three parts', despite saying it 'richly deserves to win the Whitbread' (Said 2002). Indeed, *The Amber Spyglass*, despite becoming the winner of the Whitbread Book of the Year Award, does not function well as a stand-alone book—which is per-haps inevitable for the third book in a trilogy—and is the least suc-cessfully plotted. Pullman himself, while not admitting to any faults, wrote a newspaper article explaining the delay between the publica-tion of the second and third volumes of the books, saying, 'When you get to the final volume, all your loose ends come to roost. And it takes time to tie them up neatly. That's why it took so long' (Pullman 2000c). Compared to both *Northern Lights* and *The Subtle Knife*, the plotting is much more episodic, and while there are sections of great narrative drive and power, such as the scenes when Lyra and Will enter the land of the dead, other elements are less convincing. Lyra, the much-loved heroine of the trilogy, is kept drugged and out of action for about a third of the volume. The depiction of the battle between Lord Asriel, the Magisterium and the Authority is rather frantic, with frequent switches in scene and characters. It very effectively builds up pace in the rush towards the climax of the battle, but the sharp focus on Lyra and Will is occasionally lost among the morass of characters and situations. All loose ends are not tied up. As one critic put it, however, the faults of the volume are more the result of 'overweening ambition' gone awry than lack of energy or desire to conclude the massive task set by the author for himself in the trilogy (Jones 2000).

There is a sense, then, in which Pullman's own claims to the powers of narrative simultaneously accentuate, undermine and affirm his storytelling virtuosity, depending on the strength of his writing at any given moment. As a narrative which is so much *about* narrative, Pullman enables his writing to work on a metaphorical level but at the same time to tell a story which is forcefully plot-driven. Yet his storytelling takes on another role, which he also referred to in his Carnegie Medal acceptance speech. That is the role of didacticism. In the speech, Pullman promoted the effectiveness of storytelling as a means to morality, in opposition to lessons of religion and 'moral education':

> All stories teach, whether the storyteller intends them to or not. They teach the world we create. They teach the morality we live by. They teach it much more effectively than moral precepts and instructions . . .
> We don't need a list of rights and wrongs, tables of do's and don'ts: we need books, time, and silence. Thou shalt not is soon forgotten, but Once upon a time lasts forever. (Pullman 1996b)

Pullman extended his argument in 2005 in a lecture given at the University of East Anglia in the UK, in which he again advocated literature as a 'school of morals', saying, 'I think we can learn what's good and what's bad, what's generous and unselfish, what's cruel and what's mean, from fiction' (www.philip-pullman.com: d). The morality that develops through the course of the trilogy is discussed in detail in the previous chapter. It is one that is anti-religion, anti-repression, pro-sexuality and pro-knowledge. It is also one that emphasises responsibility and values the mind that is '"open and free and curious"' (AS 520). Although these values are fully integrated into the fabric of the narrative and the development of the characters, they are undoubtedly stated with the clarity of 'moral precepts and instructions' in the closing pages of *The Amber Spyglass*, where they are made most explicit. While not contradicting his own message in the Carnegie Medal acceptance speech that stories teach better than lists of rights and wrongs, Pullman nonetheless betrays an undeniable intention to 'teach' in his clearly stated alternative morality. In his efforts to promote his anti-religion, anti-repression, pro-sexuality and pro-knowledge values, characters who represent this morality—Lyra, Will, Mary Malone—are attractively portrayed and, in the case of Mary and of Asriel and his followers, allowed to voice explicitly didactic opinions. Mary, for example, narrates to the listening Lyra and Will the story of her loss of faith and its replacement by scientific rationalism: '"I used to be a nun, you see. I thought physics could be done to the glory of God, till I saw there wasn't any God at all and that physics was more interesting anyway. The Christian religion is a very powerful and convincing mistake, that's all"' (AS 464).

Several critics of the trilogy have attacked this final sentence of Mary's speech for its overt and didactic stance. Sarah Johnson, for example, wrote in her review of *The Amber Spyglass* in *The Times* that this speech is the point at which 'Pullman's purpose crystallises' and that 'it is so safe to pick on Christianity—it never hits back. By creating in his parallel world a perfectly evil, all-powerful "Church" crammed with sadistic priests and comedy nuns crossing themselves fearfully, Pullman mocks, but avoids engaging with the meaning of that symbolic gesture' (Johnson 2000). Indeed, putting these words in Mary's mouth does seem a not very subtle act of ventriloquism on Pullman's part. Within the trilogy, there is no real debate around this issue and no room made for a discussion of some of the good the Church might conceivably have done. Pullman might argue that in Lyra's world the Church has done no good, and within his fictional frame that is possibly the case. However, this anti-religious didacticism proved highly controversial among some critics of the trilogy because of the proximity of the Christianity of the trilogy to real-world Christianity. This is the Christianity of which Mary is talking anyway, given that she comes from the Oxford of 'the universe we know' rather than Lyra's. Equally, Asriel and his followers make frequent and emphatic statements about the bad that the Church has done and the positive nature of their own philosophy, based on the primacy of the physical body and its place in the here and now. The author's own morality and belief system are very clearly transposed into his narrative, which consequently takes on a didactic role, the one that Pullman himself claimed for stories in his Carnegie Medal speech. The narrative transmits moral messages, sometimes in a far-from-subtle way.

Pullman's belief in the capacity of stories to teach morality is one explanation of his vehement dislike of C S Lewis's *The Chronicles of Narnia*, and undoubtedly informed the reception of his own trilogy. For some critics, this, and Pullman's treatment of religion generally, has been the cause of particular provocation. The *Catholic Herald* infamously described *The Amber Spyglass* as 'worthy of the bonfire' and 'the stuff of nightmares', and although the condemnation was perhaps more tongue-in-cheek than it was latterly more widely represented in the media, and by Pullman himself, the journalist Leonie Caldecott nonetheless expressed real anxiety about the anti-religious and specifically anti-Catholic nature of the trilogy (Caldecott 1999; See also Caldecott 2003). Peter Hitchens, writing in the *Mail on Sunday*, labelled him 'the most dangerous author in Britain' for his condemnation of C S Lewis and the Church (Hitchens 2002a). Pullman has also made repeated attacks in the media on the Narnia books, and *His Dark Materials* could be seen as a riposte to Lewis's series, which is also aimed at children. Pullman has condemned *The Chronicles of Narnia* for their 'pernicious' influence (Parsons and

Nicholson 1999: 131), and in 'The Dark Side of Narnia', an article published in the *Guardian* in 1998, Pullman criticised his predecessor in the strongest of terms. The series, according to Pullman, is 'one of the most ugly and poisonous things I've ever read', to be vilified for 'the misogyny, the racism, the sado-masochistic relish for violence that permeates [it]' (Pullman 1998d). More than any of these crimes, though, what Pullman contests is the Christian allegory of *The Chronicles of Narnia* and their very negative treatment of adolescence. The final volume, *The Last Battle* (1956), is heavily criticised in particular by Pullman for its assertion that the ultimate reward is to be found in heaven rather than on earth, and for its exclusion of one of the characters, Susan, from salvation because of her teenage—and female—interest in stockings and make-up. The *Chronicles'* distaste for adolescent sexuality, in Pullman's view, provides a foil to his contrasting treatment of the same theme in *His Dark Materials*. To compare the two series is ultimately to establish their very different moral stance while at the same time noting their use of the same Christian myths, although Pullman's rewriting concentrates on the Old Testament, and Lewis's on the New. The debate between the different belief systems in *His Dark Materials* and *The Chronicles of Narnia* was reignited by the release in 2005 of the first of a series of major film adaptations of *The Chronicles*, about which Pullman made a number of negative remarks to the British *Observer* (Harris 2005). Pullman's remarks were in turn refuted by various commentators, including a lengthy article in the *Chronicle of Higher Education*, and were debated fiercely by contributors to a BBC News website (Nelson 2005; BBC News 2005).

It is the establishment of an anti-religious myth in *His Dark Materials* that led Andrew Marr to comment that 'Pullman does for atheism what C S Lewis did for God' (Marr 2002). Hitchens specifically couched his condemnation of Pullman as 'the most dangerous author in Britain' in terms of the C S Lewis debate. Hitchens wrote, 'One stubborn and important pocket of Christianity survives, in the Narnia stories of C S Lewis. Now here comes an opportunity to dethrone him and supplant his books with others which proclaim the death of God to the young' (Hitchens 2002a). As Hitchens wrote of *His Dark Materials* in a later *Mail on Sunday* article, 'I think these books should carry a strong warning, pointing out that they are deliberate anti-Christian propaganda' (Hitchens 2002b). Other journalists also protested against Pullman's anti-Church stance. Claudia Fitzherbert, for example, warned, 'Christian parents beware: his books can damage your child's faith' (Fitzherbert 2002). Sarah Johnson, who has been a vocal anti-Pullman reviewer despite appreciating his storytelling abilities, wrote in *The Times* that the series is 'the most savage attack on organised religion I have ever seen' (Johnson 2000).

The anti-Church ideology of *His Dark Materials* is reflected by numerous epithets given to Pullman by reviewers. The *Guardian* named him a 'heretical fantasist' (Eccleshare 2000); Jessica Mann in the *Sunday Telegraph* called him a 'militant atheist' (Mann 2000); and Nick Thorpe dubbed him an 'anti-Christian fundamentalist' (Thorpe 2002). Michael Dirda commented, 'In another time this [*The Amber Spyglass*] is a book that would have made the Index [the Catholic list of prohibited texts], and in still another era gotten its author condemned to the stake as a heretic' (Dirda 2000). Ideological passions have been roused by the series, with reviewers making very clear the extent of Pullman's attack on the Church and organised religion.

That Pullman takes on the Church and its founding myths so centrally is an interesting paradox. In denying so thoroughly the existence of a god or an afterlife and in decrying the controlling power of religious institutions, Pullman actually spends much time concentrating on aspects of Christianity, giving new heat to debates about the place of religion in contemporary society, but also publicity to his Christian detractors. Similarly, the controversy over the Narnia films, stirred up in no small way by Pullman's commentary to the media, gave much additional press coverage to the release of *The Lion, the Witch and the Wardrobe*, as well as to his own work. This is an example of Pullman's capacity to attract attention in the public sphere to his work through provocation, as chapter 1 discussed. But Pullman also, simultaneously, attracts attention to C S Lewis's work, the new film release, and to Christianity more broadly. For a professed atheist, Pullman draws heavily on Christian tradition, and rather than ignoring it, he makes it central to his writing in *His Dark Materials*, even if it is negatively portrayed. As Pullman has put it himself, he is a Church of England atheist.

A further question that could be posed about Pullman's attack on organised religion in *His Dark Materials*, and about his broader commentary in the media, is why—at least in terms of the position of the Christian Church in the UK—he expends so much energy waging war against what is arguably a spent force. It is revealing that Dirda's review of *The Amber Spyglass* refers to how, in earlier periods, Pullman's writing would have been banned by the Catholic Church, or even resulted in his burning as a heretic. By the end of the twentieth century, however, no such dangerous judgements are meted out on Pullman. This is in contrast, for example, to the fatwa placed by Iranian Muslims in 1989 on Salman Rushdie for his controversial novel *The Satanic Verses* (1988). Fortunately, no such sanction has been pronounced on Pullman by Christian authorities. Pullman's detractors have been eager to point out that in the list of alternative names—'"The Authority, God, the Creator, the Lord, Yahweh, El, Adonai, the King, the Father, the Almighty"'—which the angel Balthamos says the Authority has given himself, that of the Muslim Allah is missing (AS 33; see, for example, Association of Christian Teachers: a). Was this an oversight or rather a response to the increasingly fraught global atmosphere between the Christian and Muslim worlds in the 1990s and 2000s, and hence an act of political correctness? Pullman denied any self-censorship on his part and angrily stated that future editions would include 'Allah', although such a change had not been made for the tenth anniversary editions of the books which were published in 2005 (Sierz 2003; Wyke 2004).

Whereas the Christian right and the evangelical Church may have a certain political and social power in the US, where Pullman is based in the UK, it would be hard to argue that his attacks are shocking to more than the most fundamental of Christians. Representatives of the Church have been willing to converse publicly with Pullman, notably in the conciliatory conversation Dr Rowan Williams, Archbishop of Canterbury and leader of the Church of

England, had with Pullman as part of the series of talks mounted by the National Theatre (Haill 2004). Williams had earlier been to Downing Street—the Prime Minister's residence and centre of the UK government—and apparently recommended the play version of *His Dark Materials*, expressing his pleasure at seeing large school parties in the audience (Haill 2004: 85).

Moreover, Pullman is referred to very favourably in a sermon entitled 'Honoring the Sexual Body' in a Christian context. However, Stephanie Paulsell, who delivered the sermon, did comment that Pullman was incorrect in maintaining that C S Lewis's negative version is representative of all Christian approaches to sexuality, citing as an alternative the deeply erotic Song of Songs from the Bible (Paulsell 2004). Paulsell's version of Christianity and sexuality is far from a fundamentalist one. She embraces gay sexuality as well as heterosexual and argues with other branches of the Church in its approach to the issue, suggesting that Christianity is certainly not the monolithic or stereotypical institution that Pullman tends to depict it as. In his book on *His Dark Materials*, Hugh Rayment-Pickard states that the author's atheism 'seemed to me to be so thoroughly *religious*' and terms Pullman's philosophy one of '"religious atheism"' (Rayment-Pickard 2004: 3).

All this would seem to suggest that Pullman's religious critique is perhaps not as controversial as it might seem, and that at least some non-fundamental Christian figures have relished the opportunity that his writing about religion has given to air their own beliefs and to discuss different versions of morality. As Rayment-Pickard concludes, 'In a strange way Pullman's counter-myth may help to keep the Christian myth alive, because it is not possible to understand *His Dark Materials* without also understanding the power and appeal of the Christian story. Like all artistic transgressors, Pullman pays homage to the sacred power that he seeks to overcome' (Rayment-Pickard 2004: 19). Stephen Thomson went so far as to reverse Blake's famous statement about Milton by commenting, 'If Milton fell unwittingly into Satan's party, I think one might say Pullman pulls the reverse stunt by falling, despite his avowals, in with God the Father' (Thomson 2004).

However, a review in the Catholic magazine *The Tablet* of Rayment-Pickard's book, and also effectively of the trilogy, suggested that Pullman's childhood and adolescent grounding in Church of England Christianity has left the adult atheist with another legacy: 'an old-fashioned Protestant caricature of the Catholic Church' (McDonagh 2004). McDonagh's argument is that the representatives of the Church in the trilogy, despite Pullman's gesture towards 'ecumenical anticlericalism' in moving the centre of Church politics from Rome to Geneva, are emphatic stereotypes of Catholic priests and certainly not of kindly Church figures such as Pullman's own grandfather or the intellectually open Rowan Williams.

There is indeed a question over Pullman's even-handedness in his portrayals of Church figures, which has been asked by both advocates of and detractors from *His Dark Materials*. Critics have made the comment that the clerics of the Magisterium are the only characters in the trilogy who are not allowed a fully rounded existence. Nick Thorpe, in his very thoughtful *Sunday Times* article, referred to 'the almost pantomime evil of his churchmen, who are conspicuously lacking in either redeeming features or consequently the nuanced psychology that make his heroes so compelling' (Thorpe 2002). In the *Daily Telegraph*, Melanie McDonagh disliked the series for its portrayal of the Catholic Church. She saw Pullman's representations in a tradition of 'Protestant-atheist polemic' in which 'the Catholic Church is seen as a diabolic institution, all Spanish Inquisition and sex-obsessed celibates' (McDonagh 2002). Claudia Fitzherbert commented that 'nearly all of his villains have moments of pathos and/or greatness, except for the priests' (Fitzherbert 2002). Erica Wagner wrote in *The Times* that 'the Church he portrays becomes so over-the-top wicked it threatens to tip into caricature' (Wagner 2000).

Such stereotyping, however, arguably fits Pullman's didactic purpose in the trilogy. As a consequence, some reviewers have been prompted to consider the extent of Pullman's didacticism, both in his dismissal of the Church and in the promotion of his own version of morality. Angelique Chrisafis termed him an 'evangelical atheist' in the *Guardian*, while Jessica Mann claimed that 'the moralising is overt' (Chrisafis 2002; Mann 2000). Wagner linked this specifically to Pullman's earlier profession as a teacher, noting that 'it is clear he has not quite lost his taste for pedagogy' (Wagner 2000). Other critics, such as Christina Hardyment, who described Pullman as a 'largely invisible moralist', seemed more forgiving about his didacticism, while others strongly applauded his moral purpose (Hardyment 1997). Andrew Marr wrote, 'What he gives me and what excites me is the sense that a post-Christian world can be as intensely filled with pity, the search for goodness, and an acute awareness of evil, as any religious universe' (Marr 2002). Indeed, the capacity for Pullman in *His Dark Materials* to address moral issues is celebrated by the critics. In the *Independent*, Natasha Walter set her reaction to *His Dark Materials* against the terrorist attacks in America in 2001, writing, 'Isn't this a great vision for the world after 11 September? Here we have a book that asks us to believe that we can build a new, highly moral world without the precepts of religion' (Walter 2002).

This is indeed a bold claim made for Pullman, but one that he has wanted to take up. In a speech made at the Edinburgh Festival of Literature in 2002 on the morality of writing in the context of terrorist threat and looming war with Iraq, Pullman stated that writers must address, as Chrisafis reported, 'larger questions of moral conduct' if they are not to 'become useless and irrelevant' (Chrisafis 2002). Whatever else the critics might have said, or still have to say, about Philip Pullman, it is apparent that with *His Dark Materials* he follows his own exhortation.

The Authority of the Storyteller

Storytelling, then, is a didactic method for Pullman, one in which he very strongly conveys his own sense of anti-Church morality, wages war against repression and kills off God in the figure of the Authority. But yet again there is a paradox here, which is intimately connected to Pullman's role as a storyteller, the function of the omniscient narrator and Pullman's controlling authorial position. The previous chapter concluded that the seeming morality of choice and responsibility that Pullman develops in *His Dark Materials* is actually dictated by the way in which the author has constructed character and the consequent logic of the narrative. Brian Alderson, who accused Pullman of 'designer theology' in the *New York Times*, detected a paradox in his position as authorial creator which is extremely unsettling for the reader: 'The author as God must lean from his heaven and direct affairs in the way he requires them to go, and we mortal readers must erect small gantries from which to suspend our varieties of disbelief' (Alderson 2000). In the conclusion of the trilogy, in which Lyra and Will are forced—through the goodness of their own characters—to renounce their love for one another only days after they have discovered it, the narrative seems a cruel one. Moreover, as fictional characters, the choices made by Lyra and Will may serve as models for real-life morality, but essentially the choices they make are always and inevitably ones external to themselves. They are fictional characters and are at the mercy of the narrator of the story, and behind the narrator, the author himself. In very real terms, the author *does* act as a creator and also, as Alderson puts it, continues to 'direct affairs' through the construction of the plot. Yet in various interviews and other commentary, Pullman has rejected such a lofty definition of his role and has instead pitched the role of the storyteller quite differently:

> My intention is to tell a story—in the first place because the story comes to me and wants to be told . . .
>
> I am the servant of the story—the medium in a spiritualist sense, if you like—and it feels as if, unless I tell this story, I will be troubled and pestered and harried by it and worried and fretted until I do something about it. (Spanner 2002)

In this description, Pullman depicts the story as having an agency external even to him, which is a surprising, even mystical way of explaining the creative process. To a writer the creative process may indeed occasionally feel as if it is mysterious and external to him- or herself. Yet the author still must make decisions about what to include in his or her text, and professing the role of the author as that of a 'medium' is in fact a denial of the responsibility that the trilogy espouses. Pullman makes the final choice about the narrative and morality of his story.

It is worth considering how the emotional impact of the ending of the trilogy would have been altered if Lyra and Will had been allowed to stay together, if Pullman had gone against the story's demands. The story undoubtedly would have lost much of its pathos and concluded with a hackneyed romantic happy ending. Beyond the end of the story, it also would have left many questions. How would such a young relationship develop? Both Lyra and Will are very young, having only just entered adolescence, and Pullman implies that both still have much to learn about themselves and their respective worlds. To even begin to imagine their lives together after the end of *The Amber Spyglass* would seem to point towards the realm of teen romance, with its trials and tribulations, petty squabbles and social pressures, a genre far from that of *His Dark Materials*. Whether Lyra and Will may in fact meet again in Pullman's projected volume *The Book of Dust* is as yet unknown, but in terms of the shape of the plot, it is undeniable that the separation of the children at the end gives a satisfying, if emotionally difficult, conclusion to the trilogy, even if it does contradict some of the overt morality transmitted via Pullman's didacticism. Although the story may not have its own volition and will, as Pullman seems to suggest in saying that he is its 'servant', the ending is nonetheless very fitting. Pullman clearly has given the ending much consideration, and in the same interview, he said that

> the reason they have to part in the end is a curious one and it's hard to explain except in terms of the compulsion of the story. I knew from the very beginning that it would have to end in that sort of renunciation. (I don't know how I know these things, but I knew.) . . .
>
> I tried all sorts of ways to prevent it, but the story made me do it. That was what had to happen. If I'd denied it, the story wouldn't have had a tenth of its power. (Spanner 2002)

The phrase 'the story made me do it' suggests an extraordinary abnegation of authorial responsibility. The compulsion is based on narrative convention. Such convention insists that an ending in which the protagonists live happily ever after is less satisfying than one in which characters must separate and continue to strive for their happiness. Elsewhere, Pullman has discussed this in terms of the 'right shape' and the 'wrong shape' for a story (Miller 2005/2006). Pullman undoubtedly made the 'right shape' choice in *His Dark Materials* in terms of the emotional and narrative impact of the separation of the children. However, in contradiction to his own assertions of servitude, it was a choice whereby he had to cast himself, the storyteller, as a godlike figure, directing action in an authoritarian way. He *chose* to follow 'the compulsion of the story'. Moreover, this 'right' choice contradicts much of what Alderson calls the 'designer theology' of the trilogy, so despite the emphasis on knowledge and the goodness of sexuality and the human body, the children nevertheless have to part in an act of renunciation. Pullman's alternative storytelling authority is as dictatorial in its didacticism as he claims the Church to be.

Loose Ends

It is perhaps in the ending of the trilogy, with the enforced separation of Lyra and Will more strongly than anywhere else, that readers have to construct their own 'small gantries' from which to suspend disbelief. In the case of some readers, the ending leads them to construct their own narrative interventions, through their fan fiction. There are numerous examples of fan fiction on the various *His Dark Materials* fan websites as well as on the generic www.fanfiction.net, which by the beginning of 2006 featured almost six hundred separate narratives (the bibliography at the end of this book gives further details). Among the many plotlines are a return to Lyra's world, where after years of study at Oxford, Lyra is controversially invited back to investigate the nature of Dust at Jordan as the Cassington Scholar. Another example is a depiction of the republic of heaven twenty-five years after the downfall of the Authority, with leading characters including Lyra's daughter and Will's son. There are also several linked stories which feature Lyra's half-sister, Elizabeth Boreal, and her powerful and evil Boreal Foundation. As is frequently the case with fan fiction, these are variable in quality, but some of the best examples demonstrate a strong imaginative engagement with and development of Pullman's own writing, probing the gaps, back histories and futures of the plots and characters of the trilogy.

One of the leading writers of such work, Ceres Wunderkind, has gone so far as to put together ten 'Commandments' of *His Dark Materials* fan fiction, noting in the very first the tendency of many fan fiction writers to reunite Lyra and Will. Pointing the putative fan fiction writer towards the material already available online, Wunderkind comments that many—if not the majority—of the stories are 'predicated on the idea that Will and Lyra will get back together again' (Wunderkind 2003). The motivation for this is explained in terms of the emotional impact of the ending of the trilogy:

> Look, people, I know *why* this happens. The ending of TAS [*The Amber Spyglass*] is brilliantly written. It has a profound effect on the sensitive reader. It can leave you feeling upset for days, and the first reaction is to try to think of ways in which this terribly unfair (or so it seems) conclusion can be reversed. The temptation to rush to the keyboard and fix Philip Pullman's ending is hard to resist. (Wunderkind 2003)

Wunderkind exhorts writers to resist this tendency and to turn to less obvious narrative interventions, to, in fact, the loose ends where Pullman

> has left any number of gaps just waiting for the enterprising writer to exploit. There's so much he hasn't told us about the society of Lyra's world; its daemonology, technology, history, geopolitics. There are many, many other characters waiting to have their stories told. Why are there so few fanfics about the Ci'gazzeans, or the Gallivespians, or Iorek Byrnisen [*sic*], or Lee and Hester, or Lord Asriel?

Please think about it. There's a whole wide multiverse out there, just waiting for you to come and play. Will and Lyra's story is only a small part of it and it's over so far as being together is concerned. Let them be. (Wunderkind 2003)

For the authors of fan fiction, the 'number of gaps' left by Pullman in the narration of *His Dark Materials* are attractive invitations to the creation of their own stories. For critics of the trilogy, they present a different sort of challenge: one to Pullman's own artistic vision. Claudia Fitzherbert picked up on this in her *Daily Telegraph* review (quoted earlier) by saying that 'threads left lying' in the first two books are not convincingly tied up by the end of the trilogy (Fitzherbert 2002). These threads derive from Pullman's attempted creation of a believable, rounded multiverse, one with a convincing history, geography and theology and woven together through the agency of narrative. The unexplored areas of the narrative and unexplained aspects of the multiverse leave questions for the reader. Some of these silences are clearly intentional: the refusal by Pullman to clarify the exact nature of Lyra and Will's sexual explorations at the end of *The Amber Spyglass* is one example; the depiction of Lord Asriel and his battle for the republic of heaven is another. As the previous chapter mentioned, throughout *The Subtle Knife*, although central to the plot, Asriel only ever appears at second hand, through the reports given by his servant Thorold and the witch Ruta Skadi. When the preparations for war become more pressing in the next volume of the trilogy, Asriel reappears in person. Yet the way in which Pullman portrays the political struggle for the universe, and the activities of Asriel, as well as those of Mrs Coulter and the Magisterium, is by shifting them in and out of focus, sometimes foregrounding them and sometimes hiding them. It is through the use of the omniscient narrator that Pullman enables himself to do this. However, this is an omniscient narrator who cannot narrate everything, indeed explicitly chooses not to narrate everything, and thus leaves open questions and 'threads left lying'. After the defeat of the Authority and his regent Metatron, but also the plunge into the abyss—and, we assume, the deaths of Lord Asriel and Mrs Coulter—to whom will governance of the worlds fall? The political structure of Lyra's world is left undetermined, although there is the briefest of mentions about the power struggles within the Church. At the end of *The Amber Spyglass*, Will and Lyra are left poised to build their own republics of heaven, but these are entities very different from the political structure envisioned by Asriel. What, then, will happen to the remaining forces of war, both on the side of Asriel and on that of the Magisterium? The dead are emancipated by Lyra and Will's actions, but these questions about the political nature of their worlds are not resolved any more than are the futures of Lyra and Will as young adults in their separate worlds.

In terms of allowing creative space for further interventions and writings of the plot, Pullman's gaps allow himself and fan writers much room. Events referred to and hinted at in the back histories of many of the characters are only briefly sketched, and action occurring during the time-space of the trilogy also is left unexplained. The adventures of Lyra and Will's dæmons after their separation from the children before entering the land of the dead is one example. Given that at the end of the trilogy, Pullman leaves his two very young protagonists with what, it may be assumed, is the majority of their lives ahead of them, the possibility of the narrative continuing beyond the trilogy is apparent. Pullman himself has already partially fulfilled this through the publication of *Lyra's Oxford*, which briefly revisits Lyra two years after the conclusion of *The Amber Spyglass*. What the projected volume *The Book of Dust* will do with these threads is at present unclear, although chapter 7 examines the hints that have been given thus far.

There are also many interesting questions that are left unanswered concerning Will's world, the 'real' world. In *The Subtle Knife*, in which this world is most thoroughly depicted, there are occasionally glimpsed characters who are trying to find out more about Will's father's discoveries in the North and who are also monitoring very carefully Mary Malone's research work into Shadows. Are these characters some part of the British government? Or are they from Will's world at all? Lord Boreal, in disguise as Sir Charles Latrom, is also very interested in Mary's research and shows up in her laboratory offering substantial funding if he were allowed to dictate the (possibly military) direction of future applications. A political sideswipe at the vagaries of the funding and use of scientific research in Pullman's own contemporary society, this scene also hints—without explaining in any depth—that Will's world is riddled with intrigue about, and power struggles over, experimental theology, just as Lyra's is. However, the extent to which the power structures and government of Will's world have any consciousness of other worlds, of Dust and of the adventures of the children and their allies is unexplained. John Parry's discovery of the 'anomaly' in the North, which he writes about, including its exact grid reference, in his letters to Will's mother before he disappears, is a connected example (SK 116). Who else in Will's world knows of the existence of this window to another world, through which not only John Parry but also reportedly two of his companions have passed?

There is much, then, left unsaid about Will's world, let alone Lyra's. But these are all loose ends that any narrative must leave, as a book—or even three books and their sequels and prequels—is a finite space in which elements of associated story cannot all be related. These are the loose ends of any fictional work, which inspire the literary detective work and creative imaginations of critics, such as John Sutherland, and readers, as fan fiction writers. That *His Dark Materials* summons into being new universes with richly imagined histories, geographies, sociologies and politics only inspires this tendency further. This is, as the introduction to this book discussed, the aspect of *His Dark Materials* which fosters readers' desires to know how dæmons are born, for example. Thus, loose ends are spaces for imaginative engagement for readers and—in the projected sequels to the trilogy—for Pullman himself.

There is, however, another type of loose end in the trilogy. This type is less to do with the unwritten stories of the characters and more to do with the paradoxes in the trilogy and the holes in its ideology. Once more, the biggest of these is to do with the choice that Lyra and Will are forced to make at the end of *The Amber Spyglass*. The morality espoused by the trilogy would seem to suggest that they should be together, but narrative logic and the lesson about sacrifice in adulthood separate them. Moreover, even though adventure and excitement are the primary modes of the trilogy, the conclusion is quiet and reflective. There is a question of why some characters are given a second chance at life in death. John Parry and Lee Scoresby are allowed further time on earth, which contradicts the pattern of death and the (lack of) afterlife that Pullman sets up in contradiction to Church ideology. There is also the issue of what the role of the subtle knife—the god-destroying knife—and of Will as its bearer, actually is. The knife is not obviously used in the battle against the Authority, who dies without violent intervention. Will is told by his father that his destiny is to take the knife to Lord Asriel and to fight on his side in the battle for power. And yet Will never delivers the knife to Lord Asriel, and so the role prophesied for the knife and told to Will by his father is not achieved by the time that Will destroys it at the end of *The Amber Spyglass*. He does use it for other purposes, however, including, notably, saving Lyra's life from the bomb. This enables her eventually to fulfil her destiny as the new Eve. But as with the resulting uncertainty about the political structure at the end of the trilogy, the precise role of the knife is undetermined.

These paradoxes are not necessarily artistic flaws, but they do hint at the impossibility of some of Pullman's vision in the construction of a perfect story and a convincing ideology. There is, though, a definite flaw in the reasoning that leads to the choice the children must make. Why, other than to force the terrible burden of choice upon the children, can only one window be left open? This explanation of Xaphania's seems cruel in the extreme: necessary, on the one hand, to sustain the good Lyra has done by emancipating the dead, but also very painful for the children. At this point, it seems that the shape of the story takes over from its ideology, contradicting it and insisting on a sad ending rather than a happy one. The storyteller is therefore in conflict with the didact, making Lyra and Will's parting not just a painful one but also an immensely frustrating one. In the end, Pullman's own storytelling virtuosity has backed him into a corner in which he must contradict either his sense of a good ending or his construction of a consistent morality. This is not to argue that the story should, or could, have ended otherwise, but it does mean that the vehemence with which the morality is conveyed is paradoxically undercut by the force of the narrative. This is a harsh lesson for his young protagonists, his readers and indeed Pullman himself to learn. The act of telling stories is beset with decisions that put both the creators and the audiences of narrative in a place which is emotionally, ideologically and technically fraught. Storytelling may be a delight, it may be exhilarating, but it is also—because of its very potential to instruct as well as entertain—a most perplexing and stern undertaking. The master storyteller discovers that his creation has achieved, if not its own autonomy, a capacity to puzzle its originator as well as its reader. Perhaps, in the end, though, this is what makes *His Dark Materials* such a powerful work. Its loose ends and its internal inconsistencies only serve to increase readers' engagement with it. The master storyteller, then, is so named not because of his ultimate control but because of a ceding of that control and the consequent opening out of the text for others.

⟨⦿ 5 ⦿⟩

Intertextuality

IN THE ACKNOWLEDGEMENTS that end *The Amber Spyglass*, and thus the entire *His Dark Materials* trilogy, Philip Pullman makes this statement about his writing process: 'I have stolen ideas from every book I have ever read. My principle in researching for a novel is "Read like a butterfly, write like a bee", and if this story contains any honey, it is entirely because of the quality of the nectar I found in the work of better writers' (AS 549). He then goes on to enumerate specific literary 'debts' that he owes, or writers from whom he has stolen, to use his own terminology. He mentions three writers in particular: Heinrich von Kleist and his essay 'On the Marionette Theatre' (1810; sometimes translated as 'The Puppet Theatre'); John Milton, for *Paradise Lost*; and William Blake. This chapter considers Pullman the literary thief or, to use more literary terminology, Pullman the intertextualist. For in writing *His Dark Materials*, Pullman uses intertextuality as a method, as a form of literary engagement and as a way of expressing his own artistic ambition. Intertextuality underpins and enriches Pullman's writing and is also the means by which he articulates many of his arguments.

Intertextuality can be simply defined as 'the relation between one text and another' (Pope 2002: 246). But what might this mean for *His Dark Materials* and its interpretation? In *The English Studies Book*, Rob Pope further breaks down his definition of intertextuality into explicit, implied and inferred forms. Explicit intertextuality consists of other texts which are 'overtly referred to' and sources which are 'demonstrably drawn on'. Implied intertextuality includes the 'passing allusions' and 'effects' inserted into the text by the author 'so as to be picked up by the alert and similarly informed reader'. Inferred intertextuality, on the other hand, refers to the texts that readers 'draw on to help their understanding of the text in hand' and may well not have been in the writer's mind at the time of writing (Pope 2002: 246). This chapter concentrates on the first two forms of intertextuality but also views the trilogy from a more reader-oriented perspective by considering the impact of intertextuality on its readers and the ways in which the rich intertextual nature of the trilogy is made apparent to these readers.

His Dark Materials has been declared a 'triumph of intertextuality', and the sources from which Pullman has drawn are numerous and varied (Scott 2005: 96). In his review of *The Amber Spyglass* in the *Washington Post*, Michael Dirda reeled off a whole list of inter-textual references, which is worth quoting at some length because of its brisk iteration of source texts:

> Besides finding hints of *Paradise Lost* and Blake's poetry, the astute will pick up echoes of the following: Christ's harrowing of Hell, Jewish Kabbalah (the legend of the god-like angel Metatron), Gnostic doctrine (Dust, our sleeping souls need-ing to be awakened), the "death of God" controversy, *Perelandra*, the Oz books (the Wheelers), Wagner's *Ring of the Nibelungs* (Siegfried's mending of the sword), Aeneas, Odysseus and Dante in the Underworld, the Grail legend and the wounded Fisher King, Peter Pan, Wordsworth's pantheis-tic "Immortality Ode," the doctrine of the hidden God and speculation about the plurality of worlds, situational ethics (actions, not people, being good or bad), the cessation of mir-acles, "Star Wars," colonialist evangelizing, the fetch of British folklore, the 17th-century doctrine of sympathies (for the Gallivespian communication device, the lodestone-resonator), the popular mythology of the Jesuits as ascetic masterminds

> of realpolitik, superhero comics and even Pullman's own
> early novel for adults, *Galatea*. Fans of science fiction and fan-
> tasy may also detect undertones of Ursula Le Guin's Earthsea
> books, Fritz Leiber's sword-and-sorcery tales of Fafhrd and
> the Gray Mouser, Jack Vance's elegant Dying Earth stories.
> (Dirda 2000)

This esoteric and eclectic list is only a start to the intertextual
source spotting that a 'similarly informed' or 'astute' (as Dirda puts
it) reader of the trilogy might undertake. Pullman's background as a
student and subsequently a teacher of literature is worth remember-
ing here. In an essay which examines *His Dark Materials* alongside
the intertexts of C S Lewis's *The Chronicles of Narnia* and J R R
Tolkien's *The Lord of the Rings*, Burton Hatlen argues that all three
authors specifically draw on literary tradition and their own biographical situation as 'scholars and teachers of English literature'
(Hatlen 2005: 76). For Pullman, as a school teacher and latterly a
university lecturer, the genres of folk story and fairy tale, as well as
the wealth of past children's literature, are added to the canonical
mix. The borrowing from, use of and engagement with other texts is
a crucial part of the creative process of *His Dark Materials*, central to
its methods and also its interpretation.

This chapter examines this literary borrowing, first in terms of
Pullman's debts and derivations and then by considering how,
through his intertextuality, Pullman both negotiates with genre and
establishes points of difference with other writers. Through intertextuality, Pullman also places a very visible marker of his own literary ambition but simultaneously continues to engage the multiple
audiences by whom his intertextuality is variably received.

Debts and Derivations

His Dark Materials, then, is an explicitly intertextual work. In addition to the 'debts' that Pullman cites in the acknowledgements, he
also makes heavy use of others' texts as epigraphs to preface his own.
The title of the entire trilogy is derived from a passage from Milton's

Paradise Lost, which is quoted in its fuller context at the beginning of *Northern Lights*. The *Amber Spyglass* has its own series of epigraphs before the text itself begins: a verse from a hymn by Robert Grant, some lines from Rilke and some from John Ashbery. Each chapter in *The Amber Spyglass* (but not in *Northern Lights* or *The Subtle Knife*) has its own epigraph, from writers including Blake, Samuel Coleridge, Emily Dickinson, Edmund Spenser, John Ruskin, John Webster, Byron, John Donne, Andrew Marvell, John Keats, George Herbert, Christina Rossetti and Pindar as well as the Bible and further quotations from Milton. (There is some divergence between various editions of the trilogy: the original and subsequent UK publications have all these epigraphs, whereas the original US edition of *The Amber Spyglass* excluded the chapter epigraphs and had a different overall epigraph from William Blake. Subsequent US editions, however, have included the chapter epigraphs from the UK edition.)

What might the role of these epigraphs be? On his website, Pullman says these epigraphs are a way of acknowledging the influence of the writers whose work he loves (www.philip-pullman.com: e). Yet their role is more than purely one of homage. Some give quite specific clues about the content of the chapter to come. The first chapter of *The Amber Spyglass*, for example, which is entitled 'The Enchanted Sleeper' and depicts the somnambulant imprisonment of Lyra by Mrs Coulter, is prefaced by a quotation from Blake that reads, 'While the beasts of prey, come from caverns deep, viewed the maid asleep' (AS 1). The chapter in which Lyra and Will's physical expression of their love occurs towards the end of *The Amber Spyglass* is prefaced by Rossetti's words, 'The birthday of my love is come, my love is come to me' (AS 480). Their parting, however, is presaged in the epigraph to the very next chapter, in which—without it being entirely clear to the reader, for whom it makes sense only retrospectively— Serafina discusses with both the children's dæmons and Mary Malone that parting. The epigraph hints at this. Marvell's words read, 'But fate does iron wedges drive, and alwaies crouds it self betwixt' (AS 498). It is worth noting that this epigraph makes reference to the theme of choice and predestination. The Marvell extract suggests that it is in fact 'fate' that will separate the children, a fate in which their choice is predetermined for them.

Other epigraphs give a more general sense of some of the themes and morality of the trilogy, even if they in addition relate specifically to the chapter to which they are appended. The quotation from Pindar exhorts, 'My soul, do not seek external life, but exhaust the realm of the possible', which is exactly the lesson that Lyra and Will must learn about the republic of heaven (AS 509). The Bible gives its lessons too, which, given Pullman's atheism, might be surprising. However, this is clearly an example of his Church of England atheism. The gospel of St John lends its words, 'And ye shall know the truth, and the truth shall make you free', to the chapter in which the deal with the harpies is struck in the land of the dead (AS 321). Such resonances are brought to a reading of the trilogy by tracing the provenance and impact of these epigraph intertexts. In terms of intertextuality, however, it is to the three specific debts that Pullman mentions in his acknowledgements that this chapter now turns.

Paradise Lost is the overarching intertext for *His Dark Materials*. As the introduction discussed, the themes and narrative structure of Milton's epic poem directly inspired Pullman's trilogy. In Pullman's narrative are rebel angels, characters readily identifiable as Adam (Will) and Eve (Lyra), a tempter figure (Mary Malone) and a stirringly portrayed Satan, leader of the rebels (Asriel). The narrative of both texts is centrally concerned with the biblical story of the Fall, which each takes as a source and then reworks. Pullman also takes into his reworking William Blake's commentary on Milton's *Paradise Lost*, as mentioned in the introduction to this book.

Paradise Lost has long been the centre of critical debate, and Pullman's trilogy brings another voice to the argument in the form of a creative intervention. Following Blake's line on Milton, that the latter was 'of the Devil's party without knowing it', Pullman sets out in the trilogy to reverse the morality of the biblical Fall and to celebrate knowledge, consciousness and sexuality. Pullman has knowingly echoed Blake's infamous statement on Milton in an interview, declaring, '"I am of the Devil's party and know it"' (de Bertodano 2002). Such statements are clearly part of the provocative persona that Pullman has developed in his commentary to the media, undoubtedly attracting increased attention to his books, leading critics such as Hitchens notoriously to name Pullman 'the most dangerous author in Britain', as the previous chapter mentioned. Yet Pullman's engagement with Milton, and with Blake's interpretation of Milton, is much more than a mere act of provocation. In *Paradise Lost*, Milton recasts the biblical story of the temptation of Eve and the Fall of humankind. Yet Milton develops the narrative beyond the frame provided by Genesis and portrays a fully imagined cosmos in which the fallen angels and Satan—Eve's tempter—are set against the autocratic power of God. The vast landscapes—or rather universe-scapes—of *Paradise Lost* are described in a grandiloquent language that profoundly impressed the young Pullman when he first studied the epic poem at school. The ongoing critical debate about *Paradise Lost*—whether it succeeds in its stated aim to 'justify the ways of God to men' or rather, as the introduction mentions, depicts God and Christianity as essentially cruel, free will as a trap for humankind and the human desire for knowledge as wrong—is a central theme in *His Dark Materials*. Yet Pullman's rewriting of the Bible and *Paradise Lost* is explicitly anti-God and pro-temptation, with the Fall as 'completely essential' and his chosen position as 'of the Devil's party' an intentional ideology. He consciously inverts the morality of the Fall and in his exploration of the rich imaginative possibilities afforded by the idea of rebel angels, Hell, and the multiple worlds travelled through by Satan in *Paradise Lost* pays a provocative homage to Milton.

In his reading of *His Dark Materials'* intertextuality, however, Tony Watkins argues that Pullman's engagement with *Paradise Lost* is partial and based on the first four of the twelve books of the poem. These, claim Watkins, are the ones in which Satan and the rebel angels are portrayed positively, whereas later sections undercut his heroism (Watkins 2004: 67–68). Carole Scott, for whom Pullman's interaction with his source texts (including the Bible as well as *Paradise Lost* and Blake) is a 'triumph of intertextuality', explores the creation of Pullman's world view through his engagement with his source texts. She argues that Pullman adds to the argument the 'relatively recent conviction' of the death of God and a 'debased church' (Scott 2004: 96), thus continuing in the dissenting tradition of Blake but, perhaps unexpectedly, remaining closer to the Church than might be imagined:

> Albeit with imaginative reconstruction, Pullman continues to employ Christianity's humanistic ethics, traditions, and values; its biblical themes and narratives; its symbolism expressed in both the Bible and church rituals; and often its diction. Finally, we find a religious, even puritanical streak in his sense of every person's ultimate responsibility to humankind, even at the expense of their own happiness. (Scott 2004: 96)

Scott's argument confirms the conclusions of the previous chapter, in which Pullman's ideology places him less in conflict with the real-life Church than might be anticipated. Some of his theology directly rewrites the Christian narrative, but the morality that he expresses is not so clearly in contradiction with Christian ethics, as implied by the appreciative commentary of some religious figures upon *His Dark Materials*. Nonetheless, Pullman's rewriting of the story of the temptation, as told in the Bible and retold in *Paradise Lost*, demonstrates how intertextual method allows the author to stir theological and ideological debate, to enrich his own narrative and to place himself—at least for consideration—alongside writers central to the canon of English literature, as this chapter later explores.

In addition to the internal references to Milton and the mention Pullman has made of the influence of *Paradise Lost* on his own work in interviews, he has also in years subsequent to the publication of *His Dark Materials* introduced an edition of the epic poem, in which he again acknowledges the poem's role in his own creative work (Pullman 2005a). Considering that C S Lewis also published a lengthy preface to the poem in 1942, based on a series of lectures, it is evident that Pullman is staking his claim for interpretive pre-eminence over Milton's work, as well as promoting his own writing over that of Lewis (Lewis 1942).

Within his introduction to *Paradise Lost*, Pullman refers to the ongoing interpretive debate surrounding the poem, making his own position clear by naming William Blake 'the greatest of Milton's interpreters' (Pullman 2005a: 8). Yet Blake is acknowledged by Pullman not only for his comments on Milton but also for his own poetic vision, particularly in *Songs of Innocence* (1789) and *Songs of Experience* (1794). Among these lyrics is to be discovered one of the possible sources of Lyra's name, as a girl 'Lyca' is both 'The Little Girl Lost' and 'The Little Girl Found'. Pullman echoes the title of the former lyric when his own Lyra first arrives with Will in the Oxford of his world. This is a place that she finds threateningly unfamiliar to her own Oxford, making her 'a lost little girl in a strange world, belonging nowhere' (SK 73). He continues his web of intertextual reference to this particular lyric in the first of the chapter epigraphs to *The Amber Spyglass*: the lines 'While the beasts of prey, come from caverns deep, viewed the maid asleep' are taken from 'The Little Girl Lost'. Beyond such specific intertextual references, however, Pullman is indebted to Blake—as he is to Milton's *Paradise Lost*—for the visual imagery and the landscapes of his work. These he has thoroughly plundered for intertextual use in *His Dark Materials*. Blake's strange, disturbing and visionary landscapes in *Songs*, and Milton's grand depiction of Satan surveying the worldscapes around him, make their way into Pullman's own creation of multiple worlds, and particularly into the depictions of Asriel forcing his way into the Aurora, Lyra's imprisonment by Mrs Coulter, the world of the dead and the cosmic battles towards the end of *The Amber Spyglass*.

Blake is influential upon *His Dark Materials* in a further, thematic way, which is signalled by the titles of his lyric sequence. Innocence and experience are central concepts in Pullman's trilogy, drawing on, as Carole Scott has it, 'Blake's perception of innocence, experience, and higher innocence as stages of maturity, both physical and spiritual' (Scott 2005: 103). In his depiction of Lyra and Will's growing consciousness and experience, Pullman makes such themes central to his own narrative and also links to the third of his major debts, the nineteenth-century German writer Heinrich von Kleist.

Kleist's 'On the Marionette Theatre' tells of the encounter between the narrator and a dancer. Their discourse on the puppet theatre and their anecdotes of a young man coming to consciousness of his own grace, and so losing it, nourish Pullman's thematics in the trilogy. Kleist's metaphors of the Fall distil in only a few thousand words the central concerns of Pullman's one-thousand, three-hundred-page trilogy. Kleist's story also supplies the inspiration for one of *His Dark Materials*' chief characters, Iorek, as the narrator of 'On the Marionette Theatre' is told of a strange encounter with a fighting bear.

There is a particular analogy between Kleist's metaphor of the young man who loses his grace through consciousness and Lyra's capacity to read the alethiometer. When she first starts to read it in *Northern Lights*, while with the gyptians, her approach is unconscious. Farder Coram enquires what she is asking it, and she is 'surprised to find that she'd actually been asking a question without realizing it' (NL 144). The method that she subsequently develops to read it is completely different from that used by the scholars trained for decades in its use. Lyra enters into a 'calm state' and experiences 'a sensation of such grace and power that [she] . . . felt like a young bird learning to fly' (NL 151, 152). Her readings are rapid, and her interpretation of its meanings swift. For the adult readers of the alethiometer, their readings are much slower. Mrs Coulter remarks when she is in Geneva at the Magisterium that Fra Pavel's understanding has sped up, as the information he has derived from it previously '"would have taken him a month at least to read all that"' (AS 343). In *The Subtle Knife*, Fra Pavel's reading process is very slow: he stops 'every minute or so to note down what he found. Then he would open one of the books, search laboriously through the index, and look up a reference before writing that down too and turning back to the instrument' (SK 35–36). The adult alethiometer readers rely on numerous interpretive books to read it correctly, whereas Lyra, in her childlike state, needs nothing other than her own mind. At the end of *The Amber Spyglass*, however, she loses this capacity shortly after she finds her love for Will, becoming in the process the new Eve. She discusses her loss with Dame Hannah Relf, the head of St Sophia's College:

'One day I knew it so well—I could move up and down the symbol-meanings and step from one to another and make all the connections—it was like . . .' She smiled, and went on, 'Well, I was like a monkey in the trees, it was so quick. Then suddenly—nothing. None of it made sense; I couldn't even remember anything except just basic meanings like the anchor means hope and the skull means death. All those thousands of meanings . . . Gone.'

'They're not gone, though, Lyra,' said Dame Hannah. 'The books are still in Bodley's Library. The scholarship to study them is alive and well.' (AS 543)

Lyra resolves to relearn how to read the alethiometer, using the methods of scholarship and knowledge. As the angel Xaphania says to her, she first read it by '"grace"' but can '"regain it by work"' (AS 520). Xaphania goes on to explain that this second form of reading will be richer as a consequence: '"Your reading will be even better then, after a lifetime of thought and effort, because it will come from conscious understanding. Grace attained like that is deeper and fuller than grace that comes freely, and furthermore, once you've gained it, it will never leave you"' (AS 520).

From both Blake and Kleist, then, Pullman derives and develops the idea of lost innocence, experience and the development of intellectual maturity, which is the mark of the adult human. The metaphor with which Lyra chooses to explain to Dame Hannah her changing relationship to the alethiometer is apt: she sees her childhood readings of the alethiometer as monkey-like in their agility and ease. Her adult readings may—at least initially—be less fluent. But like the human in relation to the monkey, her adult readings will also be more conscious, derived from knowledge and experience rather than intuition. Thus, evolutionary processes are glancingly referred to in the metaphor. Lyra is not, after all, a monkey or a bird, but a human. As a young adult human, she has gained experience and consciousness but still has much to learn. Thus, the intertextual references link the narrative of *His Dark Materials* with its ideology and its politics. The Fall from grace is developed through the Bible, through Milton, through Blake and Kleist, borrowing along the way language, imagery and stories from these sources and working towards an original creative vision.

The three sources that Pullman acknowledges above all others are of vital importance to the creation of the trilogy. Yet many more sources have gone into the making of *His Dark Materials*. While to explore these fully would be a lengthy and, moreover, potentially infinite task, given the nature of inferred intertextuality mentioned at the beginning of this chapter, the next section of this chapter treats these intertextualities under the guise of genre, arguments and engagements.

Genre, Arguments and Engagements

In *His Dark Materials*, then, Pullman cites two major sources which are canonical texts of English literature: *Paradise Lost* and the works of William Blake, as well as a less well-known essay/story hybrid by Heinrich von Kleist. Through Pullman's use of epigraphs, he extends his field of explicit intertextual references to several other major writers. His range of references, however, is not only much greater than this but also much more diverse and includes popular culture sources as well as canonical references.

Some of these different types of influence are evident from Pullman's biography, as the biographical chapter of this book discusses. The Bible, and religious imagery and language more generally, was an early influence on him via his grandfather, and even before he read *Paradise Lost* as a teenager, the biblical story of the Fall would have been known to him. The impact of the religious contexts that Pullman incorporates into *His Dark Materials* is discussed elsewhere in this book. For Pullman, however, one of the abiding impacts of his religious upbringing is not solely in the *content* but in the manner of *delivery*. Pullman's grandfather was a great storyteller, and his talent marked and inspired the young Pullman. Pullman also emphasises the importance of oral storytelling later in his life: through listening to Australian radio and relating further adventures to his brother, and then through telling stories to the children in his classes as a teacher. Pullman incorporates storytelling as a central theme of *His Dark Materials*, but he also uses its techniques in his written story. Chapters frequently end with cliff-hanging moments. In *Northern Lights*, for example, chapter 19, 'Captivity', ends with the words, 'And meanwhile Iorek, knowing nothing about it, was hurrying ever closer towards what she wished she could tell him was a fight for his life' (NL 343); and chapter 8 of *The Subtle Knife*, 'The Tower of the Angels', ends with Will's words of resolve: '"We've got to get the alethiometer back, so we'll have to steal it. That's what we're going to do"' (SK 198). Both chapter endings are a tantalising invitation to read on, to find out what will happen when Iorek arrives and the children try to steal back the alethiometer. The writing is, on the whole, dramatic and fast-paced and lends itself well to being read aloud, as anyone who has either listened to the audio versions of the trilogy or heard Pullman reading from his work in person, or in fact had it read to them by any good reader, will bear testament to. Indeed, Pullman's method of composition, in which three novels were conceived and announced from the beginning, meant that Pullman was writing the second and third volumes in the face of the expectation of the readers of *Northern Lights*. He was not able to present the whole story of the trilogy all at once, but rather, like the storyteller in his short book *Clockwork*, was in the perilous position of having to continue a story that was already in the public domain, without having fully planned the story. Fritz, the storyteller in *Clockwork*, has reason to be nervous: 'The fact was, he hadn't actually finished the story. He'd written the start all right, and it was terrific, but he hadn't been able to think of an ending. He was just going to wind up the story, set it going, and make up the end when he got there' (Pullman 1996a: 20).

Although Pullman certainly did have a sense of the overall arc of the story of *His Dark Materials* when he set out with the concept of *Paradise Lost* for teenagers, it is hard to imagine that he had plotted the entire structure of the novels. This is a further way in which his writing is linked to the genre of oral storytelling. Pullman did of course have the opportunity to redraft his work, but nonetheless, it is evident that something of the 'vertiginous delight' of storytelling remains, along with the sense, as Pullman puts it, 'that every step you take is ... on the edge of a yawning pit that you might suddenly fall into by getting the story wrong or by failing to find something' (Pullman 1999b: 187). The delay between the publication of *The Subtle Knife* and *The Amber Spyglass*—a period of three years—may at least partly be explained by this sensation and by the pressure generated by the need to create a fitting ending to the previous two volumes.

Another area of literature and storytelling which *His Dark Materials* uses as a source of intertextual material is that of folk stories and fairy tales. Again, there is a clear biographical link for these sources, as Pullman used them extensively in the classroom as a teacher and later taught them as forms of literature at Westminster Institute. There are numerous examples of places where traditional storytelling patterns and characters have been used in the trilogy. Good explanations of such intertextual reference are to be found in Parkin and Jones's *Dark Matters* (2005). David Colbert's forthcoming *The Magical Worlds of Philip Pullman* (due to be published in 2007), which promises to trace *His Dark Materials*' sources in the same way that the author has done previously with the *Harry Potter* stories, *The Chronicles of Narnia* and *The Lord of the Rings*, will also go into these references in some depth. It is not the aim of this chapter to repeat the tasks of these authors nor to provide—if it were possible—an exhaustive list of such references. Nonetheless, giving some of the more substantial examples of the trilogy at least demonstrates the range of sources that Pullman has drawn upon and the way he has adapted them to fit his own purposes.

At the beginning of *The Amber Spyglass*, Lyra is imprisoned by her mother and drugged into a deep sleep. Like Sleeping Beauty, she must await rescue by a young man, although she is not—at this stage—awoken by a kiss. The person who is keeping her hostage is her mother—a glamorous, dangerous figure who bodes as much harm to her daughter as good. This character, in her glamorous femininity, is clearly derived from Pullman's biographical memories of his own mother, as chapter 1 examined. However, Mrs Coulter is also firmly in the tradition of the evil *step*mother of folk stories and fairy tales, such as that in Cinderella.

His Dark Materials also uses many of the tropes of metamorphosis and transformation that occur in folk and fairy-tale plots. The shape-shifting of the dæmons is the obvious example of this and is explored at greater length in the epilogue to Marina Warner's *Fantastic Metamorphoses, Others Worlds* (2002). One of the most comprehensive sets of characters Pullman has developed from folk stories and fairy tale, however, is that of the witches. Yet Pullman imbues the witches with his own original vision. The witches of Lyra's world have a distinctive existence through their capacity to separate from their dæmons. They may engage in sexual relationships with short-lived human men, but because of their longevity, their partners age and die many centuries before they do. Pullman's witches are formed into separate clans, and in *The Subtle Knife* and *The Amber Spyglass*, these clans begin to take opposing sides in the war between Asriel and the Magisterium. Witches are neither good nor evil characters, but like humans can be both. The witch who kills Will's father, for example, does so not out of malevolence but because of a broken heart. The witches are also used to articulate some of Pullman's anti-religious ideology. Drawing on the real-world history of the persecution of the witches, instituted via the Catholic Inquisition in the Middle Ages and continued until the eighteenth century in England and Scotland, Pullman writes one scene in *The Subtle Knife* in which a witch is tortured, and another in which the witch Ruta Skadi relates what she has learnt from Asriel about the actions of the agents of the Authority, the '"hideous cruelties"' enacted on witches (SK 39–41, 283).

In this way, Pullman intertextually incorporates into *His Dark Materials* some of the real-world history of witches along with the vast body of folk stories and fairy tales that have witches as characters, and canonical texts including witches such as Shakespeare's *Macbeth* (1606). Into this intertextual mix he also throws anthropological knowledge. Parkin and Jones refer to the Sami people, or Lapps, of the far north of Europe, who believe in a 'goddess of the underworld called Yambe-Akka' (Parkin and Jones 2005: 255). Yambe-Akka is the name Pullman gives to the 'goddess who came to a witch when she was about to die', as indeed she comes to the tortured

witch in *The Subtle Knife* (SK 41). To continue the wealth of intertextual reference in his creation of the witches, Pullman has drawn
Serafina Pekkala's name from the Helsinki phone book (Wartofsky
2001; Ross 2002). Thus, around the frame of established literary
and fairy-tale characters, Pullman makes several other ingenious
intertextual additions in the creation of his witches. In effect, genres intermingle.

Allied to the genre of folk story and fairy tale is that of myth and
legend, which is another area that Pullman plunders extensively for
His Dark Materials, particularly in the form of Greek myth and legend. This was another area of literature from which Pullman derived
stories to tell to his own children and his school classes. The scenes
in which Lyra and Will journey to the land of the dead provides several examples of this. The living entering an underworld inhabited
by the dead is reminiscent of the tale of Orpheus and Eurydice, with
the former going in search of his dead wife, much as Lyra searches
for her lost friend Roger. In *The Amber Spyglass*, there are suburbs of
the dead (an area like Limbo), a river that must be crossed in order
to reach the land of the dead (like the river Styx), and a boatman
who ferries them across the river after explaining to them the rules
of their entrance into the underworld (like the boatman Charon).
Once in the land of the dead, Lyra and Will encounter the harpies,
also mythical creatures from Greek legend. Although these creatures
are initially presented in very negative terms, they eventually are
seen to have redeeming features. Pullman is perhaps referring here
to the originally positive but latterly negative portrayals of the physical appearance of the harpies in Greek mythology.

A further genre that *His Dark Materials* takes from and contributes to is that of children's literature generally, but it is to children's adventure stories that Pullman's writing has a particular
allegiance. As the biographical chapter in this book mentions, one of
Pullman's favourite writers from his own childhood was Arthur
Ransome, whose *Swallows and Amazons* series depicts a quality of
childhood freedom and an emphasis on moral responsibility, which
is consonant with that of *His Dark Materials*. In these novels,
Ransome created 'an idyllic playground in which children had to

behave responsibly towards each other and the environment in order to get the best out of their situation' (Eccleshare 2002a: 40). As such, *His Dark Materials* is also clearly borrowing from the form of the *Bildungsroman*, or novel of growing up. Although Pullman hints at the teen sexuality that is the central concern of his contemporaries such as Melvin Burgess, however, *His Dark Materials* is neither as explicit nor as social-realist as their writing and essentially follows a more traditional pattern. In its brave, resourceful and self-reliant child protagonists, the trilogy is almost nostalgic in its echoing of earlier writers of children's adventure stories. As the biographical chapter of this book also discussed, there are other familiar tropes of children's fiction that Pullman follows, such as the ubiquity of orphaned or near-orphaned protagonists.

Another area of both children's and adults' literature that *His Dark Materials* is aligned with is science fiction and fantasy. In the profusion of different worlds presented in the trilogy, and in particular the manner in which characters make transitions from one to another, Pullman's work clearly draws on literary precedents. In *His Dark Materials*, the most frequent means by which this transition occurs is via Will's cutting holes between worlds with the subtle knife. There are, however, holes previously cut with the knife that initially allow Will and Mary Malone to begin their adventures, as well as the results of Asriel's experiment at the end of *Northern Lights*, which creates a pathway for himself and Lyra to traverse into different worlds. Karen Patricia Smith, writing a critical essay on the fantasy models Pullman is adhering to and developing, refers to this aspect of the trilogy as 'Excursions into Invented Worlds' (Smith 2005). She records particular similarities to the work of Susan Cooper and C S Lewis in these moments of transition, and links them more generally to the 'Perilous Journeys', as she phrases it, undertaken by the characters. In the opening scenes of *Northern Lights*, there is an allusion to a transition trope as Lyra hides in the wardrobe in the Retiring Room, surrounded by academic gowns, some fur-lined. Even though this is not the point at which Lyra travels to another world (this does not happen until the end of *Northern Lights*), it is from here that she becomes irrevocably involved with

Asriel's world of high politics, and she sees his photogram of the city in the sky, after which she embarks on her world-crossing adventures. Moreover, to any reader of C S Lewis, this scene is highly reminiscent of the most famous of his 'excursion' scenes in *The Lion, the Witch and the Wardrobe* (1950), in which Lucy, one of the child protagonists, first finds an opening to the other world of Narnia through a wardrobe filled with furs. As in *The Chronicles of Narnia*, this opening scene in *His Dark Materials* leads to many pages of otherworld adventure. And yet Pullman, as earlier chapters of this book have demonstrated, occupies a stance contrary to C S Lewis and also has made remarks about his distaste for the fantasy of another Oxford writer with whom Lewis was linked and Pullman is frequently compared: J R R Tolkien. Unlike his acknowledged and appreciative debts to Milton, Blake and Kleist, then, there is another vein of Pullman's intertextuality which is more argumentative and contrarian.

It is possible to *See* Pullman's engagement with C S Lewis and J R R Tolkien, on Pullman's part at least, as a battle for supremacy. The similarities between these three writers is at least as great as their differences, and it therefore makes sense to consider how Pullman takes on his predecessors and how his arguments with them are simultaneously intertextual engagements with their writing.

The similarities between the writers are biographical, generic and textual. Lewis, Tolkien and Pullman are all writers who were, or are, based in Oxford. All three are also best known for a series of books that feature different worlds and fantastical characters, thus lending their work a generic definition as fantasy. These three series—*The Chronicles of Narnia, The Lord of the Rings* and *His Dark Materials*— share an appeal to both adults and children, and so cannot be neatly categorised as children's or adults' literature. Yet Pullman has arguments with both of these series and disputes his similarities to them.

Pullman is ideologically opposed to the Christian perspective allegorised in *The Chronicles of Narnia*. Yet *The Chronicles* are a clear source of intertextual material for *His Dark Materials*, and Pullman's commentary upon them in the media has only served to draw attention to this link. Burton Hatlen's essay on *His Dark*

Materials' 'challenge' to both Lewis and Tolkien suggests that 'rather than simply rejecting Lewis as a model, Pullman has . . . offered a kind of inverted homage to his predecessor, deliberately composing a kind of "anti-Narnia," a secular humanist alternative to Lewis's Christian fantasy' (Hatlen 2005: 82). Given the 'pernicious' influence that Pullman feels Lewis to have, it would seem that the nature of the intertextual link between Pullman's work and Lewis's is, at least in part, an intentional riposte to *The Chronicles*. This is undoubtedly a case of implied intertextuality, though one that is heavily trailed in Pullman's commentary external to the text of *His Dark Materials* itself.

Pullman also has engaged with J R R Tolkien's writing in the commentary he has made outside the trilogy itself. Such remarks have occurred in response to comments that his own writing, like that of Tolkien, belongs to the genre of fantasy. Tolkien is the acknowledged master of fantasy fiction. Pullman's trilogy is also arguably a work of fantasy, defined in *The Oxford Companion to English Literature* as a 'liberation from the constraints of what is known, coupled with a plausible and persuasive inner coherence' (Drabble 2000: 350). *His Dark Materials* certainly displays such characteristics: a knife that can cut between worlds; a vehicle that works by thought-power alone; humans accompanied by dæmons. In interview, however, Pullman has stated that '*Northern Lights* is not a fantasy. It's a work of stark realism' (Parsons and Nicholson 1999: 131). Pullman extended his argument on his website in the form of a FAQ (frequently asked question) section. The mention of elves and hobbits is undoubtedly a reference to Tolkien:

> *You once said that* His Dark Materials *is not a fantasy, but stark realism. What did you mean by that?*
> That comment got me into trouble with the fantasy people. What I mean by it was roughly this: that the story I was trying to write was about real people, not beings that don't exist like elves or hobbits. Lyra and Will and the other characters are meant to be human beings like us, and the story is about a universal human experience, namely growing up. The 'fantasy'

parts of the story were there as a picture of aspects of human nature, not as something alien and strange. (www.philip-pullman.com: h)

Pullman's own interpretation of his work is contentious—the reality of the worlds encountered in *His Dark Materials* is very different from that of our world—but perhaps what Pullman is suggesting is the conflict between fantasy and psychological realism. Elsewhere he has dismissed Tolkien's writing for being '"not interesting psychologically; there's nothing about people in it"' (de Bertodano 2002). The claim of 'stark realism' for his work is Pullman's way of promoting his own skill in developing character motivation: although the worlds of *His Dark Materials* may be unknown to us, the psychological manner in which characters traverse them is instantly recognisable. Pullman goes on to explain on his website that dæmons are a quintessential example of this: seemingly fantastical but actually an expression of human personality. Thus, in the desire to express his own creative and moral ideology, Pullman summons his predecessors Lewis and Tolkien, it would seem at first, in order to dismiss them, but in actuality to engage with them creatively. As with Milton and Blake, these intertexts inform and broaden the worlds of *His Dark Materials* but are also used as means by which Pullman has enabled himself to articulate his political and creative vision. Explicit and implied intertextuality, then, are used in appreciation, as inspiration and for argumentation.

Ambition

The initial idea for *His Dark Materials* was an ambitious one. The aim of writing '"*Paradise Lost* for teenagers in three volumes"' is a grand project, with the intention of engaging and transforming one of the central texts of the canon of English literature. In the subsequent creation of *His Dark Materials*, Pullman continued to demonstrate such intertextual ambition in the range of sources drawn upon. Susan Matthews, discussing Pullman's interaction with Blake, states that he 'echoes a writer now culturally enshrined as an authority and source of inspiration' (Matthews 2005: 127). By his intertextual negotiations with such writers, it is apparent that Pullman is, at least to some degree, associating his own writing with earlier writers' commonly perceived greatness. He signals canonical sources through his acknowledgements and his explicit use of epigraphs, and in addition he has nominated numerous influences and sources in commentary external to the text. In his arguments with C S Lewis and J R R Tolkien, he locates his work in opposition to theirs but in so doing makes the comparison inevitable, as the numerous critical commentators who have done so make evident. There is a sense, then, in which the creation of an original but nonetheless deeply intertextual work displays a writer's ambition and potentially elevates his or her work. Reviews of the trilogy, like the one towards the beginning of this chapter, note these intertextual references, using them to display the depth and range of the new creation and the author's desire to be taken seriously as a well-read writer, intelligently engaging with literary tradition. For a writer to engage with such a range of texts and, moreover, to do so explicitly is to stake a claim to his or her own literary greatness, or at least his or her own ambition to achieve literary greatness. Pullman is not so immodest in his own commentary on the trilogy to place himself alongside Milton and Blake, but in the trilogy itself his engagement and rewriting make their own claims. It is not, then, necessarily a question of judging whether Pullman has achieved the greatness of Milton and Blake, but rather it is for Pullman a method both of articulating an artistic and ideological vision and of gaining recognition via the legitimate creative process of intertextuality. Given that it was with *His Dark Materials*, rather than any of his earlier writing, that Pullman did indeed achieve widespread recognition and acclaim, it is safe to suggest that his range of intertextual reference in no small way contributed to this reception.

Such recognition has done much to draw attention to writing for children generally, as well as to Pullman in particular. The next chapter considers in greater detail the question of the role *His Dark Materials* has had in transforming perceptions of children's literature, but it is evident from Pullman's critical reception that his broad range of intertextual reference was one of the factors that particularly impressed the reviewers. And yet, as Pullman himself would say—given the evidence of his Carnegie Medal acceptance speech—it is story that is the heart of children's books, story that is at the heart of his own trilogy, and virtuoso storytelling that is the reason for *His Dark Materials'* broad appeal. The question this then begs is the extent to which a knowledge and understanding of the trilogy's intertexts is necessary to its reading experience, and how a variety of audiences might respond to the intertextuality of *His Dark Materials*.

Readers and Intertexts

His Dark Materials, then, is a richly intertextual work and, moreover, one in which the processes of reading as well as storytelling are foregrounded. In her essay '"Without Lyra We Would Understand Neither the New Nor the Old Testament": Exegesis, Allegory, and Reading *The Golden Compass*', Shelley King has argued that the alethiometer, in addition to highlighting the trilogy's concern with the issues of innocence and experience, provides a model for different patterns of reading. The trilogy, she says, is 'about reading in the broader sense of the process of textual interpretation and the role it plays in the framing of metaphysical questions within a culture' (King 2005: 106). King identifies the two different types of reading typified by Lyra and the adult scholars as that of the 'intuitive child' and the 'difficult conscious reading'. For King, this distinction is also a metaphor for the readership of *His Dark Materials*, the pairing of 'engaged child readers and literary critics, who similarly come to the text with differing modes of engagement' (King 2005: 107). Although King arguably makes too neat a separation between child and adult readers—where does the young adult fit into this pattern? and what of adult readers of the trilogy who are not literary scholars?—this section of the chapter nonetheless considers these 'differing modes of engagement' and considers the question of intertextuality from a more reader-oriented perspective.

King unearths a fascinating intertextual source for *His Dark Materials*, which additionally illuminates the metaphorical depiction of the reading and interpretive processes within the trilogy. She refers to Nicholas of Lyra, a textual scholar of the late Middle Ages whose biblical exegesis and principles of literary criticism were central to the later re-examination of received scriptural interpretation on which the Reformation was founded (King 2005: 106). Lyra's writing insisted on 'awareness of multiple levels of interpretation' (King 2005: 114), and so if transferred to *His Dark Materials* would imply that the work must be read on several levels or layers: in terms of the story; in terms of its morality; in terms of its allegory; and in terms of its mediation of the Bible and the intertexts that stand between it and Pullman (including, notably, Milton and Blake). Yet Nicholas of Lyra also emphasised the place of lay reading, or 'the accessibility of meaning to all readers, naïve and scholarly alike' (King 2005: 117). King uses the figure of Nicholas of Lyra as an analogy for the depiction of reading prefigured by Lyra and the alethiometer in *His Dark Materials*, but also to suggest that through Lyra and the alethiometer, Pullman himself builds a model for the various ways in which the trilogy can be read. For a child reader, then, or indeed a non-scholarly adult reader, much of the intertextual resonance will not be apparent, despite the explicit references in the epigraphs and acknowledgements. Indeed, any reader may bring to the text of *His Dark Materials*, as with all textual readings, a wealth of inferred intertexts which are not intentionally referred to by the author. And yet, given Pullman's emphasis on the *story*, it is important that although an understanding of the intertextual references extends and enriches the interpretation of the text, a 'naïve' reading based on the story still yields the same messages. Thus, without having read *Paradise Lost* or even having knowledge of the biblical story on which it is based, Lyra and Will's Fall, and the passage from innocence to experience, from grace to consciousness, is central to the story and is also metaphorically illustrated in the narrative through the different ways in which the alethiometer is read and through Lyra's resolve at the end of *The Amber Spyglass* to relearn her capacity to read the alethiometer. Even without any knowledge of the key intertexts, these themes are still apparent. Nevertheless, a reading of the trilogy based on a more scholarly understanding generates analyses which have an appreciation of Pullman's literary engagement; an increased sense of *His Dark Materials'* provocative tendencies, particularly with regard to its rewriting of the Bible and Church history and tradition; a critical assessment of Pullman's literary ambition; and an enriched understanding of the themes of the work.

Intertextuality, then, is an important method by which *His Dark Materials* has been constructed and can be interpreted. Source texts have been crucial in his creation of the trilogy and yield rich analysis when studied alongside the trilogy. And yet, particularly because of the dual, or rather multiple, readerships of the trilogy, the story at the heart of *His Dark Materials* conveys the meanings that Pullman has absorbed and developed from his sources. Intertextuality is vitally important in *His Dark Materials*, and yet it is also possible to sublimate it, giving precedence instead to the adventure story of Lyra and Will, and their allies of gyptians and armoured bears, witch clans and fantastical spy creatures.

6

What Type of Story Is *His Dark Materials*?

IN *HIS DARK MATERIALS*, Philip Pullman models a variety of story-telling methods and story types. During the descent into the land of the dead, this becomes apparent in No-Name's negative reaction to Lyra's made-up stories of high fantasy and in her positive reaction to the true stories that Lyra tells of her quotidian Oxford life. As the previous chapter on intertextuality emphasised, there are also a variety of story types, or genres, which are incorporated into the fabric of the trilogy. This chapter investigates in more detail some of those genres and the ways in which Pullman weaves them together in the formation of his own story type. The chapter also considers in detail the question of the trilogy's definition in terms of children's, adults' and 'crossover' literature and concludes with a consideration of how Pullman's negotiation with different story types adds to the meanings transmitted by the trilogy.

A Children's Story?

The Amber Spyglass was the first children's novel to win one of the UK's major literary prizes, the Whitbread Book of the Year. It was also, as the introduction mentioned, long-listed for the Booker Prize. The trilogy has thus received recognition for its artistic achievements in the field of fiction generally, rather than only in the restricted arena of writing for children. At the same time, Pullman's success, coupled with J K Rowling's phenomenal *Harry Potter* series and other prominent children's writers, including Jacqueline Wilson and Michael Morpurgo, has led many commentators on publishing and writing to declare that the late twentieth and early twenty-first centuries have been a 'golden age' for children's literature (Eccleshare 2002b; 2004). In terms of both sales figures and critical reception, *His Dark Materials* has been instrumental in fostering a changing perception of children's literature, and hence has negotiated with definitions of children's and adults' literature, crossing and redrawing their boundaries.

Prior to the publication of *His Dark Materials*, Pullman had written novels for adults and books for children. His first two books in the 1970s, *The Haunted Storm* and Galatea, which are discussed in more detail in the next chapter, were written for adults, but at the beginning of the 1980s, Pullman turned to writing for a younger audience, with his first published book for children being *Count Karlstein*. From then onwards, Pullman published a variety of books, but always primarily for a children's audience, all with children's publishers or via the children's imprints of general publishing houses. By the time he conceived of *His Dark Materials*, he had already acquired a reputation as an accomplished writer for children with his previous books and had been awarded several of the prizes for critically acclaimed children's writers in Britain. When Pullman initially discussed the projected *His Dark Materials* trilogy with his publisher, Pullman talked of it in terms of a teenage audience, and in the UK it was published by Scholastic Children's Books, a publisher, as the name of the company makes clear, of literature for the young. It is indisputable, then, that *His Dark Materials* was published as a work of fiction for children, or rather young adults, as Pullman's intended teenage audience could also be termed. And yet the three books went on to become emblematic not only of a purported golden age of writing for children but of a seeming 'crossover' market, in which certain books extend their appeal to an audience of both children and adults. A later title which was also widely seen in the 'crossover' genre is Mark Haddon's *The Curious*

Incident of the Dog in the Night-Time (2003). Following in Pullman's footsteps, Haddon's book also won the Whitbread Book of the Year Award, although it was entered for the Novel category award rather than the Children's Book Award.

For David Fickling, the UK publisher of both *His Dark Materials* and *The Curious Incident of the Dog in the Night-Time*, the concept of the crossover title is nothing more than an act of 'professional categorisation', a description of how and where books are sold, and particularly where they are shelved (Fickling 2006). For the producers and retailers of fiction which performs this 'crossover' between the children's and adults' market, this is then a question of whether copies of the title are located in the children's or adults' section of the bookshop, or both. The publishers of Philip Pullman and J K Rowling have encouraged marketing strategies to reach both children and adults by producing 'adult' editions of both series. The adult editions do not differ in textual terms in any way, but they do have different cover designs and cover copy. When *The Curious Incident of the Dog in the Night-Time* was published in 2003, this publishing strategy was utilised from the beginning. (The adult versions of Pullman and Rowling were produced some time after the initial publication of the children's editions.) *The Curious Incident of the Dog in the Night-Time* was published by two different imprints of the same publisher, Random House, with David Fickling Books producing the children's edition, and Jonathan Cape the adults'.

Such marketing techniques have undoubtedly added to the titles' exposure and market reach. Yet these acts of 'professional categorisation' are about the contexts in which the books are published and the manner in which they are packaged. What might there be internal to the text—in the content, in other words—that means that *His Dark Materials* might be thought of as a story for children, for teenagers or for adults?

As the previous chapter discussed, Pullman is undoubtedly writing in a tradition of children's literature. He uses tropes that reoccur in writing for children: the orphan or near-orphan; the uses of gateways or doors into other worlds; non-human characters who form strong allegiances with the child protagonists, and so on. There is a

very strongly plot-driven narrative, and despite the moral seriousness with which the trilogy is imbued, the story—for the most
part—is the primary force. And yet *His Dark Materials* is also the
vehicle for conveying a range of issues, or 'big ideas', which are as
relevant to adults as they are to children, even if at their core is the
central theme of growing up, which is particularly appropriate for a
youthful audience. The reception of the trilogy by reviewers has
emphasised this. Nick Thorpe, writing in the *Sunday Times*, commented that 'while [Pullman's] primary passion is storytelling, his
battle is nothing if not ideological' (Thorpe 2002). S F Said spoke of
the trilogy in the *Daily Telegraph* as 'prob[ing] some of the most
fundamental questions of human existence' (Said 2002). Also in the
Daily Telegraph, Andrew Marr saw Pullman as concerned with the
big ideas of 'love, moral conduct, power, nature, paradise, hell and
the existence or otherwise of God, the universe and everything'
(Marr 2002). And as Michael Dirda suggests at the end of his review
of *Northern Lights* in the *Washington Post*, the first book asks a series
of questions which 'offer moral complexity . . . What do you do
when people you love turn out to be evil? Do admirable goals ever
justify despicable means? What is the proper place of religion and
science in civil life? How does one deal with betrayal?' (Dirda 1996).

As Boyd Tonkin commented in an article in the *Independent*
about the trend for adults to read children's books, the 'more strenu-
ous theological myths' of *His Dark Materials* made the 'passion for
current children's writing intellectually watertight' (Tonkin 2002b).
Ironically, however, the intellectually engaged nature of Pullman's
work seemingly marked a distinction between it and much writing
directed at adults. As Terence Blacker phrased it in his review of *The
Subtle Knife*, 'At a time when English fiction is widely perceived as
being parochial in its concerns and domestic in its settings, one
Englishman is at work on a towering trilogy of novels' (Blacker
1997). Even more boldly, Erica Wagner proclaimed in *The Times*
that *His Dark Materials* 'looks set to pull down the whole moral
framework that has underpinned Western civilisation. Who says
English writers aren't ambitious anymore?' (Wagner 2000). Such a
claim may overstate the case a little, but it is nonetheless clear that

Pullman's intellectual and artistic ambition is simultaneously challenging and accomplished. The commentary of the critics echoed the provocative remarks made by Pullman himself in his Carnegie Medal acceptance speech, and also in the essay 'Let's Write It in Red', in which he said that 'children's books . . . at this time in our literary history, open out on wideness and amplitude—a moral and mental spaciousness—that adult fiction seems to have turned its back on' (Pullman 1998c).

The reversal of expectation inherent in Pullman's comments, and those of Wagner and Blacker, suggests that children's fiction is not only where the best storytelling can be found but also where the most intellectually demanding and daring ideas are. In *His Dark Materials*, at least, children's literature presents a challenge to writing for adults in its moral seriousness and narrative artistry. However, children's literature—along with genre literature—has traditionally been placed lower in literary hierarchies than adult literary fiction. The coverage given to various types of fiction in the pages of any newspaper demonstrates this very clearly. Books for children, or science fiction, or romance, consistently receive much less space than more 'serious' works. Pullman has attempted to address this prejudice in two ways: firstly through his comments in numerous speeches, interviews and opinion pieces, in which he elevates children's literature above the mass of adult literary fiction; and secondly, through *His Dark Materials* itself and the way in which it has been critically received. Nicolette Jones, writing in the *Sunday Times*, stated that *His Dark Materials* 'earned him a place in the firmament of children's literature' but also 'blurred distinctions between writing for children and writing for adults, and between genre fantasy and fiction of general appeal' (Jones 2000). In an article specifically addressing the question of the divide between writing for children and writing for adults, the *Observer*'s Robert McCrum stressed the need for Pullman to be 'evaluated as an important contemporary novelist who happens to write in a certain genre, a significant writer to be spoken of in the same breath as, say, Beryl Bainbridge, A S Byatt or Salman Rushdie' (McCrum 2000).

For some critics, then, Pullman has literary credentials that elevate him to the ranks of the foremost of contemporary writers of any type. For others, though, including Pullman himself, the trilogy has called into question the ranking system in which adult literary fiction would seem to be automatically valued above all other forms. Consequently, Pullman has been at the forefront of changing perceptions of children's literature and forcing critics and adult readers to take its contents, and its emphasis on story and 'big issues', seriously. The marketing strategies undertaken by publishers and retailers to promote his books as 'crossover' titles have been an important aspect in terms of bringing awareness to the virtues of children's writing, but even more crucial has been the content of the trilogy itself.

Yet children's literature is not a homogenous genre, and when asking what type of story *His Dark Materials* is, the rich variety of books written for children must be taken into account. Adventure stories have been a strong influence, but Pullman's trilogy is in a tradition of fantastical literature for children, even if, as its author would remonstrate, his work is psychologically true. Yet the trilogy is clearly not a work of social realism of the likes produced by his contemporary Melvin Burgess, for example, whose gritty stories of teenage drug-taking and sex have provided a very different sort of fiction from Pullman's. Pullman himself has written in a more social-realist genre, with his earlier novels *The Broken Bridge* (1990) and *The White Mercedes* (1992). *His Dark Materials*, although partly set in contemporary Britain through its depiction of Will's world, largely steers away from dramatising the realities of the lives of young people in the present day. There are exceptions: there is a sensitive portrayal of the relationship between Will and his mother, who would seem to be suffering from a paralysing psychological condition which means he often acts as her carer; and in *The Subtle Knife* Will's previous experience of children's cruelty to one another draws on the terrors of bullying, of which many of Pullman's child readers might have experience. Nonetheless, the fictional worlds of *His Dark Materials* are very different from that of Burgess's *Junk* (1996) or *Doing It* (2003). In his depiction of Lyra and Will's developing relationship, and their discovery of each other's bodies, Pullman is not shying away from teenage sexuality; indeed, the passage from innocence to experience and the importance of the sexual body to human life are central to the themes and plot of *His Dark Materials*. However, the soft-focus manner in which Lyra and Will's sexual relationship is described is very different from the explicitness and candour of a writer like Burgess. Nonetheless, whereas C S Lewis, for example, or J M Barrie in *Peter Pan in Kensington Gardens* (1911), portrays growing up as something to be avoided, or a painful experience in which the delights of childhood are left behind, Pullman celebrates it as a necessary part of human life. Compared to the writing of contemporary social-realist writers, though, Pullman's work could actually be seen as quite evasive about the challenges that contemporary teenagers face, other than in providing rather vague instructions about being '"cheerful and kind and curious and brave and patient"' and having '"to study and think, and work hard"' (AS 548). In fact, what Pullman seems to have written in terms of children's literature is a traditional, even old-fashioned type of children's story.

Indeed, Pullman's brave and resourceful protagonists are nostalgic in their reference to earlier children's literature characters. The challenges and moral quandaries with which they are confronted are not ones solely pertinent to the teenagers of the period in which Pullman is writing but are more universal. This is, arguably, part of the appeal of the books, perhaps in particular to adults. The timeless element of the narrative also means that its morality is more general and offers guidelines which, though vague, are transferable to a variety of situations.

The other frequent children's literature comparison made to Pullman's *His Dark Materials* is J K Rowling's *Harry Potter* series. Much of the perceived similarity between the two series derives from their position as leaders of the supposed new 'golden age' of children's fiction in the late 1990s and early 2000s. There are, though, more substantive similarities between the contents of the two series. Both are strongly intertextual, and both nostalgically refer to previous works of children's literature. Both also draw on elements of the fantasy genre. However, many comparisons of the two series have viewed Pullman, as McCrum does, as 'far superior to Rowling' (McCrum 2000). With reference to the controversy courted by *His Dark Materials*, Michael Dirda noted, 'By comparison, the agreeable and entertaining Harry Potter books look utterly innocuous' (Dirda 2000). Nick Thorpe, discussing the metaphysical concerns of the trilogy, stated that *His Dark Materials* is 'ambitious, theologically nuanced stuff which makes Harry Potter look like Noddy' (Thorpe 2002). In a similar vein, Claudia Fitzherbert, commenting on the vogue for adults reading children's books, wrote, 'Adults read J K Rowling because she is not complicated; children read Philip Pullman because he is' (Fitzherbert 2002). The inflammatory comments made in the *Catholic Herald* about *His Dark Materials* were in fact an expression of surprise that the much-less-controversial *Harry Potter* books provoked so much ire and even, in some regions of the US, censorship, whereas Pullman's books were largely overlooked (Caldecott 1999). These comments may do disservice to Rowling, but the message they transmit about *His Dark Materials* is very clear. *His Dark Materials* is defined as a complex, provocative and deeply intellectual work of literature, whether read by children or adults.

Genre, Fiction and the Sense of the Ending

In addition to appealing to a varied audience in terms of age, *His Dark Materials* also crosses boundaries of genre. It references the genres of fantasy and science fiction, as well as the thriller, particularly in scenes in *The Amber Spyglass* at Saint-Jean-les-Eaux when the bomb directed towards Lyra is detonated, only for her life to be saved by a fraction of a second. In so doing, *His Dark Materials* could potentially fall prey to the prejudices that place genre fiction, like children's literature, below adult literary fiction in a putative hierarchy of genres. And yet reviews of Pullman's trilogy have perceived this very genre-traversing tendency as one of the aspects that elevates his writing. For Michael Chabon, writing in the *New York Review of Books*, this genre traversing emphasises Pullman's intertextual sources as, he writes, 'any list of the great British works of epic fantasy must begin with *Paradise Lost*' (2004). This is a redefinition of what traditionally might be thought of as the lineage of fantasy fiction. This traditional definition, established by Tolkien's *The Lord of the Rings* and its companion volume, *The Hobbit*, involves a format 'of extensive adventures set in a world similar to that of ancient legend and fairy-tale, and populated by creatures such as elves, dwarves, trolls, wizards, and talking dragons, as well as hobbits and humans' (Shippey 2001: 43).

This is certainly the definition that Pullman rails against when claiming that *His Dark Materials*, in contrast to *The Lord of the Rings*, is a work of 'stark realism'. Chabon's redefinition of fantasy to include *Paradise Lost* thrusts Pullman's trilogy both into a more prestigious literary lineage and towards what Chabon calls 'the site of our truest contemporary narratives of the Fall: in the lives, in the bodies and souls, of our children', in other words, towards intellectual engagement rather than escapism (Chabon 2004). Chabon moreover sees any potential definition of *His Dark Materials* as science fiction, with its dabbling in concepts from quantum physics (including that of the multiverse and dark matter), primarily as a 'metaphoric' usage to promote the imaginative power of storytelling and its essential role in narrating the truth (Chabon 2004). This once more relates to Pullman's central thesis of the pre-eminence of story over all his intertexts, influences and ideology. What Pullman's engagement with different intertexts, different genres and different audiences enables him to do is to create an intellectually engaged, inventive and compelling narrative which has the capacity to surprise and to shock. What is more, Pullman's play with different story types in *His Dark Materials* allows the creation of an original work of art that simultaneously meditates on the nature of story and storytelling tradition. This literary method, like the figure of Lyra as a storytelling avatar, makes *His Dark Materials* into a metanarrative, a story about stories.

Yet there remains a puzzling question as the reader exits the story that *His Dark Materials* presents to him or her. The ending provides a resolution of sorts: not a happy ending, but one in which Lyra and Will are returned to their worlds. In the true spirit of the *Bildungsroman*, they have grown up, have gathered experience and knowledge, and thus consciously face their adult futures. For the readers, the experience of the ending of the story delivers an experience analogous to that undergone by its protagonists. Despite *His Dark Materials* being a different sort of fantasy than *The Lord of the Rings*, it does, as any compelling fictional narrative will do, create worlds in which readers can happily suspend their disbelief, even if the trilogy strives not to be a work of escapism but rather to relate its morality to normal human life. But even if a reader heeds the morality of Lyra and Will's separation and relates this to his or her own life, there is inevitably a sense of a return to the dull life of the world outside the book. To leave the trilogy is forcibly to undergo a process of growing up as a reader and to relinquish the worlds of high excitement that the trilogy has provided. Thus, the inevitability of growing up for Lyra and Will in *His Dark Materials* and the inevitability of exiting the trilogy for many of its appreciative readers are metaphorically similar. We may experience this departure as inevitable, necessary and positive, but also, as Chabon has put it,

as a thinning, a loss not so much of innocence as of wildness. In its depiction of Lyra's breathtaking liberty to roam the streets, fields, and catacombs of Oxford, free from adult supervision, and of Will's Harriet-the-Spy-like ability to pass, unnoticed and seeing everything, through the worlds of adults, a freedom and a facility that were once, but are no longer, within the reach of ordinary children; in simply taking the classic form of a novel that tells the story of children who adventure, on their own, far beyond the help or hindrance of grown-ups, *His Dark Materials* ends . . . as an invocation of the glory, and a lamentation for the loss, which I fear is irrevocable, of the idea of childhood as an adventure, a strange zone of liberty, walled, perhaps, but with plenty of holes for snakes to get in. (Chabon 2004)

His Dark Materials presents an inherent and inescapable contradiction: it celebrates most vividly and with most appeal something which has to be lost, or which is, as Chabon argues, already lost in contemporary society. The most enjoyable, the most vivid parts of *His Dark Materials* are also the most fantastical, and the ending not only tears us away from them but also teaches us that we must put them behind us. The fantastical, adventurous elements of the trilogy are then connected by analogy to the realm of the child. Leaving this realm is inevitable but also the cause of great pain and regret. Imagination and inventiveness risk being left behind in favour of intellectual engagement. Thus, *His Dark Materials* is both nostalgic and elegiac for a lost childhood, exciting and compelling in its depiction of it, didactic and contradictory in the necessary exit from it. It is here that through the narrative framework of *His Dark Materials*, Pullman puts his narrative in jeopardy. Such is the way of any fictional conclusion, but *His Dark Materials* articulates this more clearly because of its tendency towards the state of metanarrative. Because of the thematic coherence of the narrative, because of its thrilling depiction of the variety of worlds and their inhabitants, because of its vehement ideological purpose, *His Dark Materials* militates both for and against its own resolution. This is a resolution which is paradoxically unresolved, and a contradiction which is summoned by coherence. *His Dark Materials*, then, while the creation of a master storyteller, also demonstrates the inherently compromised process of artistic creation.

⟪ 7 ⟫

Other Stories

THIS BOOK CONCENTRATES, to a large degree, on the work that has brought Philip Pullman to prominence and for which he is most well-known. *His Dark Materials* is—thus far—the writing upon which Pullman's reputation rests. However, as the details of Philip Pullman's biography emphasise, the trilogy was far from his first publication. In all, Pullman has published around thirty books, ranging from his first two novels for adults in 1972 and 1978, to adaptations of traditional folk stories and fairy tales, to adventure stories and works of social realism, to several works of non-fiction. He has also published numerous essays and contributed several chapters to a variety of volumes, as well as writing a large number of articles and opinion pieces for newspapers and magazines.

This chapter looks at this variety of other publications that Philip Pullman has produced. It concentrates on his fiction but also considers some of the other developments around the worlds of *His Dark Materials* in terms of the various adaptations and extensions to the trilogy that have already appeared or are forthcoming. The chapter thus addresses the range of Pullman's writing and also explores the development of some key themes and ideologies across the range of his oeuvre. In so doing, the chapter illuminates further the meanings of *His Dark Materials* while also shedding light on some of its author's lesser known works. It begins by looking at the adaptations and extensions of *His Dark Materials* and then moves on to Pullman's adult novels, his folk stories and fairy tales, his adventure stories and his contemporary novels.

The Continuing Worlds of *His Dark Materials*: Adaptations

In addition to being published as a print version, *His Dark Materials* has already been adapted into various other media formats, and there are plans for future adaptations too. There is an unabridged audio version of the books, read by Pullman and a cast of actors voicing various characters. The trilogy was later dramatised by BBC Radio and was aired on BBC Radio 4 in January 2003. Each part of the trilogy was adapted by the scriptwriter Lavinia Murray into a two-and-a-half-hour episode, with a cast starring Lulu Popplewell as Lyra, Daniel Anthony as Will, Terence Stamp as Lord Asriel and Emma Fielding as Mrs Coulter. The adaptation remained largely faithful to the original, although to compensate for the difference of medium, the role of narration in the dramatisation was given to the angel Balthamos rather than having an omniscient and unnamed narrator, as the books do. Mrs Coulter's dæmon, which unusually for the major characters remains nameless throughout the trilogy, was baptised Ozymandias for the adaptation. Ozymandias is the title of a poem by Percy Bysshe Shelley, and undoubtedly this intertextual reference could help in providing character interpretation. However, Pullman had nothing to do with the choice of name, and moreover stated in a webchat on the BBC website that it would not have been one he would have chosen himself (BBC: a).

The National Theatre in London staged a sell-out stage version of *His Dark Materials*. First performed in December 2003, the adaptation ran through the winter season in 2003–2004, with a repeat season in 2004–2005. The trilogy was adapted for the stage by Nicholas Wright, who transformed the three books into two three-hour plays (Wright 2003). The original cast included Anna Maxwell Martin as Lyra, Dominic Cooper as Will, Timothy Dalton as Lord Asriel and Patricia Hodge as Mrs Coulter, with different actors taking their parts for the 2004–2005 season. Alongside the plays, the National Theatre also mounted a series of 'Platform Discussions', with contributions from Pullman himself and also from the director, the production team, the adapter, some of the leading actors and Rowan Williams, Archbishop of Canterbury (Haill 2004). The staging of the trilogy, which was directed by Nicholas Hytner, was documented in a book by Robert Butler, *The Art of Darkness* (2003). Much was made, both in Butler's book and more generally in the media, of the gargantuan task of compressing the one thousand, three hundred pages of the trilogy into a manageable stage version, and *The Art of Darkness* explores the technical mastery that the staging demanded. The representation of the characters' dæmons inevitably presented a particular challenge. The solution was for major dæmons, including Pantalaimon and Mrs Coulter's golden monkey, to be played by actors manipulating puppets.

In terms of the necessary excisions to reduce the length of the trilogy, Wright decided in his play text, as mentioned previously, to remove completely the world of the mulefas. The character of Mary Malone also does not exist. Her important role of tempter is given to the witch Serafina Pekkala, who relates to Lyra her love for the gyptian Farder Coram, and the way she 'lifted a blackberry and pressed it against his lips', an act repeated by Lyra before she kisses Will (Wright 2003: 143, 230). The arc of the story is convincingly carried through the plays despite this excision and, as chapter 4 debated, arguably speeds up the pace of the narrative considerably, which was no doubt an important consideration for the stage version. When questioned about the play version by Robert Butler in his Platform session, however, Pullman noted the effect of the stage adaptation and staging on the weight given to some of the themes of the trilogy above others:

> *For instance, does the Church emerge more strongly, and in darker colours, in the plays?*
> I think it probably does, yes, but that's partly because these are dramatic scenes, things you can *See* vividly, strong personalities clashing with each other, face to face. Those dramatic

things work very well on stage, so perhaps that comes out more vividly, or is more salient in the plays. *Some of the ecological themes, for example, aren't as prominent.* That's probably true, yes. For instance the character of Mary Malone, the scientist, who looks at things scientifically and wonders why the world she finds herself in has developed like this rather than like that. These are internal reflective debates and have to bear on the ecology of that world. (Haill 2004: 51)

Put concisely, the religious provocation of *His Dark Materials* was exacerbated by the stage version, whereas the environmental themes were downplayed.

The adaptation was warmly, although not universally positively, received. Alastair Macaulay in the *Financial Times* thought it 'wonderful . . . theatrically poetic . . . a staging of piercing visual beauty' (Macaulay 2004). In the *Sunday Times*, Robert Hewison called it a 'stunning spectacle' (Hewison 2004). Charles Spencer in the *Daily Telegraph*, however, was not impressed with the first season of the plays, perceiving them as 'an honourable failure rather than an exhilarating success', but by the second run he thought the staging had undergone a 'triumphant transformation' (Spencer 2004a; 2004b). In the *Guardian*, Michael Billington debated what he saw as the insuperable challenge of adapting Pullman's work:

Nothing is more tempting than the apparently impossible. But although director Nicholas Hytner and his creative team display heroic courage in turning Philip Pullman's trilogy into two three-hour plays, they are ultimately overcome by the vastness of the enterprise. There is much to admire in the staging; yet the result, inevitably, is like a clipped hedge compared to Pullman's forest. (Billington 2004)

Much of the criticism naturally focused on the perceived success or otherwise of turning Pullman's epic into two stage plays which, although lengthy, could not be expected to retain the range and complexity of material of the trilogy itself.

Like the novels, the plays also courted religious controversy. Billington wrote in his review that 'in his didactic anti-clericalism, Pullman demonises religion to the point of absurdity', a demonisation which he felt to be 'even more apparent on stage', thus confirming Pullman's own analysis of the differing impact of the stage version and the books (Billington 2004). Notoriously, a British organisation, the Association of Christian Teachers (ACT), published a press release about the National Theatre's staging of the plays that was outspoken in its condemnation. Rupert Kaye, the chief executive of the ACT, stated:

> The National Theatre as a national institution has a responsibility to put on a family play over the Christmas and New Year season which is uplifting, enjoyable and accessible to people of all ages and backgrounds. Philip Pullman's story is deeply disturbing—it is offensive to Christians and will shock and appal people of other faiths too. (Association of Christian Teachers: b)

Kaye concluded his statement with the incendiary remark, 'Ideally, I would like to See His Dark Materials books banned from every primary school in . . . England and experienced Christian counsellors made available to secondary schools where the book is being read, who can help pupils to work through the various myths and misconceptions presented. This trilogy really ought to carry a spiritual health warning!' (Association of Christian Teachers: b). Kaye's comments and the ACT's stance were widely reported upon, including mentions in the *Independent*, the *Daily Telegraph*, *The Times* and the *Times Educational Supplement*. Undoubtedly, though, as well as warning off some potential audience members, they also would have added to the publicity for the National's plays.

The ACT position was counterbalanced, however, by the endorsement seemingly offered to the plays by the Archbishop of Canterbury, the leader of the Church of England. As chapter 4 discussed, Williams was content to share a stage with Pullman during the Platform talks associated with the plays, and although the two men disagreed on key points, it is also evident from the transcript of this conversation that it was a largely amicable and respectful affair (Haill 2004). Williams also wrote an article on the stage adaptation of the trilogy for the *Guardian*. As well as calling the staging 'a near-miraculous triumph', Williams suggested that the plays, and the books, could be viewed as thought-experiments that might just have the effect of bringing non-believers to think about God (Williams 2004). Indeed, for Susannah Clapp, who reviewed the plays for the *Observer*, the depiction of Christianity, in its capacity to draw attention to religion and religious issues, was symptomatic of some of the other paradoxes that the trilogy re-enacted in its stage version: 'It takes it for granted that something is still at stake. It is drenched in Christian iconography. It takes its title from *Paradise Lost*. It is a work that sticks up for making the best of this world while spending most of its pages lusciously describing other worlds' (Clapp 2004).

The stage version, then, continued the role of the books in courting controversy about Christianity, but again gave air to the stories of Christianity. Once more, this is *His Dark Materials* as Church of England atheism.

The National Theatre's staging of the plays was a very well-staffed and highly technical affair, featuring a large team of actors and the participation of many production and backstage staff, and made full use of the theatre's drum-revolve stage to facilitate swift scene changes and to depict the numerous multiple worlds that Lyra traverses. The National Theatre has documented its full-scale production not only through Butler's book but also through a comprehensive website, www.stagework.org.uk, which charts the technical and dramatic aspects of the staging as well as issues surrounding its marketing. Further presentations of the play are forthcoming; Warwick's Playbox Theatre staged the trilogy in April 2006. Although this theatre's version was a more pared-down affair, it nonetheless featured a cast of sixty. However, this theatre does not have access to the levels of funding and technology available to the National, and the reception of subsequent versions of the plays will show to what extent a successful production relies on technical artistry and to what extent on the power of its actors, the skill of its adapter and the strength of the original story written by Pullman.

In his review of the National Theatre version, Michael Billington went on to offer words that will apply to the adapters of *His Dark Materials* for the screen. He commented, 'What I question is the adaptability of Pullman's trilogy, be it into theatre, radio or film. It seems to me the ultimate example of a literary project that achieves its fullest life at the point where the author's vision meets the reader's imagination' (Billington 2004). Indeed, the gestation of the film adaptations of the trilogy has—as is frequently the way in film—been long and complicated, and the path to production has not been smooth. However, certain elements of the trilogy's content have made this frequently troubled transition more difficult.

A film deal with New Line—the production company that made the highly successful *Lord of the Rings* trilogy—was announced early in 2002, shortly after the award of the Whitbread Book of the Year Award to Pullman. The company's previous use of CGI (computer-generated imagery) in the Tolkien adaptation promised an imaginative role for it in the creation of a convincing screen presence for the dæmons, other fantastical creatures and alternate worlds of *His Dark Materials*. The playwright and screenwriter Tom Stoppard was originally commissioned to write a screenplay, and a director, Chris Weitz, joined the project. In late 2004, however, Weitz, who had also subsequently taken over the role of screenwriter from Stoppard, stepped down from his role as director. He cited the 'technical challenges' of the project as beyond his capacities, although controversy about the anti-religious nature of the trilogy dogged the production company (www.philip-pullman.com: i). Weitz's withdrawal from directorial control occurred after comments that he had made about how he might deal with the anti-religious nature of the trilogy were aired widely in the media. An original interview with Weitz conducted by the fan website www.bridgetothestars.net was picked up several months later and reported in *The Times* under the headline 'God Is Cut from Film of Dark Materials' (Coates 2004). In the original interview, Weitz had this to say about the 'more controversial

aspects' of the trilogy, and the question of whether they would be
'toned down or removed altogether'. Weitz's response to his inter-
viewer was measured but nonetheless provocative:

> Here we are at the heart of the matter. This will certainly be
> the issue that will ignite the most controversy amongst fans
> and amongst the general public.
>
> First let me say that I have visited with Pullman and spo-
> ken with him about this subject at great length. His feeling,
> and I say this with absolute certainty that I am not unfairly
> paraphrasing him, is that the 'Authority' in question could
> represent any arbitrary establishment that curtails the free-
> dom of the individual, whether it be religious, political, total-
> itarian, fundamentalist, communist, what have you. This
> gives me a certain amount of leeway in navigating the very
> treacherous issues that beset adapting HDM for the screen.
>
> New Line is a company that makes films for economic
> returns. You would hardly expect them to be anything else.
> They have expressed worry about the possibility of HDM's
> perceived antireligiosity making it an unviable project finan-
> cially. My job is to get the film made in such a way that the
> spirit of the piece is carried through to the screen, and to do
> that I must contend not only with the difficulties of the mate-
> rial but with the fears of the studio. Needless to say, all my best
> efforts will be directed towards keeping HDM as liberating
> and iconoclastic an experience as I can. But there may be
> some modification of terms. You will probably not hear of the
> 'Church' but you will hear of the Magisterium . . . I have no
> desire to change the nature or intentions of the villains of the
> piece, but they may appear in more subtle guises.
> (www.bridgetothestars.net: a)

It was the combination of Weitz's comments about religion and
economics that was picked up on in *The Times* article, in its journalist's accusation that the production company, screenwriter/director
and author were more interested in money than in an artistically

accomplished adaptation of the trilogy. However, the intent of the article, from its headline onwards, was to provoke a reaction, and in its eagerness to do so it inserted various comments made by Pullman in an earlier interview, but out of their original context. Pullman responded to the provocation of this 'God Is Cut' article on his own website shortly after the announcement of the resignation of Weitz as director. He was emphatic in his support of Weitz and New Line and clearly very angry with the manner in which controversy had been stirred up by *The Times*' journalist, and particularly the misuse of his own words. In his riposte, Pullman stated that in the making of the film, 'there will be no betrayal of any kind. I would not have sold the rights to New Line if I thought that they were incapable of making an honest film from the story I wrote.' With regard to the religious issues, he went on to define his 'main quarrel' as with

the literalist, fundamentalist nature of absolute power, whether it's manifested in the religious police state of Saudi Arabia or the atheist police state of Soviet Russia. The difference between those powers on the one hand, and the democratic powers of the human imagination on the other, are at the very heart of *His Dark Materials* (www.philip-pullman.com: f)

This assertion echoes Weitz's understanding of the nature of the 'Authority'. Pullman then backed up New Line's capacity to share 'my understanding of the democratic nature of reading, and . . . my faith in the free play of the human imagination'. Pullman's 'quarrel' is indeed transferable to other situations, and both Weitz and Pullman correctly identify the transferability of the theme of repression and freedom. However, these other situations are *not* the contextual basis for the trilogy, which refers quite purposefully to Christianity. It cannot be denied that Pullman's repressive institution in *His Dark Materials* is *specifically* modelled on the Christian Church as is much of the intertextual rewriting in terms of the story of the Fall and the depiction of the passage from innocence to experience. Pullman's rush to New Line's defence saw him providing another layer of interpretation for his own work, and indeed his defence, as might be anticipated, is a sensitive and intelligently written one. But it is also a very didactically titled one: Pullman's retaliation is called 'Chris Weitz, New Line, "The Times", and How to Read', and there is a suggestion in Pullman's righteous anger that he protests too much in his rebuttal of *The Times'* sloppy journalism. After all, the issues brought up by the article are ones that any author would be justifiably worried about in the process of his or her work being adapted for another medium, and particularly so when an author has repeatedly been on record promoting his work's anti-Christian ideological viewpoints.

Eventually in 2005, Anand Tucker was named as the new director of the films, although Weitz continued on the team as screenwriter. Tucker has also made various comments about how the films will potentially transform Pullman's atheist and anti-Christian vision. In an interview with the *Daily Telegraph*, for example, he said, '"The books are not about pointing the finger at the Judaeo-Christian tradition . . . They're about any belief structures that try to control people and stop them from being true to themselves. That's why they work all over the world"' (Johnston 2006). Although Tucker's claims to the universality of the text are quite possibly true, and again in line with Pullman's commentary on his website, he is also very hasty to deny the specifically anti-Christian nature of the trilogy, which is clear in the text itself and has been asserted numerous times by its author in other places. When Tucker himself stepped down from the directorship of the films in May 2006, Weitz was reinstated. Tucker's departure was due, according to the New Line press release, to 'differences in creative direction', although the *Hollywood Reporter* also cited a source close to the project which referred to 'budget constraints' (www.bridgetothestars.net: c; Siegel 2006). This sudden turnaround, which occurred during the open casting auditions for Lyra, shows very clearly that the road to the film's production has been extremely rough. Moreover, in these exchanges about the film's religious content, there seems to have been an attempt to reposition interpretation of the trilogy. Pullman would vociferously deny that this repositioning is to do with the potential markets for the film, and perhaps—for Pullman at least—

this shift is more to do with a certain tiredness at the continual religious controversy that *His Dark Materials* has caused, and a desire to move the terrain of the debate. Yet both Pullman and New Line are being disingenuous to propose that the books are not quite specifically a concerted attack on organised religion and Christianity in particular, and the extent to which the final version of the films will compromise this attack will be a result of the negotiations that the production company and its director make. Bearing in mind that a large part of the projected market for the films will be in the US, where attitudes of the Christian right are a strong political and consumer force, such negotiations will inevitably have economic as well as artistic and political bases.

Pullman has stated on numerous occasions that his approach to the film adaptation—as it was to the National Theatre's stage version—will be a hands-off one. In a *Bookseller* article referring to the film deal, for example, he said, 'For me to get involved with the scripting, casting or making of the film would be a waste of time . . . It would be annoying for the film-maker, who has to have a vision that is different from the novelist's vision' (Rickett 2002: 11). It remains to be seen whether this will mean his anti-religious message will be diluted and how a new audience coming to the books via the films will react to any disparity between the versions.

There is also the question that Billington's review poses, about whether *His Dark Materials* is more powerful when directly communicated from the author via the page to the reader. Pullman himself has argued that both books and the stage allow audiences a greater level of imaginative participation than film, and yet film versions boost the exposure and sales of the books on which they are based considerably (Wagner 2003). Yet whether the films of *His Dark Materials* can give life to the same level of paradoxes, gaps and loose ends that the books have is undetermined, as is the extent of the audience's imaginative participation in the various adaptations placed before them.

The films, once released, will no doubt be the cause of the proliferation of further versions of *His Dark Materials*. An expanding fan base will increase the amount of fan fiction produced, and the films may well result in merchandising, and possibly a computer game based on the trilogy, as has been created for the *Harry Potter* series. Yet such extensions of the trilogy wrestle control of *His Dark Materials* from its author, while at the same time Pullman is actively producing further excursions into the worlds of *His Dark Materials*. The first of these excursions has been in the form of *Lyra's Oxford* (2003).

The Continuing Worlds of *His Dark Materials*: *Lyra's Oxford* and *The Book of Dust*

Described in a short promotional video by Pullman as a 'stepping stone' between *His Dark Materials* and a projected longer book, *Lyra's Oxford* is a short volume which revisits Lyra two years after the end of the trilogy and her parting from Will (www.davidfickling books.co.uk: a). The short story contained in the volume, which is called 'Lyra and the Birds', opens once more with Lyra at Jordan College, perched high on the college roof with Pantalaimon. Her growing maturity is signalled in the opening paragraph, however. She no longer needs to escape onto the roof via her bedroom window. The aging college Porter has given her a key in order that she report to him on the state of the roof four times a year, in exchange for which she can go on the roof 'whenever she wanted' (LO 3). Lyra is now, as the end of *The Amber Spyglass* foretold, a schoolgirl who lodges at the women's college St Sophia's during term-time, although her old Jordan room is kept for her. On this warm early evening, she and Pantalaimon are drawn from their college vantage point once more into adventure when they *See* a witch's bird dæmon being attacked by hundreds of other birds. They rescue the witch dæmon, whose story then leads them on a hunt for the alchemist Sebastian Makepeace, a discredited former Scholar of another of the Oxford colleges. Lyra takes the dæmon to Makepeace, leaving a trail of enquiry behind her: she mentions him to the Porter, is overheard by one of the Jordan Scholars and asks one of the St Sophia's Scholars about alchemy. The witch's dæmon tells her that he is seeking Makepeace in order to obtain an elixir for his witch, who is suffering from a new kind of sickness for which the witches have no cure.

Lyra and Pantalaimon are suspicious of the dæmon but nonetheless lead it to the street in Jericho where Makepeace lives. The dæmon insists that Lyra accompany him right to Makepeace's door. When they arrive, their suspicions are confirmed, as they have 'nearly walked into a trap' (LO 36). A witch—the dæmon's witch—is inside the house, having poisoned Makepeace. This witch, her face 'a mask of madness and hatred', comes out of the house, knife in hand, threatening Lyra's life (LO 37). Yet as Lyra prepares to do battle with the witch, and as Pantalaimon grapples with her dæmon, a swan saves Lyra by flying directly at the witch, breaking her back and killing her.

Makepeace, who is still alive, explains to Lyra that the witch had once been his lover and had borne him a son, who was killed fighting for Lord Asriel's side during the war two years ago. Blaming Lyra for this, the witch sets out to kill her, but in order also to get vengeance on Makepeace, she tries to implicate him in the murder. The plot is foiled, however, largely through the intervention of the birds in the city: the starlings who try to prevent the dæmon from reaching Lyra in the first place; the pigeons who chase the dæmon when they are making their way to Jericho; and finally the swan who saves Lyra's life at the risk of its own. It would seem, as Lyra and Pantalaimon discuss once they are safely on their way back home, '"as if the birds—and the whole city"', were protecting them (LO 48).

What does the story mean, and what is its place in the interpretation of *His Dark Materials*? The story itself asks questions about meaning and interpretation. Early on, when Lyra and Pantalaimon first sight the massed flock of birds, they wonder what its forms might be telling them:

'If it was saying something . . .' said Lyra.
'Like signalling.'
'No one would know, though. No one could ever understand what it meant.'
'Maybe it means nothing. It just is.'
'Everything means something,' Lyra said severely. 'We just have to find out how to read it.' (LO 5–6)

Later, Lyra is reminded of her own admonishment to Pantalaimon when Makepeace tells her, in response to her confusion about what the birds were doing, '"Everything has a meaning, if only we could read it"' (LO 45–46). He elaborates, '"It means something about you, and something about the city. You'll find the meaning if you search for it. Now you had better go"' (LO 46). The meaning does not become clear to Lyra and Pantalaimon during the course of the story, though they understand that somehow the city and its birds are protecting them and that they are intimately connected to and fostered by their environment. Lyra likens this interpretive puzzle to her reading of the alethiometer, with the city as a synonym for 'belonging' and 'protection' and 'home' (LO 48). The short story ends with their own jokey interpretation of the meaning of an apple pie left in the pantry through whose window they sneak back into St Sophia's. This is luck, says Lyra, although they are careful to thank the birds who saved them by leaving crumbs for them on the windowsill.

This meditation on interpretation is perhaps a warning by Pullman to critics of the trilogy, to the effect that meaning is difficult to discern and is an inherently contentious process in which intelligence as well as imagination are necessary. Indeed, it would not be difficult to overinterpret the meaning of this 'slight but tantalising after-thought' to *His Dark Materials*, as Nicholas Tucker has called *Lyra's Oxford* (Tucker 2003b). The story itself is a mere forty-six very loosely typeset pages, probably no more than the length of a single one of the chapters from *Northern Lights*, *The Subtle Knife* or *The Amber Spyglass*. However, although it is slight, it is also—as Tucker says—tantalising in its return to Lyra and Pantalaimon's world, in its suggestions of further adventures and in its hints that the fallout of the battle for the republic of heaven is ongoing, at the very least in the mind of one enraged witch. In the promotional video for the book, Pullman suggests that this 'little story' does have 'big implications, because it looks back to the trilogy and forward to the next big book' (www.davidficklingbooks.co.uk: a). Moreover, the story gives some very brief yet fascinating insights into Lyra's character development two years after her adventures in the trilogy.

Her reaction to the dæmon's story about the sickness affecting his witch is one example:

> The poor thing looked so wretched, huddled there in the cold shadow . . . ma[king] tears come to Lyra's eyes. Pan had told her she was too soft and too warm-hearted, but it was no good telling her about it. Since she and Will had parted two years before, the slightest thing had the power to move her to pity and distress; it felt as if her heart were bruised for ever. (LO 30)

Pantalaimon notes disapprovingly how Lyra's childish insouciance has turned, since her parting from Will, into a more adult empathy. Her dæmon sees this as a worrying turn, and in some ways it surely is, as it is this empathy for the mendacious witch's dæmon that leads them both into life-threatening trouble. Lyra's childhood toughness and resilience would certainly seem to have softened, continuing a process that began during the trilogy itself. Elsewhere, however, Lyra's empathy is shown as a positive virtue, as she feels sorry for the head girl whose music concert will be poorly attended (LO 22).

'Lyra and the Birds' marks, therefore, the growing socialisation of Lyra as a character. She is now far from the 'half-wild' little girl she was at the beginning of *Northern Lights* (NL 37). Instead, she feels empathy and fear, but also gains courage from her memories and from the community and comradeship that Oxford offers her. In the moment of extreme danger when the witch attacks her, it is the memory of Will that gives her courage, that makes her ready to meet the witch's force 'with all the courage she could summon' (LO 37). In some ways she is psychologically weaker and is more reliant on others. However, 'Lyra and the Birds' shows a much more grown-up Lyra, even if she is still happy to climb onto rooftops, sneak out beyond her bedtime curfew and tell tall stories in order to get out of trouble, as she does to the Scholar who overhears her trying to find out about Makepeace. This is certainly a realistic portrait of development, but whether readers warm to this older Lyra to the extent that they took to her former self is a question worth pondering. The suggestion, however, that Lyra's pain is in some ways an adolescent stage—she feels that 'her heart were bruised for ever'—hints that there is still much for Lyra to learn, and much more for her to feel, as she gradually becomes an adult.

There is more to *Lyra's Oxford* than 'Lyra and the Birds'. The story itself is illustrated with engravings by John Lawrence. There is a preface, or introduction (it is not specified which), to the book. This piece does not have Pullman's name assigned to it, but it would seem that they are words voiced by him, or at least by a narrator who is very similar to him. The preface introduces the volume, its story and its 'other things' which, the preface says, 'might be connected with the story, or they might not; they might be connected to stories that haven't appeared yet. It's not easy to tell' (LO vi). This is a tease on Pullman's part—he knows that the worldwide audience of fans and critics will scrutinise this follow-up to *His Dark Materials* with the greatest of care, and that those same readers have been patiently waiting for the long-announced companion volume to the trilogy, *The Book of Dust*, which will surely contain a host of 'stories that haven't appeared yet'. The preface once more warns about the importance and yet the risk in the hunt for meaning. As the preface concludes, 'There are many things we haven't yet learned how to read . . . The story in this book is partly about that very process' (LO vii).

Among the 'other things' that the volume includes is a page seemingly torn from a travel guide to the Oxford of Lyra's world, which describes the area of Jericho where the climax of 'Lyra and the Birds' takes place. The book also has an epigraph from Oscar Baedecker's *The Coasts of Bohemia*. Baedecker, a 'notoriously unreliable guide' according to a footnote in *Lyra's Oxford*, is an intertextual joke (LO v). The German publishing house Baedeker (note the difference in spelling) published from the early nineteenth century onwards real-world travel guides. *The Coasts of Bohemia* is an imaginary title, although it could be assumed that the page inserted into *Lyra's Oxford* ostensibly comes from this guidebook. This mirroring of our own world at a fantastical angle is similar to the depiction of Lyra's Oxford more generally in its reference to alternate existences.

Also included in the volume is a fold-out 'Globetrotter' map of the city produced by the company Smith and Strange Ltd, which—like Pullman's publisher, David Fickling—has its offices on Beaumont Street in Oxford. The map is clearly based on real-life Oxford, but some street names are subtly changed, and the key to the colleges shows that this is definitely Lyra's world. There is no Durham, Foxe, Gabriel or Queen Philippa's in the real-life Oxford, though there is a Hertford, a Magdalen and a Merton. The map, however, is a strange palimpsest of Lyra and Will's Oxfords. It indicates, in what might be construed as handwritten script, where Mary Malone lives, the direction to Sir Charles Latrom's house, and the way to Sunderland Avenue and the hornbeam trees. All these are locations that feature in Will's Oxford in *The Subtle Knife*.

The reverse of the 'Globetrotter' map details other maps available in the series, thus featuring a range of names similar to but subtly different from those in Will's world. There are maps of Mejico and the Isthmus, Central and Eastern Tartary, Corea and Nippon. Advertising for some other products aimed at explorers (cold-weather clothing, camping and navigational equipment) occupies another fold of the map. Finally, Pullman's fictitious publisher Smith and Strange gives a list of its books on 'travel, archaeology and related subjects', which, for the careful reader, offers some teasing titles. There is a book called *A Prisoner of the Bears*, written by Professor Jotham D Santelia, the Regius Professor of Cosmology at the University of Gloucester. This is the Scholar whom Lyra encounters when she is captured by the armoured bears in Svalbard towards the end of *Northern Lights*. There is also a book by Santelia's arch-rival, Professor Trelawney, whom Lyra knows from Jordan, entitled *Fraud: an Exposure of a Scientific Imposture*, a work which sounds like it would only increase the enmity between the two men. Intriguingly, there is also a very specialised sounding title, *The Bronze Clocks of Benin*, penned by none other than Marisa Coulter. One particularly esoteric-sounding volume, *Some Curious Anomalies in the Mathematics of Palladio's Quattro Libri*, is written by Nicholas Outram. This fictitious author has been given Pullman's own middle names.

In addition, there is also a reproduction of a postcard from Mary Malone to a friend written shortly after her arrival in Oxford. The postcard, as Mary jokes, features some of the less attractive locations in Oxford, though they are also ones which are very pertinent to her and the stories that unfold in *His Dark Materials*: the bench in the Botanic Gardens; a 1960s University science building; the row of hornbeam trees in Sunderland Avenue; and a section of road in Norham Gardens close to Mary's flat.

These 'other things' included in *Lyra's Oxford* are similar to some of the additional material included in the celebratory tenth-anniversary editions of *His Dark Materials*, published in 2005. The edition of *Northern Lights* includes scientific notes by Lord Asriel, in which he is obviously working his way towards creating the bridge to other worlds which he achieves by the end of the book. The anniversary edition of *The Subtle Knife* has notes and drawings by Will's father, Colonel John Parry, and *The Amber Spyglass* has papers from Mary Malone, including letters to friends and diary jottings as she goes into the world of the mulefas.

Finally, on its last pages, *Lyra's Oxford* has an advertising brochure for a sea cruise to The Levant on the S S *Zenobia*, on which someone has ringed by hand one of the stopping points in Smyrna, and written what would seem to be arrangements for a rendezvous at a café there. These pages are particularly tantalising, as the long-promised larger companion volume to *His Dark Materials*, *The Book of Dust*, will, apparently, be at least partially set in The Levant (Fickling 2006).

'Lyra and the Birds' is a story in miniature, a welcome return to some of the worlds and characters of *His Dark Materials*. Yet some of Pullman's most ardent fans expressed a certain level of disappointment at the story and the book it is contained in. Fan reviewers on the www.bridgetothestars.net website called it 'a bit of a disappointment' and 'a frightfully short book', despite Pullman's not having 'lost any of his strength as a storyteller' (www.bridgetothes-tars.net: b). But the negativity of the fan reviews stemmed largely from two connecting factors. The first was the price of the volume, £9.99 in the UK, which was perceived to be very high for such a short story, despite all the 'other things' contained in the volume. One fan reviewer went so far as to suggest, 'You can't help but think that a faint whiff of money-making enters into the equation' (www.bridgetothestars.net: b). The brevity of the story in *Lyra's Oxford* also left fans unsatisfied, with one writing, 'It's just a short story, well told, but short nonetheless. Too short, I think, to really satisfy the more dedicated fans of the trilogy.' However, another fan thought this sense of dissatisfaction, of wanting more, was part of the point of 'Lyra and the Birds' and wrote that 'thinking of *Lyra's Oxford* as a sort of appetizer before the main course really increased my enjoyment of it' (www.bridgetothestars.net: b).

Some of the professional reviews in the media echoed the sentiments of the fan reviews. John Ezard in the *Guardian* wrote:

> This captivating, slight, somewhat overpriced stocking-filler of a book has one outstanding merit for Philip Pullman's legion of readers. It answers, encouragingly, the question left hanging by the *His Dark Materials* trilogy. Having created, then parted, Lyra and Will—two of the most enticing heroes in children's or any literature—what more can Pullman do with them? (Ezard 2003)

In an interview for the *Evening Standard*, Pullman agreed with journalist Nick Curtis that the book was largely an 'appetite whetter' for his next big book based in the worlds of *His Dark Materials* (Curtis 2003). Amanda Craig also picked up on the food metaphor by seeing *Lyra's Oxford* as 'quite perfect in its way—gripping, funny, and infused with the vitality of a master-storyteller—and yet it is also no more than an amuse-gueule, a canape, a crumb offered to an audience starving for a proper Christmas dinner' (Craig 2003). There was, then, a certain air of disappointment around the publication of *Lyra's Oxford*, but also a growing sense of expectation for *The Book of Dust*, in addition to some thought-provoking questions left unanswered at the conclusion of 'Lyra and the Birds'. What is the nature of Lyra's relationship to the city of Oxford? What is the true nature of Makepeace's work: is he really an alchemist? Or was he made to leave his college because of investigations into Dust? He is clearly not the deranged individual whom other Scholars think him to be.

Such questions may well be answered in Pullman's projected longer book, *The Book of Dust*. Pullman first began mentioning this book shortly after the publication of the final volume of the trilogy, and from then onwards he has dropped several hints and clues about what the book might contain. In an interview with Alona Wartofsky in the *Washington Post* in February 2001, he discussed the possibility that the book would be a prequel, detailing the early life of Lee Scoresby and his friendship with Iorek, or possibly relate the love story of Serafina Pekkala (Wartofsky 2001). Later mentions of the book suggested that it would be a sequel rather than a prequel, picking up Lyra's story four years after the end of *The Amber Spyglass* and two years after 'Lyra and the Birds' (Wagner 2003). Following accusations that the Christianity attacked in *His Dark Materials* is largely an Old Testament Christianity without the redemption offered in the New Testament, Pullman has also, perhaps jokingly, mentioned that the figure of Jesus may contribute to the theology and morality of *The Book of Dust* (Haill 2004: 86). As mentioned earlier, and heavily hinted by the advertisement for the cruise in *Lyra's Oxford*, The Levant will feature as a location for this volume (Fickling 2006).

Until the volume itself appears, however, and no date has yet been announced for its publication, it is worth bearing in mind Pullman's own comment that '"there are all kinds of stories, thousands of stories, that could be set in this world . . . And I may write them"' (Wartofsky 2001). There is a warning here not to speculate too far about an as yet unwritten book. Once more, though, Pullman's words do reiterate the unfolding possibilities for stories and story-telling in the worlds he has already created, which is undoubtedly something that fans and fan fiction writers, as earlier chapters in this book have discussed, have taken to heart. The gaps and the loose ends in the trilogy engender spaces for further creativity, but the thousands of fans of the trilogy will have to wait a little longer for a more concerted exploration of them from Pullman himself.

Novels for Adults

Despite its adult audience, *His Dark Materials* is still largely thought of as a work of fiction for younger readers, featuring child protagonists and many of the conventions of traditional literature for children. Pullman began his writing career, however, with the publication of two specifically adult novels which, as well as being currently out of print with no seeming plans for republication, would be very unlikely to appeal to younger readers. Pullman himself, while professing an affection for the second of the two, *Galatea* (1978), dismisses them both as youthful and flawed works, and he rarely refers to the first novel, *The Haunted Storm* (1972), by name. Nevertheless, these two novels are a part of Pullman's oeuvre, and while some of the books he wrote later on, with children specifically in mind, bear a stronger relation to *His Dark Materials*, this chapter still considers them in brief, particularly as neither of these two books is easy to get hold of, and so they have not generally been discussed by critics in relation to his later writing.

The Haunted Storm, published by Pullman under the name Philip N Pullman, is a peculiar, angst-ridden story that combines theological investigation with a sexually charged narrative. It concentrates on the life of Matthew Cortez, a troubled young man who thinks he has '"a sort of God-mania, or religion-mania"' (Pullman 1972: 68). He is waiting for a sign, possibly a sign from God, in order to achieve 'emotional and mental and sexual relief' (Pullman 1972: 10). He is wracked with existential despair at the lack of meaning in the world.

In an erotic encounter, a young woman whom he meets on the beach tells him about her lover. The two young people part without exchanging names but meet again several months later when Matthew comes to stay with his great-uncle, an evangelical preacher. Matthew attends a service at the village church and asks the priest to talk to him about his Gnostic beliefs. The priest, it transpires, is the father of the young woman he met several months previously, and thus Matthew and Elizabeth begin an intense relationship.

Two girls are murdered on separate nights in the village, and Matthew is concerned that his headaches and blackouts coincide with the nights of the deaths. It would also seem that Elizabeth's previous lover might be his own elder brother, who was thrown out of the family home by his parents when Matthew was a child. Alan, the elder brother, is a brooding presence, connected to a radical political organisation and in fierce dispute with Elizabeth's father for literal and figurative possession of a well near the village. On the night of the eclipse, the narrative comes to a head as Matthew, Elizabeth, Alan and Canon Cole all gather at the site of the well.

The Haunted Storm is a text that bristles with meanings that are difficult to discern. It is not plot-driven, although the insistent threat of sexual violence adds a strong undertow to the novel. Instead, it places philosophical and moral enquiry at its centre, dramatising it through the characters and their highly pitched discussions. The novel contains lengthy passages from one of Canon Cole's sermons and explores Matthew's own feelings towards God, whom 'he came to regard . . . as an ironical ghost whose existence was in no doubt, but who has little or no effective power' (Pullman 1972: 46). Although the form of Pullman's first published work is therefore very far from his later success with *His Dark Materials*, *The Haunted Storm* nonetheless displays a similar fascination with questions of religion, morality and sexuality. The concept of God as an 'ironical ghost' with 'little or no effective power' is perhaps the kernel of an idea that would later resurface as the dying impotent Authority in *The Amber Spyglass*.

Pullman's second novel, *Galatea*, is similarly concerned with questions of being, matter and sexuality, but is a very different sort of narrative from *The Haunted Storm*. It is a baroque, magic realist story populated by a series of strange creatures and laced together with meditations on the construction of humans and their societies. At its heart is a quest: that of the concert flautist Martin Browning to find his missing wife. Catherine Browning has disappeared, and in his hunt for her, he is first drawn to a city in the warm south, Valencia. In Valencia—a city which may or may not be the real-life Valencia—Browning makes the acquaintance of a number of characters. Among them are the banker Lionel Pretorius, dubbed the 'broker of reality' (Pullman 1978: 7), his beautiful daughter Mary, the rich cyclist Johnny Hamid, and an androgynous messenger, Galatea. In the search for his wife, he then journeys to Venezuela, from where there are murmurings of a strange business, the Anderson Valley Project. Along the way, Browning comes across a variety of strange beings: dead people brought back to life as zombies; the 'Electric Whores'; unreal people; angels; and automata. Eventually he arrives at the 'Perfect City of the Unreal People', an experimental city presided over by his own wife and populated by perfect automata. Along the way, he and his friends are beset by danger and challenges to their own being, rationality and sense of self.

The plot of *Galatea* is complex and picaresque, reminiscent of the writing of Pullman's contemporary Angela Carter, whose early novel *The Infernal Desire Machines of Doctor Hoffman* (1972) is similar in scope, structure and theme. Included in Pullman's narrative is an evident interest in sexuality, in questions of matter and being and of the constructedness of human nature. All this is set within exotic, fantastical locations which nonetheless bear strong similarities to reality. Galatea, as the narrator of the novel explains, is the name given in legend by the king of Cyprus to a statue he carved and fell in love with. The goddess Aphrodite takes pity on the king and brings this 'artificial girl' to life (Pullman 1978: 285).

Pullman's second novel is as far from *His Dark Materials* as *The Haunted Storm* is. However, there are, once more, ways in which Pullman's interest in certain themes is clearly developing in his early adult work. The rich variety of different beings that populate Martin Browning's world is reminiscent of the array of creatures that Pullman devises in the trilogy. The theme of matter and being that the artificial and constructed nature of these beings brings forth points forwards to the questions that Pullman's later creation of Dust poses. There is also a passage in which some threatening ecclesiastical characters headed by a bishop threaten to put Browning and his friends to death in order to ascertain whether they are angels or not, creatures of '"gross matter"' or '"condensed light"' (Pullman 1978: 149). This perverse act at the hands of the Church also looks towards the criticism that Pullman would later make of institutionalised religion in *His Dark Materials*. When the attempt to kill them is thwarted, Browning instead professes, '"The true doctrine is that good works alone are the measure of goodness!"' a sentiment which is directly translated into the morality of *His Dark Materials* (Pullman 1978: 154).

Folk Stories and Fairy Tales

After publishing his first two adult novels with no great degree of success, Pullman devoted his writing energies to the creation of plays for the Oxford schools in which he was employed in the 1970s and 1980s. He later rewrote some of these plays as books. His first novel for children, *Count Karlstein* (1982), was conceived in this way, as the author's note to the 2002 edition recounts. *Count Karlstein* was also the first of a number of books which could be described as folk stories and fairy tales. Some of these books are really adaptations: his versions of Aladdin (*The Wonderful World of Aladdin and the Enchanted Lamp* (1993)), *Mossycoat* (1998) and *Puss in Boots* (2000) are less original creations than retellings. Nonetheless, it is clear that Pullman characteristically revels in, for example, Puss's consummate storytelling abilities. Thus, his recurring themes and character traits are essential components of these retellings. However, this section of the chapter concentrates on the more extended fairy tales and folk stories created by Pullman: *Count Karlstein*, *Spring-Heeled Jack* (1989), *The Firework-Maker's Daughter* (1995), *Clockwork* (1996), *I Was a Rat!* (1999) and *The Scarecrow and the Servant* (2004).

   Count Karlstein is set in a mountainous region in Europe and is the melodramatic tale of a man who makes a pact with Zamiel, the Demon Huntsman. In return for being made the Count Karlstein, he must deliver to the Huntsman after ten years a human—for very unpleasant purposes, it may be assumed. He decides to give the Huntsman his orphan nieces Charlotte and Lucy, and the ensuing story details the girls' attempts to escape and features a host of humorous secondary characters. It also plays with the conventions of the gothic novel, a form of which the two girls—like Jane Austen's heroine Catherine Morland in *Northanger Abbey* (1818)—

are excessively fond. Another version of the story was published in 1991 as *Count Karlstein: Or The Ride of the Demon Huntsman*, in which the story is retold in words and pictures, with comic-strip sections which are integral to the story.

Spring-Heeled Jack also uses both words and images to convey the story of a hero in the time before Superman and Batman (as the opening paragraph has it). Once again, the central characters are orphans, and the first chapter sees them escaping the orphanage in Victorian London, a reference, perhaps, to Dickens's *Oliver Twist* (1837–38). The character of Spring-Heeled Jack was a popular legend in Britain in the nineteenth century and made a transfer from widespread sightings and rumours to the pages of penny dreadfuls, and later comic books. The pages of Pullman's version of *Spring-Heeled Jack* are bursting with invention and storytelling playfulness: footnotes, diagrams, epigraphs and a menu are added to illustrations and comic-strip sections, as well as the more conventional textual relation of the narrative.

Both of these early illustrated stories indicate Pullman's interest in the 'picture story' and the interaction between images and text, which is something he has written about in two essays examining texts and their writer/artists, including *Rupert*, the *Beano*, *Dan Dare*, Raymond Briggs, and Art Spiegelman's *Maus* (Pullman 1989b; 1998b). Pullman's next book in the genre of folk stories and fairy tales, *The Firework-Maker's Daughter*, is also illustrated, although this time the pictures are not so fully integrated into the storytelling. In this story, set in the Far East, Lila—the daughter of the title—sets out on a quest to become a Firework Maker herself, during which she meets a range of characters including an elephant used as a roving advertisement hoarding. Lila eventually achieves her ambition and proves herself to have the attributes of all true Firework Makers: talent, courage and willpower, luck, wisdom and love. These attributes are not specific to the career of the Firework Maker, however, and in the story, Lila—like Lyra will later—proves herself a worthy child heroine.

Clockwork: Or All Wound Up again features images on its pages, though their use is slightly different from either the supplementary illustration of *The Firework-Maker's Daughter* or the integrated story lines of *Count Karlstein* and *Spring-Heeled Jack*. It has a number of boxed images implanted in the text, with accompanying words which either provide quirky moral messages, additional information or a commentary from the narrator. Set in a little German town during a hard winter, *Clockwork* is populated by folk-tale-like characters and situations. One of these is a clockmaker's apprentice, Karl, who is anxious and embittered because he hasn't managed to make a figure for the town clock, the act which signals the end of his apprenticeship. Towards the beginning of the narrative, he gets into a discussion with Fritz, a 'talented storyteller' (Pullman 1996a: 15). In return for Fritz's kindly advice, Karl turns on his friend:

> 'You don't understand,' said Karl passionately. 'Everything's so easy for you! You just sit at your desk and put pen to paper, and stories come pouring out! You don't know what it is to sweat and strain for hours on end with no ideas at all, or to struggle with materials that break, and tools that go blunt, or to tear your hair out trying to find a new variation on the same old theme—I tell you, Fritz, it's a wonder I haven't blown my brains out long before this!' (Pullman 1996a: 17–18)

What Karl doesn't know, and Fritz does not admit, is that he does not yet have an ending to the story that he has been relating to the eager customers in the inn. What Karl describes as the torment of the clockwork maker's task could equally be applied to that of the writer, as Fritz knows all too well. Pullman's voice can be clearly heard through Fritz's thoughts: 'Stories are just as hard as clocks to put together, and they can go wrong just as easily—as we shall *See* with Fritz's own story in a page or two' (Pullman 1996a: 18). When Fritz starts to relate his story, he is interrupted by a visitor to the inn, who, terrifyingly for Fritz, is one of the characters from his own story. *Clockwork* is another of Pullman's metanarratives, telling stories within stories that comment upon the responsibilities of the storyteller, and using the inexorable mechanism of clockwork as a metaphor for the unstoppable powers of story.

I Was a Rat! . . . *or The Scarlet Slippers* is a rewriting of the Cinderella story. Its protagonist is a pageboy rat who fails to make it back to Cinderella's carriage on time. Once more, this is an illustrated story, featuring several pages of pastiche tabloid newspaper inserted into the text. These pages, and the intervention of the newspapers in the lives of the protagonists, make for a satirical commentary upon celebrity and the role of the media in forming public opinion, while at the same time being wrapped in a humorous, human story. The first page from the *Daily Scourge* reports on the engagement of the Prince to the mysterious Lady Aurelia (the Cinderella character), and promises a 'fact-file' of the Prince's 'previous girlfriends' on numerous pages. Another page reports on the interior design makeover that the palace is undergoing under the new Princess's influence, coming to the opinion-forming conclusion that this is taxpayers' money well spent (Pullman 1999a: 5, 32). The documenting of the role of the Princess in public life draws substantially on the ways in which the UK's Princess Diana was portrayed in the media. The newspaper pages and the intertextual references combine to provide a multi-layered narration, demonstrating Pullman's awareness of the different audiences for his books, so that the commentary upon tabloid journalism appeals to children and adults alike, but with different awareness of the contexts to which that commentary satirically refers.

The Scarecrow and the Servant brings together the two protagonists of its title in a beguiling tale of companionship, storytelling and justice. The scarecrow is a literally pea-brained but well-intentioned character who falls in love with a broom. The 'servant' is a boy, Jack, who has a character type beloved of Pullman: honest, straightforward, loyal and yet a startlingly clever storyteller whose talents get himself and the scarecrow out of numerous scrapes. In a thrilling courtroom finale, Jack successfully fights for the true ownership of Spring Valley and its water supplies against the unscrupulous Buffaloni brothers. Despite the Buffalonis' attempts to claim that the scarecrow is no longer the same scarecrow as the one originally created, as '"every component particle of him has been scattered to the four winds"', the jury decides in the scarecrow's favour: '"Don't matter if he is all different bits from what he was, he's still the same Scarecrow"' (Pullman 2004a: 201, 211). The jury establishes the essential humanity of the scarecrow against the Buffalonis. This is a fairy tale, and—unlike in *His Dark Materials*—the scarecrow and Jack then live happily ever after.

In these folk stories and fairy tales, be they adaptations, more concerted rewritings or stories drawing on genre traditions, Pullman demonstrates a fascination with the mechanisms of storytelling, incorporates a variety of intertextual sources and techniques to enhance his narrative, uses a mix of image and text to convey and comment on the story, and plays with different audiences. On the one hand, the stories seem simpler ones than the complex narrative of *His Dark Materials*, but on the other hand, their multi-functionality merits attention for these books.

Adventure Stories

A second broad category into which Pullman's writing outside of *His Dark Materials* can be placed is his stories of adventure, which divide into two sets of books: *The New Cut Gang* and the *Sally Lockhart* series. The stories of *The New Cut Gang* appear in two books, *The New Cut Gang: Thunderbolt's Waxwork* (1994) and *The New Cut Gang: The Gas-Fitter's Ball* (1995). The two published books are set in the London borough of Lambeth in 1894, and have as their central characters a gang of cheeky crime-solving children who happily play truant from school, preferring to roam the streets of south London. The first book concerns a story of counterfeit money and waxwork figures, the second the theft of silver-ware from the Gas-Fitters' Hall. The tone of the books is cheerful, and the mischievous children win out against both the wrongdoers in society and the bumbling forces of the law. There are some notable secondary characters: in *Thunderbolt's Waxwork*, there is a woman named Mary Malone (though she bears little resemblance to her namesake in *His Dark Materials*); and *The Gas-Fitter's Ball* features a star turn from the Prince of Wales. The books are enjoyable pastiches of the crime story, set in a London reminiscent of the writing of Arthur Conan Doyle and Charles Dickens, but with children as protagonists.

The *Sally Lockhart Quartet*—*The Ruby in the Smoke* (1985), *The Shadow in the Plate* (1986; later published under the title *The Shadow in the North*), *The Tiger in the Well* (1991) and *The Tin Princess* (1994)—are also set in Victorian London, although the final title in the series moves the action to a fictitious central European country. This is a major series of novels which, while not rivalling *His Dark Materials* in thematic complexity or artistic invention, nonetheless presents in Sally Lockhart a heroine as lively as Lyra, and in many ways the series is a forerunner of the later trilogy. All four novels are tales of high adventure, with independent young people as the protagonists who must use their virtues of bravery, loyalty and resourcefulness to overcome very real evil. The characters, although not as young as Lyra and Will, have unsettled family backgrounds. Sally comes into conflict with the mores of her society, initially by setting up her own financial consultancy business—a very unusual occupation for a young Victorian woman—and then by becoming an unmarried mother. Upon the young shoulders of these characters, who are coming to terms with questions of moral responsibility, their sexual feelings and treachery in many forms, lies an urgent need to defeat wrongdoing, to protect the disadvantaged and even, in *The Tin Princess*, to juggle the destinies of nation-states. In the series, Pullman, while spinning fast-paced yarns of high excitement, is uncompromising in his refusal to provide happy endings. In *The Shadow in the North*, one of the heroes is killed, and *The Tin Princess* closes with a violent scene of twisted love, where innocence and experience collide in a dreadful fate.

The *Ruby in the Smoke* opens with an introduction to the heroine of the series, Sally Lockhart. Sally is sixteen, 'alone, and uncommonly pretty'. Pullman immediately creates suspense by announcing at the end of the second paragraph that 'within fifteen minutes, she was going to kill a man' (Pullman 1985: 7). On the opening page Pullman also gives a clue to one of the main genres on which the Sally Lockhart books are based. The porter is 'guiltily' reading the office-boy's penny dreadful magazine, a form of cheap and sensational literature prevalent in the 1800s. True to the sensational promise, in a couple of pages Sally does indeed kill a man, though it was neither her intention nor her actions but rather her words that caused this death. She tells Mr Higgs, the Company Secretary of Lockhart and Selby, that she wants to know more about '"The Seven Blessings"'. Higgs drops down dead in shock, and Sally sets out on an adventure to discover the meaning of a phrase that would strike so much fear in the heart of a man that he would die hearing it (Pullman 1985: 10). Sally's mother died when she was a baby, and so the death of her father three months before the beginning of the book under—as she discovers—suspicious circumstances makes her an orphan. Sally's upbringing, like Lyra's, has been unconventional. She knows nearly nothing of traditional academic subjects, but

> she had a thorough grounding in the principles of military tactics and book-keeping, a close acquaintance with the affairs of the Stock Market, and a working knowledge of Hindustani. Furthermore she could ride well . . . ; and for her fourteenth birthday her father had bought her a little Belgian pistol, the one she carried everywhere, and taught her to shoot. (Pullman 1985: 16)

This resourceful and brave girl gathers a number of loyal friends to her, including the office-boy Jim, the photographer Fred and his sister Rosa. Together, they solve the mystery of her father's death and enable Sally to discover her father's fortune, but only after murderous encounters with villains and the drug opium.

The next book in the quartet, *The Shadow in the North*, sees Sally, Fred and Jim swept once more into adventure against the ominous businessman Axel Bellmann. The book also documents the stormy but growing love between Sally and Fred, which is tragically curtailed by Fred's death in a raging fire. At the end of the book, Sally is left older, wiser but also pregnant—she is carrying Fred's child.

At the beginning of *The Tiger in the Well*, Sally has recovered from her tragic loss. She has a little daughter, Harriet, and a happy life. Her happiness is menaced, however, by an arch-villain in the shape of the *Tzaddik*. The book opens with a disturbing plot to take Sally's child away from her, which she eventually thwarts, but her life takes a happier turn when she meets, and begins a new relationship with, the Jewish political journalist Daniel Goldberg. *The Tiger in the Well* also has a character with a prototype for the dæmons of *His Dark Materials*. However, this proto-dæmon—a servant monkey—is not the playful companion that Pantalaimon is to Lyra, but an emanation of the brooding, sick, malign presence of its owner. The monkey appears to many as a supernatural being, 'a little imp from hell that waits on him' (Pullman 1991b: 26).

The Tin Princess shifts in focus from Sally Lockhart and London to the imaginary central European country of Razkavia. Jim and a new character, Becky Winter, are drawn into the high politics of state when they come across Adelaide, a character from *The Ruby in the Smoke*, who is now married to the crown prince of Razkavia.

Throughout the Sally Lockhart series, storytelling is privileged as it is in *His Dark Materials*. It is the narratives of nationhood that Adelaide calls upon when she becomes the ruler of Razkavia, and for the badly injured Daniel Goldberg, faced by a hostile, anti-Semitic crowd in *The Tiger in the Well*, these narratives are both a lifesaver and a clarion call to racial tolerance:

> And Goldberg felt a moment of pure, clear-headed elation. It was a kind of religious glee: holy mischief. He was weak with loss of blood, he was exhausted, his arm throbbed with an abominable pain, and there was an armed crowd in front of him that the slightest miscalculation would send mad. He thought: is there anywhere else I'd rather be? Anything else I'd rather be doing now than this?
>
> What a lucky bugger I am, he said to himself. Talk for your life, Danny boy. Tell 'em a story. (Pullman 1991b: 347)

Daniel's bravery in the face of danger and, moreover, his love of the challenge of talking for his life, align him with Pullman's parade of talented storytellers, which culminates in the figure of Lyra.

Contemporary Novels

In addition to the adventure stories and fairy tales that Pullman has written, he has also published two novels which have in common a contemporary setting, largely realist narratives, divided families and teenage protagonists. In the list of Pullman's further publications now included in new editions of his work, these books are grouped as 'Contemporary Novels' and are quite distinct from his earlier and later work for children.

The first of these, *The Broken Bridge*, was initially published in 1990. A revised edition, in which some of the ordering of the story had been changed, was later published under the same title. It is the story of Ginny, a sixteen-year-old girl who lives with her father in a Welsh seaside town. Her father is white, but her mother, who she believes died when she was a baby, was a black Haitian, and so Ginny is of mixed race. At the beginning of the book, Ginny and her father have a peaceable existence, marred for Ginny only by not yet having a boyfriend and by sometimes feeling out of place in an overwhelmingly white society. When she falls for Andy, the only other black person in the area, she is later embarrassed that she did not realise, as all her friends did, that he was gay. This calm existence, though, is disrupted by the visit of a social worker to Ginny's home, and an ensuing set of events that leads Ginny to question her origins. It transpires that Ginny has a half-brother the same age as her. Robert, this brother, comes to live with them when his mother—Ginny's father's estranged wife—dies. Ginny's mother was never married to her father, but also, as Ginny finds out, never in fact died. Instead, the promising young artist gave her unwanted baby to the care of nuns, from whom her father kidnapped her. For this, her father was imprisoned for several months before his proper parentage was established and he was allowed to take Ginny home legally.

In the course of the novel, Ginny goes through several stages of discovery about her background, believing at various points that she may have been fostered and that she was the baby supposedly abandoned in a car crash (in the 'broken bridge' of the title). She has memories of vivid scenes from her early life that intrude upon her settled existence with her father, which begin to make sense as her story unfolds. Eventually she finds out that her mother is still alive, a successful artist, with her work featuring in an exhibition that Ginny attends. However, at the launch of the exhibition, Ginny's mother rejects her a second time. Interwoven into the plot is a subtext of insistent rumours of violence and murder and of mental imbalance and voodoo. It blends these with contemporary social realism and is a portrait of self-discovery and growing up as a teenager.

The second of Pullman's contemporary novels is *The White Mercedes* (1992), or, as it was later renamed, *The Butterfly Tattoo* (1998). This book is set in Oxford, but it is the Oxford of the real world rather than Lyra's fantastical Oxford. The protagonist is Chris Marshall, a seventeen-year-old who takes on a summer job with a company that provides entertainment systems for parties and events. At an Oxford college ball, Chris meets a terrified girl, Jenny, whom he hides from three male pursuers. Jenny has gate-crashed the college ball, and Chris's act of charity leads to their growing friendship and a sexual relationship. Eventually, however, Chris will unknowingly betray Jenny and lead her to her death—a death which is presaged in the very first line of the novel, 'Chris Marshall met the girl he was going to kill on a warm night in early June' (Pullman 1992: 7). Pullman's suspenseful opening line is reminiscent of the opening paragraphs of *The Ruby in the Smoke*.

Through Barry, the boss of his company, Chris is swept into a criminal underworld. Barry is a man with a capacity to spin tall tales as effectively as Lyra, but he is far from having learnt the moral responsibility of storytelling. He is being remorselessly hunted down by the youngest brother of two men with whom he was previously connected. In a bungled robbery job, one of the brothers died, and Barry gave evidence at the trial of the second while secretly keeping the proceeds of the crime. When the youngest brother turns up in the white Mercedes of the original title of the book, he convinces Chris to lead him to Barry's hiding place. However, due to a series of miscommunications, Jenny is shot dead by the brother, and Chris is left at the end of the novel to continue his life older, wiser and sadder, and with the heavy burden of his betrayal.

The rather clunky plotting of this novel demonstrates if nothing else how far Pullman's storytelling abilities would later develop in the achievement of *His Dark Materials*. However, there are again thematic similarities between this earlier work and Pullman's later writing. There is a story of young love at the centre of the story, although it is one in which the sexual nature of the relationship is more explicitly described than in *The Amber Spyglass*: there is no doubt what the young protagonists are doing during the scene in which they make love, as Pullman explains how Jenny puts a condom on Chris. In terms of other similarities, there is the central betrayal of Jenny by Chris, which is reminiscent of the way in which Lyra unknowingly leads Roger to his death at the hands of Lord Asriel. Moreover, there is a philosophical undercurrent in the story that would not look out of place in *His Dark Materials*. When the younger, vengeful brother masquerades as a Special Branch officer in order to convince Chris to give him information about Barry, he talks to him in biblical terms about innocence and wisdom:

> 'We're not innocent; we *know*. I don't know if you're religious. The Garden of Eden—you know that story? The tree of knowledge of good and evil. Remember that? Before you eat the fruit you're innocent, whatever you do is innocent, because you don't understand. Then you eat it. And you're never innocent again. You *know* now. And that's painful; it's a terrible thing. I know what I'm asking you, Chris. I'm asking you to betray a man you thought was a friend. I'm asking you to taste the fruit.
>
> 'But I'll tell you something. Losing that innocence is the first step on the road to *real* knowledge. To wisdom, if you like. You can't get wisdom till you lose that innocence . . . So

it's paradoxical, isn't it? You can't do good unless you stop being innocent. All the real good in the world is done by people who've tasted the fruit of that tree. And found it bitter and painful.' (Pullman 1992: 134)

The irony in this speech, which would fit directly into the thematics of *His Dark Materials*, is that it is done as a lie, not for the sake of good. Instead, it is for the evil represented by the figure of the vengeful younger brother. Chris will betray his friend Barry and also lead Jenny to her death. At the end of the novel, Chris meditates on what has happened and the words used to convince him to commit his act of betrayal:

It was very strange. Carson had appealed to the highest part of him, not the lowest, and although the wisdom he spoke came from the tongue of a liar, still it was the truest wisdom Chris had ever heard. He knew he'd be living with it for a long time to come, perhaps for a lifetime, until it became part of his own self. He might never find anything truer. (Pullman 1992: 158–59)

There is one further children's book by Pullman which does not fit very well into any of the categories of his other books. It is also the only one of his children's books currently out of print in the UK, the novel *How to Be Cool* (1987). In tone, it is closest to *The New Cut Gang* books, although it is set in 1980s Britain rather than the Victorian 1890s. It is the zany story of a set of secondary school children who have aspirations to be 'cool'. They inadvertently discover that there is a secret wing of the government, the 'National Cool Board', which decides and promotes forthcoming trends through its Agents. Disturbed by this manufacturing of trends, the children decide to set up their own alternative organisation, which they call How to Be Cool. The range of reference of the book is very specific to the 1980s, naming particular pop stars of the period such as Sade, who has since faded from view. It also features none of the technological gadgetry that a 1990s or 2000s teenager would aspire to or have access to—mobile phones, the Internet, MP3 players—and thus the book seems very dated, probably explaining its lack of availability to Pullman's readers in the bookshops.

Other Publications and Adaptations

In addition to his fiction, Pullman has published a range of essays and opinion pieces, the major examples of which are mentioned in the bibliography at the end of this book. The topics he has covered are wide, ranging from his thoughts on science, religion and education, to the importance of free speech and storytelling, to soap operas and the book publishing industry. Pullman has said that it is likely a selection of these writings will be published as a collected volume in the future (www.philip-pullman.com: j).

Pullman has also published some non-fiction books early in his writing career: a guide to *Using the Oxford Junior Dictionary* (1979), which is a short book of exercises and games, and a book entitled *Ancient Civilizations* (1981). He has also published a play based on Arthur Conan Doyle's writing, *Sherlock Holmes and the Limehouse Horror* (1982), and a stage adaptation of Mary Shelley's *Frankenstein* (1990). In addition, several of his books beyond *His Dark Materials* have also been adapted for the stage, including versions of *I Was a Rat!*, *The Firework-Maker's Daughter* and *Aladdin*.

It is clear that Pullman's reputation as a master storyteller rests upon *His Dark Materials*, but his writing career has been lengthy, diverse and—for both Pullman's many fans and his critical readers— worth exploring as well.

◖◖ Conclusion ◗◗

Pullman the Master Storyteller

HIS DARK MATERIALS CONCLUDES with a new beginning. The Authority is no more. Lyra and Will have liberated the dead, re-enacted the Fall and restored environmental equilibrium. They have also begun a transition from childhood to adulthood and, as part of that process, foreseen their return, separately, to their own worlds. The story also ends with Lyra's promise to herself and her dæmon that they will begin the building of '"the republic of heaven"'.

After three volumes of high adventure, political wrangling and moral quest, then, Philip Pullman's trilogy comes to a conclusion in which readers are invited to imagine a new beginning. This is a new beginning founded on the basis of a moral philosophy which has developed throughout the course of the trilogy and which this book has examined in some detail. It is one that is not dependent on rules laid down by external authorities, and especially not on the repressive codes of institutionalised religion. Instead, *His Dark Materials* promotes an individual engagement which prioritises an ethos of hard work and imaginative engagement. Pullman is not prescriptive about the form that this ethos will take, and, indeed, a criticism that could be made of this moral philosophy is that it is too vague to be of any practical use.

Yet the lessons that we derive from fiction are learnt in a very different way from more explicit attempts to instil morality. The lessons of fiction are, if they are learnt at all, achieved only through dialogue between the author and the reader, and particularly by the ways in which the author manages to inspire the imaginative engagement of the reader. Michael Billington, in discussing the difficulties of adapting *His Dark Materials* into other artistic media, comments that the trilogy is 'the ultimate example of a literary project that achieves its fullest life at the point where the author's vision meets the reader's imagination' (2004).

Pullman also maintains that the way in which we learn from fiction is much subtler than the provision of a moral code. In a speech given at the University of East Anglia in 2005 entitled 'Miss Goddard's Grave', in which he opposed the 'school of morals' that literature can offer to both 'theocratic absolutism' and the postmodern unravelling of meaning inherent in 'theory', he asserted that stories have the capacity to

> show us human beings like ourselves acting in recognisably human ways, and they affect our emotions and our intelligence as life itself affects us; that the stories that we call the greatest are great because they are most like life, and the ones we think not so good are correspondingly less so—the characters in one are rich and complex and unpredictable, like real people, those in the other are two-dimensional and cardboard-like, stereotypes ... And our moral understanding is deepened and enriched by the awakening of our imaginative sympathy. (www.philip-pullman.com: d)

Moreover, art prompts us to *See* meanings as 'ambiguous, complex, subject to development, and arrived at by experience and by imaginative sympathy' (www.philip-pullman.com: d). This is precisely the activity that Lyra realises at the end of *His Dark Materials* will constitute the republic of heaven. In other words, the republic of heaven is a profound plea for intelligent and empathetic reading and for democratic dialogue. As Pullman puts it, 'The book proposes, the reader questions; the book responds, the reader considers.' This is an 'active' process in which we are not forced to 'read in a way determined by someone else—even by the author' (www.philip-pullman.com: d).

Putting Pullman's own work to this process, as *Philip Pullman, Master Storyteller* has done, and as countless other readers and critics have done, is an entrance into dialogue with the trilogy. Depending on the nature of the individual reading, this dialogue has been in turns appreciative and critical, rapturous and hostile. As Pullman suggested in his speech, readers have the right to dissent. One of the areas which has caused most dissent in *His Dark Materials* is, of course, its religious controversy. Although this battle against religion and 'theocratic absolutism' is represented in intellectually subtle ways, it is interesting to note that it is also in the depiction of anti-religious views that Pullman is at his most didactic, providing priests who are 'two-dimensional and cardboard-like', to turn the words of his own speech against him. By creating stereotypical characters, Pullman ironically undermines the potential of his own text for positive dialogue, and his occasional desire to preach rather than tell stories undoubtedly weakens the capacity of the trilogy to engage readers' imaginations. Indeed, it is here, where his art falters and didacticism takes over, that he has received the most negative criticism. Where his vision allows readers to participate, however, is where the trilogy has been most thoroughly praised.

In 'Miss Goddard's Grave', Pullman is also emphatic in his defence of morality and art from a more contemporary brand of theoretical relativism. In this, he says, 'truth is provisional and there is no such thing as human nature . . . meanings shift and are contingent'. This is a stance against a particular form of deconstructive criticism aligned with postmodernism and 'an endlessly playful dialectic' (www.philip-pullman.com: d). For although Pullman's narrative tells of the death of god, it does not foretell the death of morality and meaning. Rather, *His Dark Materials* actively promotes both meaning and morality. In the speech, and arguably in the trilogy itself, Pullman makes a stand against some of the incursions of the modern world: against what he terms 'the sheer relentless *busyness* of modern life . . . the commercial pressures . . . the obsession with targets and testing and league tables' (www.philip-pullman.com: d).

Perhaps, in the final analysis, this is one of the reasons the trilogy has been so successful. While it is perfectly aware that it exists within a postmodern world which has pronounced the death of god and rejected religious authority and is struggling with a host of other pressures, *His Dark Materials* is rather attractively old-fashioned in its call for 'the marriage of responsibility and delight' (www.philip-pullman.com: d). For Pullman's work is a very fine contribution to a continuing tradition of literature providing moral guidance and debate, but with the added complication of attempting to do so in a postmodern world. The trilogy takes on some of the biggest issues of our time: the death of god and how to establish an alternative morality within a secular society. Simultaneously, though, and above all, *His Dark Materials* is a riveting story populated by memorable characters and thrilling landscapes.

The introduction to this book discussed how numerous critics of *His Dark Materials* have already made comparisons between the trilogy and various classics of children's and fantasy literature. Although some might argue that too little time has passed since the publication of the final volume of the trilogy to make such an assessment, and that only time can determine true classics from the pretenders, it is evident that many others have already elevated Pullman's work to the literary pantheon. Certainly, the evidence of the growing level of critical interest that Pullman has aroused, including the publication of this book, would suggest that readers will continue to engage with his work for many decades to come. For through *His Dark Materials*, Philip Pullman has undoubtedly managed to convey an accomplished, captivating, sometimes provocative vision to a legion of readers who have responded imaginatively, whether in excitement, in anger, in appreciation or in wonder. For this, the master storyteller of *His Dark Materials* has already engaged, and will continue to do so, with million of readers, provoking them, delighting them and making them think.

◖ Bibliography ◗
and Further Reading

THIS BIBLIOGRAPHY CONTAINS all the books, articles and websites referred to in *Philip Pullman, Master Storyteller*, as well as including some additional items for further reading. It is divided into two parts: first are works by Philip Pullman, including books, essays and articles. Second is a list of secondary sources, including books, essays and articles on Pullman, interviews with him and other miscellaneous resources referred to in this book. It concludes with a selection of websites relating to Philip Pullman and *His Dark Materials*. It is not an exhaustive bibliography—so much has been written on and by Pullman that to list them all would take up an extraordinary amount of space. It does, however, include major reviews, interviews and resources. The references to Pullman's books are to the first UK publications.

Works by Philip Pullman

Books

The Haunted Storm. 1972. London: NEL.
Galatea. 1978. London: Victor Gollancz.
Using the Oxford English Dictionary: A Book of Exercises and Games.
    1979. Oxford: Oxford University Press. Illustrated by Ivan Ripley.

Ancient Civilizations. 1981. Exeter: Wheaton. Illustrated by Gary Long.

Count Karlstein. 1982. London: Chatto & Windus.

The Ruby in the Smoke. 1985. Oxford: Oxford University Press.

The Shadow in the Plate. 1986. Oxford: Oxford University Press. (Later published as *The Shadow in the North.*)

Spring-Heeled Jack: A Story of Bravery and Evil. 1989a. London: Doubleday. Illustrated by David Mostyn.

The Broken Bridge. 1990a. London: Macmillan.

How to Be Cool. 1990b. London: Macmillan.

Frankenstein. 1990c. Oxford: Oxford University Press. Adapted from the novel by Mary Shelley.

Count Karlstein: Or The Ride of the Demon Huntsman. 1991a. London: Doubleday. Illustrated by Patrice Aggs.

The Tiger in the Well. 1991b. London: Penguin.

The White Mercedes. 1992a. London: Pan Macmillan. (Later published as *The Butterfly Tattoo.*)

Sherlock Holmes and the Limehouse Horror. 1992b. Walton-on-Thames: Thomas Nelson.

The Wonderful World of Aladdin and the Enchanted Lamp. 1993. London: Scholastic. Illustrated by David Wyatt.

The New Cut Gang: Thunderbolt's Waxwork. 1994a. London: Viking. Illustrated by Mark Thomas.

The Tin Princess. 1994b. London: Penguin.

The Firework-Maker's Daughter. 1995a. London: Doubleday. Illustrated by Nick Harris.

The New Cut Gang: The Gas-Fitter's Ball. 1995b. London: Viking. Illustrated by Mark Thomas.

Northern Lights. 1995c. London: Scholastic. (Published in the US as *The Golden Compass.*)

Clockwork: Or All Wound Up. 1996a. London: Doubleday. Illustrated by Peter Bailey.

The Subtle Knife. 1997. London: Scholastic.

Mossycoat. 1998a. London: Scholastic. Illustrated by Peter Bailey.

I Was a Rat! . . . or The Scarlet Slippers. 1999a. London: Doubleday. Illustrated by Peter Bailey.

The Amber Spyglass. 2000a. London: Scholastic.

Puss in Boots. 2000b. London: Doubleday. Illustrated by Ian Beck.

Lyra's Oxford. 2003a. Oxford: David Fickling Books. Engravings by John Lawrence.

The Scarecrow and the Servant. 2004a. London: Doubleday. Illustrated by Peter Bailey.

Selected Essays and Articles

'Invisible Pictures'. 1989b. *Signal.* 60. September. 160–86.

'Carnegie Medal Acceptance Speech'. 1996b. http://www.random-house.com/features/pullman/philippullman/speech.html.

'The Moral's in the Story, Not the Stern Lecture'. 1996c. *Independent.* 18 July.

'Printout'. 1996d. *New Statesman.* 19 July.

'Picture Stories and Graphic Novels'. 1998b. In Kimberley Reynolds and Nicholas Tucker, eds. *Children's Book Publishing Since 1945.* Aldershot: Scolar Press. 110–32.

'Let's Write It in Red: The Patrick Hardy Lecture'. 1998c. *Signal.* 85. January. 44–62.

'The Dark Side of Narnia'. 1998d. *Guardian.* 1 October.

'Introduction'. 1998e. In Philip Pullman, ed. *Detective Stories.* London: Kingfisher. Illustrated by Nick Hardcastle.

'An Introduction to . . . Philip Pullman'. 1999b. In James Carter, ed. *Talking Books: Children's Authors Talk about the Craft, Creativity and Process of Writing.* London: Routledge. 178–95.

'Gotterdammerung or Bust'. 1999c. *Horn Book Magazine.* 75: 1. January–February. 31–34.

'Writing Children's Fiction: Or You Cannot Be Serious'. 1999d. In Barry Turner, ed. *The Writer's Handbook 2000.* London: Macmillan. 216–18.

'Blame it on the Loose Ends'. 2000c. *Scotsman.* 21 October.

'The Republic of Heaven'. 2001. *Horn Book Magazine.* 77: 6. November–December. 655–67.

'Dreaming of Spires'. 2002a. *Guardian.* 27 July.

'From Exeter to Jordan'. 2002b. *Oxford Today.* Trinity issue. 20–22.

'Voluntary Service'. 2002c. *Guardian.* 28 December. 4–6.

'The Responsible Storyteller'. 2002d. *Guardian.* 28 December.

'Responsibility and the Storyteller'. 2002e. *New Humanist.* Spring. 6–7.

'Science: A Very Short Introduction'. 2003b. In Mary Gribbin and John Gribbin. *The Science of Philip Pullman's* His Dark Materials. London: Hodder Children's Books. xiii–xix.

'Teaching and Testing'. 2003c. In Bernard Ashley, Anne Fine, Jamila Gavin, Chris Powling and Philip Pullman. *Meetings with the Minister: Five Children's Authors on the National Literacy Strategy.* Reading: National Centre for Language and Literacy. 8–10.

'Lost the Plot'. 2003d. *Guardian.* 30 September.

'All around You Is Silence'. 2003e. *Guardian.* 5 June.

'Reading in Colour'. 2004b. *Index on Censorship.* 33: 4. October. 156–63.

'Theatre—The True Key Stage'. 2004c. *Guardian.* 30 March.

'Let's Pretend'. 2004d. *Guardian.* 24 November.

'Introduction'. 2005a. In John Milton. *Paradise Lost.* Oxford: Oxford University Press. 1–10.

'Against "Identity"'. 2005b. In Lisa Appignanesi, ed. *Free Expression Is No Offence: An English PEN Book.* London: Penguin Books. 105–15.

'Aye, There's the Rub'. 2005c. *Guardian.* 27 November.

Secondary Material

Books on Philip Pullman

Butler, Robert. 2003. *The Art of Darkness: Staging the Philip Pullman Trilogy.* London: National Theatre and Oberon Books.

Gifford, Clive. 2006. *So You Think You Know* His Dark Materials? London: Hodder Children's Books.

Gribbin, Mary, and John Gribbin. 2003. *The Science of Philip Pullman's* His Dark Materials. London: Hodder Children's Books.

Haill, Lyn, ed. 2004. *Darkness Illuminated: Platform Discussions on 'His Dark Materials' at the National Theatre.* London: National Theatre and Oberon Books.

Houghton, John. 2004. *A Closer Look at* His Dark Materials. Eastbourne: Victor.

Lenz, Millicent, and Carole Scott, eds. 2005. His Dark Materials *Illuminated: Critical Essays on Philip Pullman's Trilogy.* Detroit: Wayne State University Press.

Parkin, Lance, and Mark Jones. 2005. *Dark Matters: An Unofficial and Unauthorised Guide to Philip Pullman's Internationally Bestselling* His Dark Materials *Trilogy.* London: Virgin Books.

Rayment-Pickard, Hugh. 2004. *The Devil's Account: Philip Pullman and Christianity.* London: Darton, Longman & Todd.

Squires, Claire. 2003. *Philip Pullman's* His Dark Materials *Trilogy: A Reader's Guide.* London: Continuum.

Tucker, Nicholas. 2003a. *Darkness Visible: Inside the World of Philip Pullman.* Cambridge: Wizard Books.

Watkins, Tony. 2004. *Dark Matter: A Thinking Fan's Guide to Philip Pullman.* Southampton: Damaris Publishing.

Wright, Nicholas. 2003. *His Dark Materials.* London: Nick Hern Books.

Yeffeth, Glen, ed. 2005. *Navigating the Golden Compass: Religion, Science and Daemonology in* His Dark Materials. Dallas: Benbella Books.

Articles, Interviews and Other Resources on Philip Pullman

Adronik, Catherine M. 2001. 'Philip Pullman: His Wonderful Materials'. *Book Report.* 20: 3. November–December. 40–44.

Alderson, Brian. 2000. 'Compass, Knife and Spyglass'. *New York Times.* 19 November.

Association of Christian Teachers. a. 'Philip Pullman'. http://www.christian-teachers.org.uk/news/PhilipPullman.htm.
———. b. '*His Dark Materials*'. www.christian-teachers.org.uk/news/HisDarkMaterials.htm.

Bawden, Nina. 1995. 'It's Not Just Kids' Stuff'. *Evening Standard.* 18 December.

BBC. a. 'Philip Pullman Webchat'. http://www.bbc.co.uk/radio4/arts/hisdarkmaterials/pullman_webchat.shtml.

BBC News. 2005. 'Pullman Attacks Narnia Film Plans'. *BBC News.* 16 October.

Berman, Matt. 2000. 'Heaven Can't Wait'. *Times-Picayune (New Orleans)*. 5 November.

Bethune, Brian. 1996. 'Dæmons and Dust'. *Maclean's*. 109: 30. 22 July. 58.

Billington, Michael. 2004. 'Pullman's Trilogy Feels the Squeeze'. *Guardian*. 5 January.

Bird, Anne-Marie. 2000. 'Dust, Dæmons and Soul States: Reading Philip Pullman's *His Dark Materials*'. *British Association of Lecturers in Children's Literature Bulletin*. 7. June. 3–12.

———. 2001. ' "Without Contraries Is No Progression": Dust as an All-Inclusive, Multifunctional Metaphor in Philip Pullman's *"His Dark Materials"*'. *Children's Literature in Education*. 32: 2. June. 111–23.

Blacker, Terence. 1997. 'At the Cutting Edge of Good and Evil'. *Mail on Sunday*. 7 December.

Blake, William. 1998. *Selected Poetry*. Oxford: Oxford University Press. Edited with an introduction and notes by Michael Mason.

Boehning, Julie C. 1996. 'Philip Pullman's Paradise'. *Library Journal*. 121: 3. 15 February. 175.

Bradbury, Malcolm. 1996. 'Have Today's Writers Really Lost the Plot?' *Evening Standard*. 18 July.

Bradley, A C. 1904. *Shakespearean Tragedy*. London: Macmillan.

Briggs, Julia. 2000. 'Fighting the Forces of Evil'. *Times Literary Supplement*. 22 December.

Caldecott, Léonie. 1999. 'The Stuff of Nightmares'. *Catholic Herald*. 29 October.

———. 2003. 'The Big Read and the Big Lie'. *Catholic Herald*. 26 December.

Carey, Joanna. 1996. 'The Pullman Engine'. *Guardian*. 23 April.

Chabon, Michael. 2004. 'Dust and Dæmons'. *New York Review of Books*. 25 March.

Chrisafis, Angelique. 2002. 'Edinburgh 2002: Pullman Lays Down a Moral Challenge for Writers'. *Guardian*. 12 August.

Clapp, Susannah. 2004. 'Dæmons Are Forever'. *Observer*. 11 January.

Coates, Sam. 2004. 'God Is Cut from Film of Dark Materials'. *The Times*. 8 December.

Costa, Maddy. 2001. 'Kid's Stuff'. *Guardian.* 22 August.

Craig, Amanda. 1997. 'Windows into Souls'. *New Statesman.* 26 September.

———. 2003. 'Dreaming Spires of Unreality'. *The Times.* 13 December.

Curtis, Nick. 2003. 'His Dark Material'. *Evening Standard.* 5 December.

de Bertodano, Helena. 2002. '"I Am of the Devil's Party"'. *Sunday Telegraph.* 27 January.

Dederer, Claire. 2000. 'Fantasy with Polar Bears'. *Newsday.* 12 November.

Dickson, E Jane. 2001. 'Telling Stories'. *The Times.* 2 June.

Dirda, Michael. 1996. 'A World Elsewhere'. *Washington Post.* 5 May.

———. 1997. 'The Edge of the World'. *Washington Post.* 3 August.

———. 2000. 'The Amber Spyglass'. *Washington Post.* 29 October.

Drabble, Margaret, ed. 2000. *The Oxford Companion to English Literature.* Oxford: Oxford University Press. 6th ed.

Eccleshare, Julia. 2000. 'Rational Magic'. *Guardian.* 28 October.

———. 2002a. *Beatrix Potter to Harry Potter: Portraits of Children's Writers.* London: National Portrait Gallery Publications.

———. 2002b. 'A Golden Time for Children's Books'. *Publishers Weekly.* 18 February.

———. 2004. 'A Fast Track for Children's Books'. *Publishers Weekly.* 8 March.

Ezard, John. 2003. 'Pullman Pulls It Off'. *Guardian.* 20 December.

Feay, Suzi. 2001. 'A Winner—If He Gets His Evil Way'. *Independent on Sunday.* 19 August.

Fickling, David. 2005. 'It's the Story, Stupid! (Money and Books)'. *Publishing Research Seminar Series.* Oxford International Centre for Publishing Studies, Oxford Brookes University. 1 November.

———. 2006. Personal communication. 25 January.

Fitzherbert, Claudia. 2002. 'This Author Is Original and Also Dangerous'. *Daily Telegraph.* 23 January.

Flesch, William. 2004. 'Childish Things'. *Boston Globe.* 13 June.

Fraser, Lindsey. 1995. 'Reigning Cats and Dogs at Bedtime'. *Scotsman.* 16 September.

Fried, Kerry. 2003. 'Lyra's Oxford'. *New York Times Book Review*. 21 December.

Gardiner, Juliet. 2000a. 'Recuperating the Author: Consuming Fictions of the 1990s'. *The Papers of the Bibliographical Society of America*. 94: 2. 255–74.

———. 2000b. ' "What Is an Author?" Contemporary Publishing Discourse and the Author Figure'. *Publishing Research Quarterly*. 16: 1. Spring. 63–76.

Gooderham, David. 2003. 'Fantasizing It as It Is: Religious Language in Philip Pullman's Trilogy, *His Dark Materials*'. *Children's Literature*. 31. 155–75.

Hardyment, Christina. 1996. 'Grown-up Talent in the Juvenile World'. *Independent*. 6 July.

———. 1997. 'Children's Books: Hip History and Fierce Fables'. *Independent*. 1 December.

Harris, Mary Russell. 2003. 'Ethical Plots, Ethical Endings in Philip Pullman's *His Dark Materials*'. *Foundation*. 32: 88. Summer. 68–74.

Harris, Paul. 2005. 'Holy War Looms over Disney's Narnia Epic'. *Observer*. 16 October.

Hatlen, Burton. 2005. 'Pullman's *His Dark Materials*, a Challenge to the Fantasies of J R R Tolkien and C S Lewis, with an Epilogue on Pullman's Neo-Romantic Reading of *Paradise Lost*'. In Millicent Lenz and Carole Scott, eds. His Dark Materials *Illuminated: Critical Essays on Philip Pullman's Trilogy*. Detroit: Wayne State University Press. 75–94.

Hewison, Robert. 2004. 'When Worlds Collide'. *Sunday Times*. 11 January.

Hitchens, Peter. 2002a. 'The Most Dangerous Author in Britain'. *Mail on Sunday*. 27 January.

———. 2002b. 'Karl Marx Would Be Proud of Blair Smear Merchants'. *Mail on Sunday*. 9 June.

———. 2003. 'A Labour of Loathing'. *Spectator*. 18 January.

Howker, Janni. 1997. 'Turmoil on the Edge of Time'. *Times Educational Supplement*. 19 September.

Hunt, Peter. 2001. 'Philip Pullman (1946–)'. *Children's Literature*. Oxford: Blackwell. 113–15.

Independent. 1996. 'Why Modern Literary Culture Has Lost the Plot'. *Independent*. 18 July.

Jefferson, Margo. 2002. 'On Writers and Writing: Harry Potter for Grown-ups'. *New York Times*. 20 January.

Johnson, Sarah. 1997. '*His Dark Materials*: The Subtle Knife'. *The Times*. 18 October.

———. 2000. 'On the Dark Edge of Imagination'. *The Times*. 18 October.

Johnston, Sheila. 2006. 'Film-Makers on Film: Anand Tucker'. *Daily Telegraph*. 4 February.

Jones, Dudley. 1999. 'Only Make-Believe? Lies, Fictions, and Metafictions in Geraldine McCaughrean's *A Pack of Lies* and Philip Pullman's *Clockwork*'. *The Lion and the Unicorn*. 23: 1. January. 86–92.

Jones, Malcolm. 2000. 'Pullman's Progress'. *Newsweek*. 30 October.

Jones, Nicolette. 1996. 'What Shall We Tell the Children?' *The Times*. 18 July.

———. 2000. 'The Garden of Earthly Delights'. *Sunday Times*. 29 October.

Katbamna, Mira. 2003. 'Crisis of Creativity'. *Guardian*. 30 September.

Kellaway, Kate. 2000. 'A Wizard with Words'. *Observer*. 22 October.

Kemp, Peter. 1997. 'Master of His Universe'. *Sunday Times*. 19 October.

Kimball, Melanie A. 1999. 'From Folktales to Fiction: Orphan Characters in Children's Literature'. *Library Trends*. 47: 3. 558–79.

King, Shelley. 2005. ' "Without Lyra We Would Understand Neither the New Nor the Old Testament": Exegesis, Allegory, and Reading *The Golden Compass*'. In Millicent Lenz and Carole Scott, eds. His Dark Materials *Illuminated: Critical Essays on Philip Pullman's Trilogy*. Detroit: Wayne State University Press. 106–24.

Knights, L C. 1945. *Explorations: Essays in Criticism Mainly on the Literature of the Seventeenth Century*. London: Chatto & Windus.

Langton, Jane. 1996. 'What Is Dust?' *New York Times.* 19 May.

Lenz, Millicent. 2001. 'Philip Pullman'. In Peter Hunt and Millicent Lenz, eds. *Alternative Worlds in Fantasy Fiction.* London: Continuum. 122–69.

———. 2003. 'Story as a Bridge to Transformation: The Way beyond Death in Philip Pullman's *The Amber Spyglass'. Children's Literature in Education.* 34: 1. March. 47–55.

Lewis, C S. 1942. *A Preface to Paradise Lost.* London: Oxford University Press.

Lister, David. 1996. 'Children's Author Accuses Novelists of Losing the Plot'. *Independent.* 18 July.

Loer, Stephanie. 2000. 'Author's Trilogy Inspired by Milton's "Paradise Lost"'. *Boston Globe.* 3 December.

Lyall, Sarah. 2000. 'The Man Who Dared Make Religion the Villain'. *New York Times.* 7 November.

Macaulay, Alastair. 2004. 'Visit to Parallel Universes Is Out of this World'. *Financial Times.* 11 December.

MacPherson, Karen. 2000. 'Pullman Writes Grand Finale for Trilogy'. *Pittsburgh Post Gazette.* 10 October.

Maguire, Gregory. 1998. 'Children's Books'. *New York Times.* 19 April.

———. 2000. 'The Amber Spyglass'. *Horn Book Magazine.* 76: 6. November–December. 735–38.

Mann, Jessica. 2000. 'A Paradise without God'. *Sunday Telegraph.* 5 November.

Markham, Arthur B. 2005. 'Science, Technology and the Danger of Dæmons'. In Glen Yeffeth, ed. *Navigating the Golden Compass: Religion, Science and Daemonology in* His Dark Materials. Dallas: Benbella Books. 61–69.

Marr, Andrew. 2002. 'Pullman Does for Atheism What C S Lewis Did for God'. *Daily Telegraph.* 24 January.

Matthews, Susan. 2005. 'Rouzing the Faculties to Act: Pullman's Blake for Children'. In Millicent Lenz and Carole Scott, eds. His Dark Materials *Illuminated: Critical Essays on Philip Pullman's Trilogy.* Detroit: Wayne State University Press. 125–34.

McCrum, Robert. 2000. 'The World of Books: Pullman Gives His Readers Precisely the Satisfactions They Look For in a Novel'. *Observer.* 22 October.

———. 2002. 'Dæmon Geezer'. *Observer.* 27 January.

McDonagh, Melanie. 2002. 'Once upon a Time, Children's Books Were Looked Down On'. *Daily Telegraph.* 13 April.

———. 2004. 'His Dark Prejudices'. *The Tablet.* 27 November.

Mckay, Carla. 2000. 'Tempted by This Dark Spirited Fantasy'. *Daily Mail.* 1 December.

Metzger, Robert A. 'Philip Pullman, Research Scientist'. In Glen Yeffeth, ed. *Navigating the Golden Compass: Religion, Science and Daemonology in* His Dark Materials. Dallas: Benbella Books. 49–59.

Miller, Laura. 2005/2006. 'Far from Narnia'. *New Yorker.* 26 December and 2 January.

Milton, John. 2000. *Paradise Lost.* London: Penguin. Edited with an introduction by John Leonard.

Moloney, Daniel P. 2001. 'The Golden Compass/The Subtle Knife/The Amber Spyglass'. *First Things.* 113. May. 45–49.

———. 2005. 'Show Me, Don't Tell Me: Pullman's Imperfectly Christian Story (and How He Lost His Way)'. In Glen Yeffeth, ed. 2005. *Navigating the Golden Compass: Religion, Science and Daemonology in* His Dark Materials. Dallas: Benbella Books. 171–85.

Moore, Emily. 1996. 'Talkback: Philip Pullman'. *Guardian.* 16 April.

Moran, Joe. 2000. *Star Authors: Literary Celebrity in America.* London: Pluto Press.

Moruzi, Kristine. 2005. 'Missed Opportunities: The Subordination of Children in Philip Pullman's *His Dark Materials*'. *Children's Literature in Education.* 36: 1. March. 55–68.

Nelson, Michael. 2005. 'For the Love of Narnia'. *Chronicle of Higher Education.* 2 December.

Nikolajeva, Maria. 1999. 'Children's, Adult, Human . . . ?' In Sandra L Beckett, ed. *Transcending Boundaries: Writing for a Dual Audience of Children and Adults.* New York: Garland Publishing. 63–80.

Odean, Kathleen. 2000. 'The Story Master'. *School Library Journal.* 46: 10. 50–54.

Parsons, Wendy, and Catriona Nicholson. 1999. 'Talking to Philip Pullman: An Interview'. *The Lion and the Unicorn.* 23: 1. January. 116–34.

Paulsell, Stephanie. 2004. 'Honoring the Sexual Body'. http://www.covenantnetwork.org/sermon&papers/Paulsell-04.html. 5 November.

Poole, Richard. 2001. 'Philip Pullman and the Republic of Heaven'. *New Welsh Review.* 14: 1. Summer. 15–22.

Pope, Rob. 2002. *The English Studies Book: An Introduction to Language, Literature and Culture.* London: Routledge. 2nd ed.

Potton, Ed. 2002. 'Garden-Shed Visionary'. *The Times.* 24 January.

Rickett, Joel. 2002. 'Behind the Headlines'. *The Bookseller.* 8 February. 11.

Robinson, Karen. 2002. 'Dark Art of Writing Books That Win Minds'. *Sunday Times.* 27 January.

Ross, Deborah. 2002. 'Soap and the Serious Writer'. *Independent.* 4 February.

Rustin, Margaret, and Michael Rustin. 2003a. 'Where Is Home? An Essay on Philip Pullman's *Northern Lights*'. *Journal of Child Psychotherapy.* 29: 1. April. 93–105.

———. 2003b. 'A New Kind of Friendship: An Essay on Philip Pullman's *The Subtle Knife*'. *Journal of Child Psychotherapy.* 29: 2. August. 227–41.

———. 2003c. 'Learning to Say Goodbye: An Essay on Philip Pullman's *The Amber Spyglass*'. *Journal of Child Psychotherapy.* 29: 3. December. 415–28.

Rustin, Susanna. 2000. 'Heaven Is a Place on Earth'. *Financial Times.* 4 November.

Said, S F. 2002. 'Why Philip Pullman Should Win the Whitbread Tonight'. *Daily Telegraph.* 22 January.

Scott, Carole. 2005. 'Pullman's Enigmatic Ontology: Revamping Old Traditions in *His Dark Materials*'. In Millicent Lenz and Carole Scott, eds. His Dark Materials *Illuminated: Critical Essays on Philip Pullman's Trilogy.* Detroit: Wayne State University Press. 95–105.

Sharkey, Alix. 1998. 'Heaven, Hell, and the Hut at the Bottom of the Garden'. *Independent on Sunday*. 6 December.

Shippey, Tom. 2001. 'Fantasy'. In Jane Rogers, ed. *Good Fiction Guide*. Oxford: Oxford University Press. 43–46.

Siegel, Tatiana. 2006. 'Weitz returns to "Compass" for New Line'. *The Hollywood Reporter*. 8 May.

Sierz, Aleks. 2003. 'Enter the Dæmons'. *Independent*. 12 December.

Smith, Karen Patricia. 2005. 'Tradition, Transformation, and the Bold Emergence: Fantastic Legacy and Pullman's *His Dark Materials*'. In Millicent Lenz and Carole Scott, eds. His Dark Materials *Illuminated: Critical Essays on Philip Pullman's Trilogy*. Detroit: Wayne State University Press. 135–51.

Spanner, Huw. 2002. 'Heat and Dust'. *Third Way*. http://www.third-way.org.uk/past/showpage.asp?page=3949. April.

Spencer, Charles. 2004a. 'Working with the Wrong Material'. *Daily Telegraph*. 5 January.

———. 2004b. 'Triumphant Transformation'. *Daily Telegraph*. 10 December.

Stanistreet, Michelle. 2002. 'Bestseller Philip Pullman Told Dark Tales Even as a Boy'. *Sunday Express*. 17 March.

Sutherland, John. 1996. *Is Heathcliff a Murderer? Great Puzzles in Nineteenth-Century Fiction*. Oxford: Oxford University Press.

———. 1997. *Can Jane Eyre Be Happy? More Puzzles in Classic Fiction*. Oxford: Oxford University Press.

Thomson, Stephen. 2004. 'The Child, the Family, the Relationship. Familiar Stories: Family, Storytelling, and Ideology in Philip Pullman's *His Dark Materials*'. In Karín Lesnik-Oberstein, ed. *Children's Literature: New Approaches*. Basingstoke: Palgrave Macmillan.

Thorpe, Nick. 2002. 'The Anti-Christian Fundamentalist'. *Sunday Times*. 4 August.

Tonkin, Boyd. 2002a. 'An Inevitable Victory for a Dark and Complex Fable'. *Independent*. 23 January.

———. 2002b. 'Once upon a Time in the Marketing Department . . .' *Independent*. 6 November.

Townsend, John Rowe. 2002. 'Paradise Reshaped'. *Horn Book Magazine*. 78: 4. July–August. 415–21.

Traviss, Karen. 2005. 'I Gotta Get Me One of Those: Why Dæmons Might Make the World a Better Place'. In Glen Yeffeth, ed. *Navigating the Golden Compass: Religion, Science and Daemonology in* His Dark Materials. Dallas: Benbella Books. 81–88.

Tucker, Nicholas. 2000. 'Paradise Lost and Freedom Won'. *Independent*. 28 October.

———. 2003b. 'Philip Pullman—The Dæmon King'. *Independent on Sunday*. 30 November.

von Kleist, Heinrich. 1810. 'On the Marionette Theatre'. In Nicholas Tucker. 2003. *Darkness Visible: Inside the World of Philip Pullman*. Cambridge: Wizard Books. Translated by Idris Parry. 197–207.

Wagner, Erica. 2000. 'Divinely Inspired'. *The Times*. 18 October.

———. 2002. 'Courageous and Dangerous: A Writer for All Ages'. *The Times*. 23 January.

———. 2003. 'Welcome to My Worlds'. *The Times*. 27 October.

Walsh, Clare. 2003. 'From "Capping" to Intercision: Metaphors/Metonyms of Mind Control in the Young Adult Fiction of John Christopher and Philip Pullman'. *Language and Literature*. 12: 3. August. 233–51.

Walter, Natasha. 2002. 'A Moral Vision for the Modern Age'. *Independent*. 24 January.

Warner, Marina. 2002. *Fantastic Metamorphoses: Other Worlds: Ways of Telling the Self*. Oxford: Oxford University Press.

Wartofsky, Alona. 2001. 'The Last Word'. *Washington Post*. 19 February.

Wavell, Stuart. 2001. 'The Lost Children'. *Sunday Times*. 11 November.

Weich, Dave. 2000. 'Philip Pullman Reaches the Garden'. *Powells.com*. http://www.powells.com/authors/pullman.html.

Welch, Frances. 2000. 'Jesus Was Like the Buddha and Galileo'. *Sunday Telegraph*. 19 November.

Wernick, Andrew. 1993. 'Authorship and the Supplement of Promotion'. In Maurice Biriotti and Nicola Miller, eds. *What Is an Author?* Manchester: Manchester University Press. 85–103.

Whitehouse, Anne. 2003. 'Honorary Graduate Philip Pullman Shares His Thoughts on Education'. *The Oak*. Summer. 2.

Wickens, Barbara. 1998. 'Sympathy for the Rebel Angels'. *Maclean's*. 111: 2. 12 January. 64.

Williams, Rowan. 2004. 'A Near-Miraculous Triumph'. *Guardian*. 10 March.

Wood, Naomi. 2001. 'Paradise Lost and Found: Obedience, Disobedience, and Storytelling in C S Lewis and Philip Pullman'. *Children's Literature in Education*. 32: 4. 237–59.

————. 2004. '(Em)Bracing Icy Mothers: Ideology, Identity, and Environment in Children's Fantasy'. In Sidney I Dobrin and Kenneth B Kidd, eds. *Wild Things: Children's Culture and Ecocriticism*. Detroit: Wayne State University Press. 198–214.

Wunderkind, Ceres. 2003. 'The Commandments of HDM Fanfic'. http://www.geocities.com/ceres_wunderkind/c_all.htm.

Wyke, Nick. 2004. 'An Audience with Atheism's Answer to C S Lewis'. *The Times*. 10 January.

Websites and Online Resources

www.philip-pullman.com
Philip Pullman's website
References:

a: http://www.philip-pullman.com/pages/content/index.asp?PageID=84

b: http://www.philip-pullman.com/about_the_author.asp

c: http://www.philip-pullman.com/pages/content/index.asp?PageID=119

d: http://www.philip-pullman.com/pages/content/index.asp?PageID=113

e: http://www.philip-pullman.com/pages/content/index.asp?PageID=36

f: http://www.philip-pullman.com/pages/content/index.asp?PageID=118

g: http://www.philip-pullman.com/pages/content/index.asp?PageID=12

h: http://www.philip-pullman.com/about_the_writing.asp

i: http://www.philip-
pullman.com/pages/content/index.asp?PageID=107
j: http://www.philip-
pullman.com/pages/content/index.asp?PageID=121

www.bbc.co.uk/radio4/arts/hisdarkmaterials
Material connected to the BBC Radio 4 adaptation of *His Dark Materials*

www.bookcollection.i8.com
Fan website

www.bridgetothestars.net
Fan website
References:

a: www.bridgetothestars.net/index.php?p=weitzinterview
b: www.bridgetothestars.net/index.php?p=loreviews
c. www.bridgetothestars.net/news/1146880843

www.darkmaterials.com
Fan website

www.davidficklingbooks.co.uk
Philip Pullman's UK publisher
References:

a: Promotional video for *Lyra's Oxford*

www.fanfiction.net
Fan Fiction website including *His Dark Materials* stories

www.geocities.com/darkadamant
Fan website

www.hisdarkmaterials.org
Fan website

www.randomhouse.com/features/pullman
Philip Pullman's US publisher

http://tts.inkypot.com
His Dark Materials online role-playing game

www.stagework.org.uk
National Theatre's educational website documenting its stage production of *His Dark Materials*

❀ Index ❀

207